A Brief Study of Paul
and
His Epistles

A Brief Study of Paul
and
His Epistles

O.M. Rao

2011

A Brief Study of Paul and His Epistles – Published by the Rev. Dr. Ashish Amos of the Indian Society for Promoting Christian Knowledge (ISPCK), Post Box 1585, 1654, Madarsa Road, Kashmere Gate, Delhi-110006.

ISBN: 978-81-8465-124-9

Laser typeset by
ISPCK, Post Box 1585, 1654, Madarsa Road, Kashmere Gate, Delhi-110006 • *Tel:* 23866323

e-mail: ashish@ispck.org.in • ella@ispck.org.in
website: www.ispck.org.in

Contents

Part - II
The 13 Epistles (of Paul)

 vii

Foreword

1. The Pattern of Writing

As the regular books in general have passage of exegetical notes and contain long discussions of arguments of the topics , here I have felt for students chiefly (and other readers also)for better grasp of the subject in a brief outline form, so as to retain in their minds well what they have read here in catching the main ideas.

2. Thanks

a) My thanks go to first **Mr. C.Benjamin**(Rtd.Asst.Chief Engineer of Vizag Dockyard, an M.Div graduate of our William Carey Christian Collage of Vizag) for his repeated mention to me to write on the Epistles of the New Testament also, which finally made me launch this project. I must mention that he took pains to translate into Telugu some books for the benefit of the local people of Andhra Pradesh .I am sure his reward wll be from the Lord .

b) I wish to thank **Prof.Bilmoria Rani** for bringing out the typed fair copy to repeated revisions and in my bad hand-writing too.In fact she was the one who helped me in for many of my books. May God richly bless her.

c) I need to thank **Mr. M.Kishore Kumar** our neighbour at Vizag residence at the Ark apartments at the C.B.M Compound with his overload of work at the local collage at Vizag as the lecturer, he patiently typed into the fair copies both these above volume and a shorter one of Acts, Hebrews and James books of the New Testament and other epistles of St. Paul.

I must say it is my bounden duty to offer my thanks and also my prayer for his family for God's help to them in all matters.

d) I need to thank **Prof. O. Deenammal**,that inspite of heavy work of running the William Carey Christian Institute as it's president, in her spare time to look into the preparation of manuscripts into proper printing level. May God richly bless her.

My special thanks to **Ms.Ella Sonawane** the Mission Secretary Manager of the **ISPCK** at Delhi, for her strenuous job in bringing out this volume,infact preceded by many of my writings earlier. May God bless her and the General Secretary **Rev. Dr. Ashish Amos**, Asst. Secretary (Ecumenical Relations) **Mr. Chowdhury** and others there in the Christian literature ministry all over India and abroad.

– O. M. Rao

Part - I
About Paul

Chapter -1

The Life of Paul

A. THE TWO SOURCES FOR PAUL'S LIFE

There are two sources to gather information about Paul's life:

I.   Paul's letters: Rom.11.1; 15.22-28.

(Acts 7.58; 8.1-3;9.1-30;11.25-30;12.25;13.1-28,31)

I Cor. 7.7; 16.5-11.

II Cor. 2.1;9.13; 11.32-33; 12.2-4; 13.1, 10; 14.21.

Gal. 1.15-23; 2.1-14.

Phil. 3.5-6; 4.16.

(From Pastoral Epistles also information can be used, if the information from these corresponds to known N.T. History).

II. External events which help to correlate with the events in Paul's life. There are five such points:

a.   Lucious Vitellus sent Pilate (Prefect of Judea) to Rome in A.D. 36 to answer for his conduct. The replacement of Pilate by Marcellus was the time of Stephen's martyrdom (Acts 6.8-7.60) and the persecution of the church at Jerusalem (Acts.8.1ff.) Paul's conversion was at this time (Josephus Antiquities 18.4 etc.).

b.   The famine in the time of Emperor Claudius (Acts 11.28-30), which according to Josephus affected the eastern area of the Mediterranean. This occurred during the time of the procurator Tiberius Julius Alexander, A.D. 46-48. So A.D. 46 could be the probable year for this famine.

c.   The expulsion of the Jews from Rome by the edict of Emperor Claudius in his 9th year of his reign, A.D.49. This was promulgated as there were regular disturbances between the Jews and the Christians over the 'Christos' issue. This could be the time for the return of Aquila and Priscilla to Corinth from Rome, when Paul arrived there during his second missionary journey (Acts 18.2ff.).

d.   Paul was brought before the Proconsul Junius Gallio Annaeus in Achaia in A.D.52, which was in the second missionary journey of Paul at Corinth (Acts 18.12). Prior to his arrest, Paul lived 18 months there. Paul must have left Antioch from where he came here, 15 months before, which must be after the Jerusalem Council.

e.   Porcius Antonius Festus, was procurator of Judea in A.D. 60 after Felix (Acts 24.27; 25.9,10). This was the time Paul appealed to Caesar.

B.   THE NAME

i.   Prior to Acts 13.9 he was called 'Saulos' (Acts 7.58; 8.13;9.1). This was the same name of the first king in the **O.T. Saul** in Hebrew means **'asked of God'**(I Sam.9.2,17;10.1 etc.).

ii.   In the conversion episodes, he uses 'Saul' as his name (Acts 9.4,17; 22.7,13; 26.14).

iii. a. In Paul's 13 letters, he uses 'Paulos' which is the Greek form of the well known Roman family's name. We know that he hails from Tarsus of Asia Minor, which gave him Roman citizenship (Acts 16.39; 22.27f; 25.10).

b. 'Paulos' also occurs in II Peter 3.15 (Acts 13.9ff).

It is possible that Paul had two *names* being *bi-lingual*: Paul from his *Sematic background* and Saulos from his *Roman background*. Though Luke marks it as a change in his faith from Acts 13.9ff and it is possible that he gave up Saulos then. Some say the change could be due to two different sources Luke was drawing, in writing Acts.

C.   THE BACKGROUND OF PAUL'S LIFE

Paul must have been born some time around the A.D. first decade. He must have been at the stoning of Stephen (Acts 7.58), probably around 30 years or above. He calls himself old in Phlm. 9. He was born in Tarsus of Cilicia (Acts 22.3). He was from the tribe of Benjamin (Rom. 11.1; Phil. 3.5). He had a sister (Acts 23.16). In 66 B.C; when Pompey re-organised

Asia Minor after his conquests, he made Tarsus capital of Cilcia province. Mark Anthony granted it, during his time, freedom, immunity and citizenship to it which was confirmed by Emperor Augustus. The city was noted for the Stoic and Epicurean philosophers in it. Paul must have had his early education from here, so that he could boast that 'he was a citizen of no mean city' (Acts 21.29).

Being a Hellinized town, he knew Greek well so that he used the Greek Old Testament (LXX), in spite of the fact that he calls himself a Hebrew (Phil. 3.6). This was Normal with a Diaspora Jew like Paul. The rhetoric of Stoic diatribe in his letters seems to exhibit this Background.

Paul seems to be boasting of his Jewish background:

A Jew	-	(Acts 21.39; 22.3).
An Israelite	-	(II Cor. 11.22; Rom.11.1).
A Hebrew, born of the Hebrews	-	(Acts 23.6; Phil. 3.6).
A Pharisee, (the strictest party of his religion)	-	(Acts 26.5Gal. 1.14).
Educated at the feet of Gamaliel	-	(Acts 22.3).

These references show that he was a Greek speaking Jew, who could also speak Aramaic. His native tongue could be Aramaic and his thought pattern was Semitic. The fact that he was getting trained at the feet of Gamaliel shows that Paul was training himself to become a Rabbi. He was at his conversion not only a disciple, but a teacher with the right to make legal decisions which enabled him to travel to Damacus (Acts 9.1-2 etc.) and confirm with the exercise of his casting a vote against the Christians; most likely as a member of the Sanhedrin Council (Acts 26.10). If so, by then he must be above 40 years of age for such a position. So the conversion could be at his middle age and from such a position, and most likely he was married as it was required of Rabbis. I Cor. 7.8 refers to his status as single and out of the two options – unmarried or widowed, the latter could be the one he was referring to here. The *background* of Paul is thus, both strictly Jewish faith and Diaspora Hellenistic Judaism.

a.   The reference to his strict *Judaism* was not so much a boast, but deference to the high esteem the Jews were held and listened to among the Pagans. If one asks why the Jewish faith is regarded so highly? The answer is that its belief in one God, its strict laws – ethical and ritual observance, its uniform life through out the Roman world. It was a new stream in the old pagan religions.

b. *Hellenistic Judaism* (outside of Palestine) where the Synagogue replaced the Temple, the exposition of the Torah instead of sacrifices and the Greek thought entered into one living God, minimum of ritual commandments, and basic ethical code (circumcision not required). This was in contrast to the strict orthodox Jews of Palestine who demanded strict observance of the full Law.

So we see two schools of thought about circumcision which arose among the Jews:

i. Jerusalem Jews   ii. Diaspora Jews.

Though Paul was a Pharisee, yet he was a Diaspora Jew as seen in his attitude. He has traces of both. His Diaspora Jewish influence shows his liberal attitude to the Law and circumcision on the one hand, and the openness to Greek reason and the influence of the extraordinary missionary zeal – world wide – of Judaism in the pagan world which he used for the Gospel propagation.

D. PAUL'S CONVERSION

Most of the N.T. Scholars see the relation of the martyrdom of Stephen and the conversion of Paul. The killers placed their garments at the feet of Paul (Acts 7.58f.), which could be A.D.36 (if 30 years from A.D.5). There seems to be 14 years lapse between his conversion and the Council visit to Jerusalem (Gal.2.1) which could be A.D. 49.

Both Luke in Acts and Paul himself describe the Damascus road experience, as the turning point in Paul's life and career. This led him to preach the Gospel to the Gentiles (Gal. 1.15-16). With this he always associated his apostleship (I Cor. 9.1; Cf. 15.8). In II Cor. 5.16, he gives the impression that once he regarded Christ from a human point of view. Did Paul meet Jesus when he was educated at Jerusalem under Gamaliel? This reference could be to the tradition the church received from Jesus Christ, which Paul inherited when he became the disciple of Christ. The reference in I Cor. 9.1 to 'Have I not seen Jesus our Lord?' could be to his meeting the risen Christ on the road to Damascus. The reference in I Cor. 15.8 about the risen Christ's appearances which he narrated beginning with Cephas

(Peter) down to James, the Lord's brother, he places himself at the last for Christ's appearances referring to the Damascus road appearance.

After his Damascus road experience, he was led to the disciples at Damascus where Ananias prayed for him, when his sight was restored. According to Acts 9.19, Paul was baptized in the fellowship at Damascus and he left from there.

E. PAUL'S ACTIVE MINISTRY

I. Prior to his active ministry

According to Gal. 1.17, Paul left for Arabia, which some identify with the Nabatean kingdom of Transjordan of Aretas IV, most probably for solitude from the Jewish opposition to meditate and prepare for the future ministry. After returning from there, Paul spent three years at Damascus where he was baptized (Gal. 1.18) which could be A.D. 36-37. This period corresponds with "Considerable time" referred to in Acts 9.23.

Paul began to witness boldly to the Jews there which led to their opposition supported by king Aretas IV of Damascus (II Cor. 11.32). So Paul left the city. He went to Jerusalem the first time after his conversion (Acts 9.26; Gal.1.18). It must be around A.D. 40.

It was Barnabas who introduced Paul to believers there at Jerusalem (Acts 9.27). He met Cephas and others and the Hellenist Jews plot against him made him to leave to his native city Tarsus (Acts 9.30; Gal. 1.21). From A.D. 40 to 44, Paul seems to have stayed there as nothing is known about him. It was Barnabas who went and took him to Antioch where they stayed a whole year (Acts 11.25-26).

During this time, a prophet named Agabus from Jerusalem announced the impending famine there (Acts 11.28). This could be the widespread famine that affected the eastern Mediterranean region during the reign of Claudius in A.D. 46. So Paul took the collection to Jerusalem (Acts 11.29-30; 12.25). As Luke has several council visits of Paul, and as we do not find this in Galatian account, all we can say is that this visit must have been a very brief one and he must have returned to Antioch.

From now on Paul and Barnabas were commissioned by the church at Antioch to launch on their missionary travels which covers the period A.D. 46-58.

II. **Paul's active ministry: From the book of Acts:**

    a. Acts 7.1ff. – The martyrdom of Stephen 9.1-31 – Paul's conversion. His visions tallied with that of Ananias.

    b. **The spread of the Gospel**

        i. From Antioch to Asia Minor (Acts 11.26).

        ii. Christians got the name here (Acts 11.26).

        iii. Relief sent to Jerusalem through Paul etc. (Acts 11.27-30) from Macedonia (II Cor. 8.3).

    c. **Spread of the Gospel to Macedonia and Greece: (Acts 16.1- 19, 20)**

       1. Acts 16.4-40 :   Gospel to Philippi.

       2. Acts 17.1-15 :   Gospel to Thessalonica and Beroea.

       3. Acts 18.1-28 :   Paul at Corinth.

       4. Acts 19.1-20 :   Paul at Ephesus and Asia Province.

    d. **Paul's desire to take the Gospel to Rome realized: (Acts 19.21-28,31)**

       1. Acts 19.21-20.38 : Paul set out for Palestine.

       2. Acts 21.1-14 : From Miletus to Caesarea.

       3. Acts 21.15-23.35 : Paul at Jerusalem.

       4. Acts 24.1-26.32 : Paul taken prisoner to Caesarea.

       5. Acts 27.1-28.31 : Paul taken prisoner to Rome.

The book of Acts was regarded by some as actually an account of Paul's conversion and his missionary activities. The author, a close companion of Paul: the 'We' Sections (Acts 16.10-17; 20.5-15; 21.1-18; 27.1-28.16) show that as these 'We' sections come in the latter half of the book, some hold that 1-12 chapters is a sort of introduction to the book taken chiefly from Peter. We have to note that it is not a biography of Paul. Paul was emphatic that he was the chief apostle to the Gentiles.

From Acts, we find that the Gospel spread only to Samaria and the Sharon valley prior to Paul.

Prior to Paul: It was Philip, one of the seven Deacons, who spearheaded the Gospel to these two regions followed by Peter and John.

Acts 8.4-13	:	Philip takes the Gospel to Samaria.
Acts 8.14-25	:	Peter and John at Samaria.
Acts 8.40	:	Shows Philip at Azotus to Caesarea.

(Acts 21.8-9 shows Philip being settled here with his 4 daughters). Acts9.32-10.1ff. Peter at Lydda (9.32), at Joppa (9.36), at Caesarea (10.1ff.). (This was the coastal Sharon valley region).

Chapter -2

Paul's Three Mission Journeys

A. PAUL'S FIRST MISSIONARY JOURNEY (ACTS 13-14 CHAPTERS) A.D. 46- 48.

From Antioch (of Syria) by sea to Salamis and Paphos (of Cyprus) to Perga (of Pamphylia) by land to Antioch (of Pisidia) to Iconium, Lystra, and Derbe (of Lycaonia).

B. PAUL'S SECOND MISSIONARY JOURNEY (ACTS 15.39-18.22) A.D. 49-52.

From Jerusalem from land route to Antioch (of Syria) to Tarsus (of Cilicia to Derbe, Lystra and Iconium (of Lycaonia) to Troas (of Mysia), by sea to Philippi and by land to Thessalonica and Beroea (of Macedonia), by sea to Athens and by land to Corinth (of Greece), by sea to Ephesus (of Asia) and by sea via Rhode island to Caesarea and Jerusalem (of Palestine).

C. PAUL'S THIRD MISSIONARY JOURNEY (ACTS 18.22-21.16) A.D. 53-57

From Antioch (of Syria) by land to Tarsus, Iconium, Ephesus, Thessalonica, Corinth, then back to Thessalonica, Philippi, Troas, Assos, Mitylene, Cos, Rhodes, Patara, Paphos, Tyre, Ptolemais, Caesarea and Jerusalem.

These three missionary journeys cover the four Roman provinces: Galatia, Asia, Macedonia and Achaia. In a sense, Paul made Christianity a world religion and we can say he was one of the most successful evangelists of the Gospel and also a great strategist.

The Missionary Methods of Paul

1. He worked within the Roman empire – from Galatia (next to his own province Cilicia). The Roman administration, the Greek

civilization, travel facilities on commercial routes helped spreading the Gospel.

2. He established centres (2 or 3) in each province like Corinth in Achaia, of Ephesus in Asia Minor etc. From there, he spread the Gospel to the whole province (Rom. 15.19).

3. Paul did miracles (5 times recorded – Acts 14.3, 8-18; 16.18;19.11-12; 20.9-1) not to win converts though he did, but as the manifestation of the power of the Holy Spirit.

4. He preached convincingly

   i. *at Antioch of Pisidia*: The Jews as divinely ordained for the preparation for the Gospel (Acts 13.16ff.).

   ii. *at Lystra*: the crucifixion of Jesus is the result of the rejection of the Jews(Acts 14.15-17).

   iii. *at Athens*: Forgiveness to all who receive the Gospel but judgment on those who reject it (Acts 17.22-31).

5. In each place he won converts, he planted churches in baptizing them and ordaining elders to be in-charge of that fellowship (I Cor. 1.14,16; Acts 18.8 etc.).

6. Of the three missionary journeys from A.D. 46 to 58, his actual time for the travels was only three years. He had long halts, like around two years at Corinth (1 ½ years the first time and around three months, the second time (Acts 18.11; 19.8) and two years at Ephesus (Acts 19.10) etc.

If we include up to A.D. 64, till the time of his death, we find that of the 20 years in active ministry, if we minus the three years actual travel, 17 years are left. What was he doing in these years?

The answer is that he was organizing the churches, in instructing them in the basic doctrines of the Christian faith, by writing letters and advising them on practical issues.

This shows that for every year of his travel, he was spending six years in organizing those churches he established. This shows that though many missionaries won more converts than Paul, yet none planted or organized churches like Paul. In this lies Paul's successful mission endeavours. He always toured in company and thus, drew strength to cope with the struggles and stress, and to be joyous.

Chapter -3

Paul's Sufferings for the Sake of the Gospel Proclamation (II Cor. 11. 23-28)

1. *5 times* he was given – 39 lashes.

2.. *3 times* beaten with rods.

3. *One time* – he was *stoned*. The opponents dragged him out of the city of Lystra, thinking he was dead, but when the disciples gathered around he got up (Acts 14.19-20).

4. *3 times* ship wrecked (The last was when Paul was sent from Caesarea by Festus, the Governor of Caesarea (Acts 27.39ff.). They swam to the island and later knew it was Malta south of Italy shore (Acts 28.1).

5. A night and day – adrift at sea.

6. Dangers faced in his journeys – by land and rivers and sea.

    A. i. From robbers.

        ii. From Gentiles.

        iii. From the Jews

        iv. From false brethren

    B. i. Danger in wilderness.

        ii. Danger at the city

        iii. Danger at the sea

7. Physical and mental strains.

        i. Sleepless nights.

        ii. In hunger and thirst.

        iii. In cold and exposure.

        iv. Daily pressure in anxiety about all the churches.

8. Paul was let down in a basket through a window at the Damascus city fort wall to escape from the hands of the governor under king Aretas (Acts 11.32).

9. Paul's boast: He says he will boast of the things that show his weakness or sufferings (Acts 11.30).

Paul says that a great endurance is needed for those in the Christian ministry: 9 trials listed here, which are classified into 3 categories by one of the N.T. Scholars.

I. i.   Afflictions - Physical, mental and spiritual pressures.

ii. Hardships – physical.

iii. Calamities – in different situations.

II. There are second group of difficult situations created by the people.

i.   Beatings (11.24).

ii. Imprisonment (Acts 16.23 etc.).

iii. Uprisings or tumults (Acts 13.55; 14.5).

III. The third group of hardships is for the sake of the Gospel spreading and the resulting establishment of Christian fellowships.

i.   Physical and mental hardships in labours.

ii. Sleepless or restless nights (Acts 20.31).

iii. Hungry, at times starving etc.

We in return can see the *spiritual qualities of Paul*, which enabled him to endure these above hardships.

1. *Holy life* with single-minded purpose in the ministry.

2. Holding to the *Truth* of the Gospel – the knowledge.

3. *Forbearance* in terms of not easily provoked to fight.

4. With *kindness* (*forbearance* associated) (Gal. 2.22; I Cor. 13.4).

5   The gift or quality of Christian life aided by the Holy Spirit.

6. *The righteousness resulting quality of life.*

vs. 8-10: Paul's enemies in the ministry

i.   As *"unknown"* or "he is not worth noticing" (*yet* "well known" in truth).

ii. As *"dying"* i.e., "he is finished", (*yet* "keep on serving") (Acts 14.19).

iii. As one *"punished"* (*yet* "always rejoicing in the *Lord*") (Rom. 8.3f.; Phil.4.4).

iv. As "poor" yet

    a. "making many rich in divine knowledge" (Eph. 3.14; Phil. 3.7f.).

    b. "Possessing everything" (I Cor. 3.2ff; Rom. 8.17 etc.).

Chapter - 4

Paul's Espistles (Or) Letters

From Christ's ascension, around A.D. 30; after conversion in A.D.36, after which could be the time for the commencement of Paul's ministry around A.D. 46. We know that Paul was beheaded in A.D. 64 at Rome, after two years of imprisonment there. So Paul ministered around 20 years from A.D. 46-64.

Paul fought to emancipate the Gospel from the narrow confines of the Jewish nation. But for Paul, Christianity would have been a mere sect of the Jewish religion and would have died within a few centuries. Paul made Christianity a world religion. Some even say that the real founder of Christianity was Paul, though Christ ushered it into this world. He was as a Bengali said, like Vivekananda to Ramakrishna Paramahansa for the Ramkrishna Mission.

We find that only three years were spent for the three missionary actual travel. He had long stops at various centres for teaching, writing letters etc.

1. **Acts 18.11:** Paul spent 1 year 6 months at Corinth.

    Acts 19.8: Paul spent 3 months again at Corinth.

2. **Acts 19.10:** 2 years at Ephesus.

The epistles of Paul are divided traditionally into **three categories**:

a. The General Epistles,

b. The Prison Epistles,

c. The Pastoral Epistles.

The theological emphasis is different from each group: The Generals deal with Christology while the Pastorals deal with Ecclesiology. The General epistles trace their origin to Corinth and few other centres, while the Prison epistles from Rome (Philippians may be from Ephesus, if so they date much earlier, around A.D. 50), and the Pastoral epistles from three different centres (Titus may be from Ephesus). Along with the dates, we can show in the following table about these three categories of epistles:

Sr. No.	Name of the Letter	Date	Group	Origin	Theological Emphasis
a.	Galatians	48	General	Antioch	Soteriological & Eschatological
b.	1st and 2nd Thessalonians	50	General	Corinth	– do –
c.	1st and 2nd Corinthians	55	General	1st Ephesus and 2nd Macedonia	– do –
d.	Romans	57	General	Corinth	– do –
e.	Ephesians	60 or 62	Prison	Rome	Christological
f.	Colossians	-do-	-do -	-do-	-do-
g.	Phelemon	-do-	-do-	-do-	-do-
h.	Philippians	63 or 50	-do-	Rome or Ephesus	do
i	Timothy	62	Pastoral	Macedonia	Esclesiological
j.	Titus	62	-do-	Corinth (or Ephesus)	-do-
k.	2nd Timothy	64	-do-	Rome	-do-

Those who put Ephesian origin of 1st Corinthians and Philippians, give the date at an early time to A.D.50. For Titus, the date is almost the same, around A.D. 62 but some give the origin to Ephesus instead of Corinth.

F.F. Bruce makes the following tentative groupings of these letters:

Group I:

Galatians.... written from Antioch (of Syria), A.D. 48.

I and II Thessalonians ... from Corinth A.D. 50.

Group II:

I Corinthians and Philippians .... from Ephesus A.D. 50.

II Corinthians (10-13 chapters) ....from Ephesus A.D. 55.

                    (1-9 chapters) .... from Macedonia A.D.55 or 56.

Romans ... from Corinth A.D. 57.

Group III:

Colossians ... from Rome A.D. 60 or 61.

Philemon ... from Rome A.D. 60 or 61.

Ephesians ... from Rome A.D. 60 or 61.

Group IV:

Titus ... from Ephesus after A.D. 62.

I Timothy ... from Macedonia after A.D. 62.

II Timothy ... from Rome A.D. 64.

Of course, F.F.Bruce points out the questions that arise with regard to such placing, like the position of Galatians among the letters of Paul, the arrangement of the Corithians correspondence, the date and province of the Captivity epistles (Phil., Eph., Col., and Phlm.), even the authenticity of Ephesians and the pastoral epistles (I and II Tim. and Titus).

The letters of Paul are 13, out of the 27 New Testament books. This shows half of the number of N.T. writings and ¼ of the volume of writing in the N.T. is ascribed to Paul. The majority of these letters were written far before the gospels were put into writing. Thus, Pauline letters carry the original action or sayings of Jesus, for Mark supposed to be the earliest Gospel was written around A.D. 70 after Paul's death, while Paul wrote his first epistle in A.D. 48 (Galatians). The best example of the reference to the earliest tradition was the institution of the Last Supper given in I Cor. 11.23ff. The epistle to the Hebrews, being traditionally ascribed to Paul was bound up with Pauline letters since 3rd century but now it is no longer so associated.

Letter writing was a slow process in ancient times. Paul used amanuenses, and the fact that an individual style being found in Paul's letters, shows that he dictated them. Only Tertius' name we know of the scribes Paul used (Rom. 16.22). It is assumed that the frequency with which Timothy's name occurs in his letters and greetings, he might have been used often as one of the amanuenses by Paul (II Cor; Phil; Col., I and II Tim.,Philm.).

As these letters were not intended for publication, naturally they were intended for whom they were addressed. At times, Paul develops careful argument in a calm mood, or at times he erupts into a torrent of thought. We do find that some of his letters were exchanged (Col. 4.16 etc.).

Chapter - 5

Paul and the Gospel of the Primitive Church

Jesus Christ preached of the Kingdom of God, while Paul made the Death, Resurrection, and the Exaltation of Jesus, the subject of his preaching (I Cor. 1.18; Acts 17.18 etc.). Some say that Paul was the real founder of Christianity we have today and but for Paul, Christianity would have been a sect within Judaism and not the world-wide religion it is today.

It is pointed out that Paul does not make the slightest effort to expound the teachings of Christ. He makes no reference to the Jesus, the Rabbi from Nazareth, or as a prophet or as the one who did so many miracles during his ministry. Nor does Paul refer to Jesus' association with the tax-collectors, sinful people etc. He does not refer to the famous so-called Sermon on the Mount (Matt. 5-7 chapters), or the innumerable parables Jesus used in his preaching (Matt. 13 and Mk. 4 chapters). Nor does he refer to the constant hostility of the Jewish leaders and his encounters with the Pharisees and Scribes, over the interpretation of the Mosaic Law; Paul does not even mention the Lord's Prayer which Jesus taught at the request of his disciples.

Paul's Gospel (I Cor.4.15) is filled with Jewish ideas and Hellenistic mythologies. It is true that to the Post-Easter Church, the death and Resurrection of Christ is the starting point of their proclamation as distinguished from the teachings of Jesus Christ. Jesus' life assumed greater dimensions than his proclamation, in the early Church. The same shift we find in Paul.

Paul does quote from the words of Christ in his letters:

I Cor. 7.10f   :   the wife should not separate from the husband.

I Cor. 9.14   :   to get their living for preaching the Gospel.

| I Cor. 11.23ff | : | the institution of the Last Supper. |
| I Thess. 4.15 | : | we who are alive shall not precede those who have fallen asleep. |

At least these two epistles (I Thess. and I Cor.) were the earliest ones (A.D. 50 and 54), and Paul must have a fresh memory of what he heard about Jesus and his teachings from other disciples; so from memory he quotes. Paul knows only a certain amount of tradition about Jesus. If Christ's ascension took place around A.D.30 and Paul's conversion, around A.D 36, he must have missed the historical Jesus by 6 years. It is possible that when he was at the feet of Gamaliel at Jerusalem, prior to his conversion he must have heard about him, for Jesus ministered chiefly in the northern province of Galilee, and came only to Jerusalem for his final week of ministry and his passion. Paul might not have met Jesus except at the time of the encounter with the risen Christ on the road to Damascus (I Cor. 15.5-8).

On this basis that Paul never met Jesus in person, he tells in II Cor. 5.16 that "he regarded Jesus no longer from a human point of view". In a sense, the historical Jesus was replaced by a divine mythological being. Is it the same way the historians turn the great historical figures emphasizing their moral and religious concepts? As the faith of the primitive Church was based on the Post-Calvary and Post-Easter incidents, naturally it was the death and resurrection of Jesus which gave the impetus to convey to the world, what Jesus has accomplished for man's salvation.

In the second instance, we notice that the Gentile church which came into existence through the labours of Paul and his colleagues had in a sense taken over the Jewish believers' church, centered at Jerusalem and gave its character to Christianity. Thus, there was a shift, from the Jewish Christian early church, to the Pauline church in terms of the understanding of the Law. God's dealings with the Jews and Gentiles.

To some extent, the nature of Pauline Christology is the result of his own personal experience (Rom. 7 and Gal. 2). Paul does quote the O.T. and the church's tradition, and that of his own day (I Cor. 15.3ff, 11.23 etc.).

In Romans (Rom. 1.16-17), we get Paul's emphasis on the Gospel of justification by faith. There is an apocalyptic note in the finality of God's call in Christ, and in the present it has already dawned. His doctrine was given in detail in Galatians, Romans and Philippians, though the basic theme worked out logically in Romans. In contrast, we do not find the primitive church, treating its faith this way. Paul seems to combine the Christological concepts from the tradition of the primitive church and moulding it in the light of his own personal experience, along with the Soteriological understanding of his own interpretation. This he proclaims as the Gospel.

Chapter - 6

Paul's Attitude Towards the Law

Paul held firmly to the theme that righteousness is attained only by the grace of God and through faith. Law cannot make a man righteous (Rom. 1.18-3.20-31).

Paul grew up as a Jew under the law, but after his Damascus experience he came to a new understanding of salvation through Jesus Christ. His changed attitude towards the law did not discard the law.

We see that Jesus Christ also gave a new interpretation of the Mosaic Law, but he did not give up the law. He said that he came to fulfill the law (Matt. 5.17). It is to bring to perfection or finality what the law contained. In a similar way, Paul spoke of establishing the law, for it is the oracle of God (Rom.7.12, 16). He even holds that the law is spiritual (Rom.7.14). It is said that as a Jew, Paul understood that men should keep the law in order that they might be saved, but now as a Christian he understood that men must be saved that they might keep the law (Ander-Scott).

The Mosaic Law to Paul was spiritual if it can be obeyed. The chief work of the law is not to give salvation but to reveal sin: "if it has not been for the law, I would not have known sin" (Rom.3.20). So the true function of the law is moral informer. The moral demand of God is essential for human conduct, or else there will be chaos.

To Paul, the law not only reveals sin but also promotes sin. When the law prohibited something, it became a challenge for man to commit it. Mosaic Law promised life to those who observe it (Lev.18.5). But in the personal experience, Paul found that what was intended for life brought death: "The very commandment which promised life proved to be death to me" (Rom.7.10,13; I Cor. 15.56; II Cor. 3.7-9).

Paul did not say that law begets sin. In that case God who is the author of the law would be the cause for sin. Sin was present before the coming of the law and when the law came, it identified it as sin and in this way a sense of guilt was created through the law. This was quite the opposite of the traditional Jewish view, in that it restrained man from expedient which was superseded by Christ. Thus Christ puts an end to the law's reign.

To Paul, the law found its fulfillment in Christ (Rom.10.4; Gal.4.4). Paul used as illustration, the existing practice of slave tutors for the children of the well-to-do people, when he wrote, "The Law was our custodian until Christ came" (Gal. 3.24). Just as the children, when they come to the adult age dispense with the custodian slave, so too with the revelation of Jesus Christ. In effect, the law was in preparation for the coming of Christ.

According to the Rabbinical tradition, that God reached Moses through the angels when he gave the law, or else Moses would have died on the spot, for no man can see God and live (Ex.33.20; Is.6.5). To Paul, this indirect mode of revelation of the law showed its inferiority, which was thus replaced by a superior direct revelation of God in Jesus Christ. Freedom from law was attained through faith in Christ, for Christ is the end of the law (Rom. 10.4).

In Rom. 2.12-17, Paul refers to three periods in human history:
  i.   **The first one** from Adam to Moses which was prior to the giving of the law. So there was no law then.
  ii. **In the second period** from Moses to Christ, the law reigned and the imputation of transgression was put to men.
  iii. **In the third period** from Christ onwards, which put an end to the law as Christ was the perfection of the law (Gal. 3.24).

Chapter - 7

Justification by Faith

JUSTIFICATION

The Greek word for "justification" is "Dikaiosis", and the verb "Dikaiao" to "justify" occurs 15 times in the epistles of Romans and Galatians. It is a metaphor from the Law courts where a person at the end was acquitted from the charge of a crime. It is also translated as "righteousness" from the Greek word "Dikaiosune". It is God's righteousness to declare a man righteous or just, on the basis of what Christ has done on our behalf.

It is justification by faith, that is, when a person believes in Christ he is declared just on the basis of the atoning work done by Christ Jesus. This expresses God's grace for man and is opposed to the Jewish idea of justification by works, in observing the commandments of God. God forgives the sinner and like in the law courts, declares him acquitted of all his or her crimes. What is important to believe here is, that a man through faith in Christ is regarded a just person in spite of his sin (Phil. 3.8-9).

It does not mean that sin is condoned. On the other hand, God's justice demands that sin be punished. For this, on behalf of man, the Son of God by becoming man has paid the penalty for sin by his death on the Cross through his blood. So it is a costly payment to set us free from sin (Rom.5.9). By faith man appropriates what Christ has done for him. By this we understand that **the work of salvation is entirely divine and by grace**. Man only responds to this divine grace by faith. This is justification by faith according to Paul. So this is a gift of God and not a reward of man's works.

The O.T. understanding of God as the stern judge has the basic premise that all are sinners, for no one can be just before God (Ps. 143.2). In such a situation only God can pardon sinners, for man sins against God's laws.

Though God was the judge, yet in the O.T. he showed favour to the Israelites without condoning their sins. This was the hope of Israel that one day in the future, a Redeemer or Messiah would come to establish justice of God in the world (Is.59.15-20). Paul shows that in Christ this expectation was fulfilled.

Redemption

In Rom.3.24, Paul speaks of the other term "redemption" from the Greek word "Apolutrosis". Here also, we find Paul, using another metaphor which is of the slave market. By paying the slave price "**lutron**", the "**ransom**", a slave is freed from his bondage. Similarly, it is liberation for man from the bondage of sin.

In the O.T. we find that the Hebrews were freed from the Egyptian bondage. This was seen as the redeeming of Israel by their God (Is.41.14;43.14 etc.) and their freedom was the redemption (Ex.15.16; Is.43.21). In a similar manner, Paul refers that we are bought with a price like the ransom money, the blood of Christ (I Cor.6.20; 7.22). To Paul, God is the Redeemer and Christ is the redemption (I Cor.1.30). Though redemption is offered freely, yet a costly price was paid by Christ on man's behalf. So the atoning work of Christ is seen as **substitutionary** on behalf of man (Titus 2.14). Paul regarded the Law, Sin and Death as hostile forces which were overcome by Christ.

The question of **to whom the price was paid** engaged the early church fathers quite a bit, whether to Satan, and how Christ redeemed man from the bondage of Satan (Irenaeus, Origen etc.,). Even the **illustration of angling** was used by Gregory of Nazyanzus to show how with a hook inside the bait, the fish was caught, so too Christ caught Satan by overcoming death by his divinity, like the hook behind his humanity. But if man sinned against God, as sin is different from the crime, naturally Anselm argued that it was to God the price has to be paid, for the reconciliation has to be with God. But then other church leaders questioned the very idea of "payment" and showed that what is important, is that the justice of God was satisfied by Christ's obedience and in Christ man was forgiven.

Expiation

In Rom. 3.25, Paul talks of Christ offering of His blood as "expiation" for our sake from the Greek word "hilasterion". Some translate "hilasterion" as "propitiation" which gives the wrong idea that God has to be pacified from his anger with us. The A.V. used that term in English.

The Greek O.T., called the Septuagint translated Hebrew "kipper" as "hilasterion". "Kipper" refers to the "mercy seat" in the Tabernacle or the Temple at Jerusalem. It carries the idea of "covering" of sins, as used in the O.T. purification rites (Lev. 8.15; 9.15). Paul's idea seems to be, that just as the blood of the sacrificial victims covered or cleansed the sins of the worshippers at the temple sacrifices, likewise the blood of Christ cleanses us from our sins.

So we, in faith, appropriate what God has done for us in terms of forgiving our sins through the shed blood of Christ on our behalf.

Chapter - 8

The Concept of God

Paul has the Jewish background of *monotheism*, that God is one and no other gods beside him, which is the first commandment (Ex.20.1ff.). God is also the *Creator*, that the whole universe owes its existence to him, as it is the created matter (organic like living beings; the inorganic or the dead matter) it is different from God (Gen.1.3ff.). The *transcendence* of God, is one high above. Even some Rabbis held that God could not have come in contact with the sinful world; as such it was his Sekhenah, or his presence which was directly involved in creation of this world; and not God himself, similar to the Gnostic views that matter is less good and God being spirit is good, and so could not come in contact with this world. To the Jew the *holiness* of God was behind such views (Is.31.1f.).

God was also seen in *anthropomorphic* terms and expressing his *emotions* like that of a human being either positive or negative traits, yet God was contrasted with man as quite different, 'in that he is spirit and not flesh like humans' (Is. 31.3; Hos.11.9). On the basis of transcendence and being spirit, representation of God in terms of creatures, the Jews were prohibited to make (Ex. 20.2ff.). In *relation to the Jewish people*, God was the *Redeemer*. *God* since the time he redeemed them from the *Egyptian bondage*, yet being a *God of justice* he demands that they fulfill the covenant obligations or else his wrath will fall on them, in meeting out his judgment at present and on the final day (Amos 8.9ff. etc.).

On this above background, Paul, makes the necessary adaptations in the context of the Christ-event and brings out his views about God. It is in the *context of Jesus Christ* that God is revealed to human beings, the God who is the *creator* and *sovereign* of the whole universe.

It was Jesus Christ, the *agent of creation* (I Cor. 8.6; Eph. 3.9; Col.1.15 etc.). Though God is holy, yet it is the Holy Spirit which was ascribed this holiness, to be called "the Holy Spirit", one of the persons of the Triune God (Rom. 8.13-17).

God is held as *holy* and of justice for which Christ has to die on our behalf. This *substitutionary* act was ascribed in the analogies of the *law courts* and *slave markets* (Rom.3.25etc.). So sin was not condoned but paid for with the precious life of God's own Son. In this, God *as redeemer* was brought out and Christ was the redemption (Rom.5.6-9). The *wrath of God* which should have fallen upon us is now no longer a thing to be afraid of (Rom.3.5, 5.9 etc.).

Like the teaching of Christ about the *fatherhood* of God, Paul also brought out the *love of God* shown in Jesus Christ for the sinners (Rom. 5.8etc.). For this Paul addressed God as the Father (Gal.1.3; Eph.1.2; II Thess. 1.2 etc.). The believers are adopted to be the *sons* and *joint heirs* with Jesus Christ into the family of God (Rom. 8.14, 17; Gal. 4.5-7; Eph.1.5 etc.).

The *Sovereignty* of God is expressed in the analogy of "the potter and the clay" used by prophets like Jeremiah, Isaiah et.al. in the Old Testament (Jer.18.5ff; Is. 29.16) The emphasis was in *relation to the saving act* of God, though the negative side also shows up. Terms like *predestination* (five times of the six times in the entire N.T. was used by Paul (Rom. 8.20,30; I Cor. 2.7; Eph. 1.5,11), *foreknowing* (Rom. 8.29; 11.2 etc.), *elect* or to *choose* or *call* (Eph. 1.4; I Thess. 1.4; Rom.1.7, 8.28 etc.) to be God's people, adoption to sonship (Rom.8.14-17; Eph.1.5 etc.) are used to convey that history moves according to God's will and purpose and God carries out his plan of salvation of mankind (Eph. 1.9-11 etc.).

God's sovereign will is revealed *in Jesus Christ* in showing his gracious intentions in man's salvation (Rom.1.16-17; I Cor. 2.20; II Cor. 12.7). This was a mystery from ages ago, but now revealed to Paul directly (Gal. 1.12 etc.), and so also to the church.

Chapter - 9

Jesus Christ

If the date of the conversion of Paul was put around A.D. 36, then Paul must have missed Jesus by six years, if the date of Jesus' ascension was put at A.D. 30. Paul knows only a certain amount of tradition about Jesus. The first Thessalonians (A.D. 50) and first Corinthians (A.D.54) were held to be the earliest epistles of Paul which only preserve references to the *historical Jesus*, chiefly *his sayings* (I Cor.7.10f., 9.14,11.23; I Thess. 4.15 etc). These preserve what Paul heard from the other disciples and had fresh memory by then. As Paul never met Jesus in person, he tells in II Cor. 5.16 that "he regarded Jesus no longer from a human point of view".

As the faith of the early church was based on the post-Calvary and post-Easter experience of the *risen Christ*, naturally the death and resurrection of Christ was prominent in their preaching. Paul too takes it up in the same way, to convey to the world what Jesus had accomplished for man's salvation. In a sense, the historical Jesus was replaced by a divine mythological being. The Damascus experience of Paul's conversion added to this fact that it was the risen Christ whom he met (Acts 9.1-9; I Cor. 15.5-8).

The *humanity of Jesus* on the other hand, Paul did not reject. Rather, he maintained that Jesus was born of a woman (Gal. 4.4), and he physically descended from David (Rom. 1.3; II Tim. 2.8). He referred to Jesus as the real paschal lamb slain for the sin of mankind (I Cor. 5.7). As such, Jesus' physical body was necessary for the work of redemption (Phil. 2.7; II Cor. 8.9). As it was a sinless victim needed for the sacrifice, so Jesus committed no sin and was without sin (II Cor. 5.21; Rom. 8.3), though he came in the likeness of sinful flesh. He came as man to undo the work and consequences of Adam's disobedience. In this Jesus was referred to as the Second Adam (I Cor. 15.21; Rom. 5.15 etc.).

The *deity of Jesus* was the dominant theme in Paul's writings. Paul wrote that God was in Christ (II Cor. 5.19), and the fullness of Godhead resided in him bodily (Col. 2.9). As such, Jesus was the revelation of the nature and the being of God on earth (Col. 1.15f.).

Titles like *"Son of God"* and *"Lord'"* were used by Paul to express the deity of Jesus, which were already in use in the early church. In referring to Jesus, Paul did not identify Jesus, the Son of God, the same as God. The fact is, that he came from Judaism which held to strict monotheism. Paul maintained the distinctiveness of the three persons in the Godhead and yet one God. This Trinitarian formula, we find clear expression in Rom.8.9-11. A *certain amount of subordination* is noticeable in Paul's writings (I Cor. 3.21ff., 11.3;15.28 etc.), but this has to be understood in the sense of *obedience* of the *earthly Jesus*, the Son, to God, the Father. There was oneness between them.

The other term *"Lord"* which was used for God in the Old Testament as the Greek version of Hebrew "Adonai" in the Septuagint, was now applied to Jesus in addressing him by the early church. Paul himself addressed the risen Christ as "Lord" when he met him on the road to Damascus (Acts 9.3ff.). The Lordship refers to the *sovereignty of God* and so now that of Jesus, both over the created world and of his people (Rom. 10.9; 14.9; II Cor. 4.5; Eph.4.3 etc.). On the whole it expresses the *deity of Christ* (Rom. 10.9; I Cor. 12.3; Phil.2.9; I Tim.2.15 etc.). This designation occurs 114 times in the writings of Paul, and with the name Jesus Christ 95 times.

Paul even uses the term "God" or "our God" for Jesus Christ (Rom.9.5;Titus 2.13, etc.) to identify Jesus as divine and God himself, who appears in human form for our salvation. The pre-existence of Christ and his divine essence, as one who descended from heaven and not just of human origin, is the basis for this expression.

Chapter - 10

The Holy Spirit

The Holy Spirit was received by the disciples after the ascension of the risen Christ (Acts 2.1ff.), as promised by Christ before his Passion and also after his resurrection (Jn. 14.7f., Acts 1.8 etc.). In the fourth Gospel in the teaching of Christ, it was very clear that Holy Spirit was distinct from Christ, and also in its function (Jn. 14.16-17; 15.26; 16.7-14). But in the epistles of Paul there is such an interchange between the *Holy Spirit and the spirit of Christ*, that sometimes it is hard to distinguish between the two (II Cor. 3.11; Rom. 8.9,11 etc.). So the question that was raised was "Is the Spirit actually the spirit of the risen Christ or distinct from him?"

Inspite of the fact that the Holy Spirit was referred to as the Counselor similar to Jesus, yet he was referred to as *"another Counselon"* (Jn. 14.16; 16.12ff.) in the Fourth Gospel so as to distinguish him from the person of Christ. Though the "Spirit" is used in *neuter* in Greek Language, yet we find that the *masculine pronouns* in the Greek "Ho" and "ekenos" (meaning "he") or the *relative pronoun* "Hos", used both by John in the *fourth Gospel* (Jn. 14.26, 16.14) *and by Paul* (Eph. 1.14 etc). This shows the Holy Spirit is a *person* . Though the Holy Spirit was never embodied in *flesh* like the Son, yet that does not mean he is not a person. Personality is the inner self which characterizes each one as an individual.

In tune with the ascription of personality, the Holy Spirit is shown having *personal characteristics* as seen from the letters of Paul; he *searches* the truth of God (I Cor. 2.10ff.); in distributing his gifts as he wills (I Cor. 12.11) shows that he possesses a *mind* of his own (Rom. 8.27); he has an *emotion* of his own in that he can be grieved (Eph. 4.30); he is *one of the three persons in the Triune God*, in that he *indwells* in the hearts of the believers with them (Rom. 8.9-11). The Trinitarian formula in the Christian benediction endorses this view (II Cor. 13.14). *Inspired* by the Spirit, we approach God as the Father through Jesus Christ, thus confirming the *Trinitarian belief* in God (Rom. 8.15; Gal. 4.6; Eph. 2.16).

The *functions* of the Holy Spirit, Paul clearly mentions in his epistles: Paul exhorted the Ephesians "be filled with the Spirit" (Eph. 5.18) meaning the *indwelling* function of the Spirit in the lives of the believers (Rom. 8.9; I Cor.12.7, etc.). The Holy Spirit acts as the *seal* of God in marking the believers as those who belong to God (Eph. 1.13; 4.10). He enables the believers to acknowledge Jesus Christ as Lord of their lives (I Cor. 12.3). The Holy Spirit *pledges* us or guarantees now of what we can expect later of the fullness of our inheritance with God (II Cor. 1.22; 5.5; Eph. 1.14 etc.). The Holy Spirit *distributes spiritual gifts* as he sees fit to the believers (I Cor. 12.4ff. etc.).

Paul categorises men according to the *reception of the Holy Spirit;* those who are *in the flesh* or natural men versus *those in the spirit* (Rom. 8.9-10; 12.13; Gal. 3.3-4; 5.16ff.). So the way of *life in spirit* is according to the will of God. As such these are the ones who receive the *sonship with* God the Father and who could address God *in intimate* terms like "Abba, Father" (Rom. 8.14-15; Gal.4.6 etc.). By this the believers are made *joint heirs* with Christ (Rom. 8.17; Gal. 4.7 etc.) *Love* is the basic ingredient of all activities of the believers and the source of this is traced to the working of the indwelling Holy Spirit (Rom. 5.5 etc.).

Chapter - 11

The Church

Paul regards the Church as the result of the response to the preaching of the Gospel (Rom.15.14-21). There is the Hebrew background where people called by God respond in action. The Hebrew term "Qahal" refers to this summoning (Lev. 10.17' I King. 8.4 etc.). The other is the Greek general term "Ecclesia" used for calling together the people of the city state for an assembly to discuss matters of the city state. The Septuagint (LXX) translated the Hebrew "Qahal" as "Ecclesia" in Greek. Paul uses it in the Hebrew background of "Qahal", when he calls the Church as the "Israel of God" in Gal. 6.16.

Etymologically, the English word "Church" is a modification of the Greek term "Kuriakon", which is translated as that belonging to the Lord or as the house of the Lord, for "Kurios" in Greek means the Lord and "Oikos" means house. So it was similar to the Jewish reference to the temple as the "house of God" (Is. 5.7; Jn. 8.35 etc.). As this Greek word traveled through Europe, the Germans modified it to "Kirche", the Dutch still changed it to "Kerk", the Scots to "Kirk", the English to "Church".

'Ecclesia' term was used 58 times in Pauline letters

Romans	-	5 times
I and II Corinthians	-	36 times.
Galatians	-	3 times
Ephesian	-	9 times.
Philippians	-	1 time
I and II Thessalonians	-	3 times.
Philemon	-	1 time.
Total	-	58

"Ecclesia" comes from two words: "Ek" – out "Kaleo" – to call.

Thus, it means "called out" people to a fellowship out of the world. The word "Saints" from the Greek word "Hagioi" (Rom. 1.7; 15.26; II Cor. 1.1 etc.) means the same as those set apart or consecrated for a holy task which term Paul uses for the believers.

So what was a general Greek term for the "assembly" of the citizens was applied for the fellowship by the followers of Christ. Eventually, by **connotation** it became a Christian term. Though in Matthew 16.18, it refers to the Christian term "Church", many N.T. Scholars think that the next use in Matt. 18.17 was listed in general terms. So by naming the Christians as the followers of Christ (Rom. 15.20), it takes on the Christian connotation.

The use of similar terms and analogies show that in the thinking of Paul and other early disciples, there exists a close relationship between the old Israel and the Church, so as to call the church as "the Israel of God" (Gal. 6.16). We also find in I Pet. 2.9, where the Christians were referred as the chosen race, holy nation, God's own people etc., which was used for Israel in the Old Testament (Ex.19.5; 7.6; 10.15; Is.43.20 etc.). In a similar way Paul refers to baptism as the circumcision of the Jewish rite, but of the heart and not of the flesh (Rom. 4.11; 9.6-8; Phil. 3.3). Likewise the use of the O.T. analogies like 'Son' (Ex. 4.24; Is.1.2; Jer. 31.9; Hos.11.1 etc.), we find Paul using for the believers (Rom.8.17, 23; Gal.4.5; Eph.1.5 etc.), or the use of the term "bride" for believers (Rom. 7.14; II Cor. 11.2 Eph. 5.22-32) which was common usage for Israel in the O.T. (Is. 54.5; Jer.3.8, 14,20; Hos.2.19-20 etc). All this shows the clear association of the Church with the O.T. Israel and the N.T. Israel, the Church, is that in the old Israel it was exclusively applied to the descendents of Jacob, to the twelve tribes of Israel. In the case of the N.T. Israel, it crosses such boundaries. To Paul the new community breaks down the racial, social and cultural barriers (Gal. 3.28; Col. 3.11 etc.). It is a fellowship of believers from both the Jews and Gentiles who become the fellow-heirs with Christ (Rom. 8.14-15; Eph. 3.6 etc.).

Paul has seen the *local family* in each place he went, as the nucleus to work with, for the formation of the local Church in that locality, like **'house churches'** of Priscilla and Aquila (Rom.16.3; II Cor.16.19), of Nympha (Col. 4.15), of Archippus (Phlm. 2. etc.). The reference to the church in the singular, identifying with a certain area comes under this category of local churches, like Church at Cenchrea (Rom. 16.1), at Corinth (I Cor. 1.2; II Cor. 1.1) at Thessalonica (I Thes. 1.1-2), at Colossi. 1.1 etc.).

Paul also sees the Church as the universal Church comprised of all believers (I Cor. 6.4; 12.29; Eph. 1.22; 3.10; 5.23, 27,32 etc.). Paul also refers to the group of churches in a locality, like churches in Judea (I Thess. 2.14), in Galatia (Gal. 1.2); in Asia (I Cor. 16.19); in Macedonia (II Cor. 8.1) etc.

Paul refers to the Church as the Body of Christ (I Cor. 12.27). The Greek term he uses for the body is "Soma" which refers to the whole person of Christ. The metaphor highlights the unity between believers and Christ, which becomes the basis for appeal to the members to act in harmony with one another (Phil. 2.2). This analogy Paul brings out after he has discussed the Lord's Supper (I Cor. 10.16-17; 11.17-34).

By this Paul tries to convey that unitedly the Church has to respond to Christ, her head (Col. 1.18) in carrying His mission in the world with the life-giving Spirit available from the risen Christ (Rom. 8.11 etc.). We have also analogies like the household (Rom. 8.23), the Temple building (I Cor. 6.16; Eph. 2.21 etc.), bride (Eph. 5.21-23; II Cor. 11.2 etc.), which all refer to the nature of the Church in its unity, dependence on Christ and its mission in the world.

Chapter - 12

The Last Things

The Jewish belief of the Day of Judgment was taken up by Paul, that at the end *God will* judge *mankind* according to *their works*. The term he used for this was the *Wrath of God*. His extensive use of this term is seen in 21 times as against the 15 times in the rest of the New Testament. It is in the first instance, the present retributive judgment for the rejection of Christ (Rom. 1.18) upon the unbelieving world. Paul also refers to the definite future time when this judgment of God takes place "the day of wrath" (Rom.2.5-6), when the wrath (or anger) of God falls on those who did evil deeds, for it will be according to their works.

At this time, the *"man of lawlessness"* will be revealed (II Thess. 2.4-8), who will deceive the people, even tempt the very elect by his miracles. This is in tune with that voiced forth by Christ himself about the anti-Christ (Mk. 13.14, 22). But at the Second Advent of Christ, he will destroy him (II Thess. 2.8).

In Romans, Paul was much concerned about the future state of Israel. Paul expresses great sorrow at the state of Israel that inspite of the many privileges it had, Israel rejected Christ (Rom. 9.1-5). Paul maintains their *disbelief* is *partial*, as already 'a remnant' believed in Christ (Rom. 11.1-10) and *temporary* (Rom. 11.11-24). At the end Paul hopes that all Israel will be saved, who will turn to Christ in faith when the Messiah will return, who will be the deliverer from Zion and who will remove ungodliness from them (Rom. 11.26).

In the epistles to Thessalonians, the major discussion was related to the believers who passed away before the Second Coming of Christ. In the first century itself the disciples expected that the *second coming of Jesus* would take place in that very generation (I Thess. 4.13-17; Jas.5.8 etc.).

This was probably based on Jesus' statement in Matt. 16.28. Many of the first generation of disciples began to pass away but the expected return of Christ had not taken place. So some of the early Christians were concerned as to what happens to the dead. Paul answers this question in I Thess. 4.13-17. In this context Paul talks about the resurrection of the saints followed by the translation of the living believers, who together will meet Christ in mid air. This is a special resurrection, the *rapture of the saints*. This is different from the general resurrection when every one had to stand before the judgment seat of Christ to answer to the deeds done during their life time (II Cor. 5.10). The belief in this special resurrection is rooted in the fact of the *resurrection of Christ*, who becomes the first fruits of those believers already dead, who will rise in their own order (I Cor. 15.20-23).

This is a radical belief Paul expressed here, though hinted at in the Old Testament but never as a definite doctrine. So some of the believers raised questions like "how are the dead raised?" or "with what kind of body do they come?" (I Cor. 15.35). Paul argues that as flesh and blood cannot inherit the kingdom of God (I Cor. 15.30), that the resurrected body will be a "spiritual body" or "glorious body" similar to that of the resurrected body of Christ Jesus (I Cor. 15.44; cf. Phil. 3.21; I Jn. 3.2 etc.).

Paul holds, that immediately after death the souls of the believers will be with the Lord, i.e., *to die is to be with Christ* (Phil. 1.23). That means that after death the *souls* of the believers will be in a *conscious state*. They will wait for the return of Christ for their resurrection, and then in the final judgment for their rewards.

Chapter -13
The Probable Time Frame

1. Paul's salvation - 32 A.D.
2. Paul in Arabia - 32-36 A.D.
3. Paul back at Tarsus - 36-42 A.D.
4. Antioch Church's Establishment - 44 A.D.
5. The 1st Mission Journey - 46-48 A.D.
6. The 2nd Mission Journey - 49-52 A.D.
7. The 3rd Mission Journey - 53-57 A.D.
8. Imprisonment in Caesarea - 57-59 A.D.
9. Imprisonment at Rome - 60-62 A.D.
10. Probable Release - 63-67 A.D.
11. Probable Re-arrest and Execution - 67 A.D.
12. Jerusalem Destruction - 70 A.D.

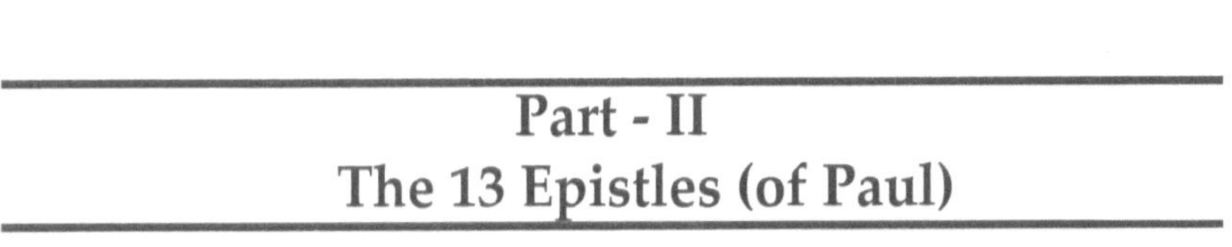

Part - II
The 13 Epistles (of Paul)

1
Romans

I. INTRODUCTION

A. The Occasion for Writing the Epistle

Romans (along with Galatians and to some extent Philippians) was a letter written (unlike the swift pouring of his emotional expressions like in Corinthians) in a calm mood where he develops his careful arguments as it deals with doctrinal matters.

Though Paul was using amanuensis to put in writing his thoughts, we do not have any record of who they were, except in Rom.16.22, the name of Tertius who also sends his greetings. In Rom.15.23b he informs that he longed to come to Rome, but so far he did not, because his motto was not to encroach into another's field of ministry where Christ had already been named, but to new fields (Rom.15.20).

Now he finds that not much room is left there for unevangelised areas (Rom.15.23a) and so he plans to have a preaching mission in Spain and enroute he wished to stop for a while at Rome (Rom.15.24). Paul did not start the church at Rome.

The epistle to Romans is said to have been written from Corinth around A.D. 57 on the 3rd mission journey of Paul. From Rom. 16.1 we find this letter was given to Phoebe, the deaconess at Cenchrea, the eastern sea port of Corinth, to carry it. Paul seems to be residing in the house of Gaius of Corinth (I Cor. 1.14) in whose house the Corinthian Christians met for fellowship (Rom.16.23).

Though Paul longed to stop at Rome on his way to Spain, yet he was not sure whether he would make it. He had to first take the collections to the poor at Jerusalem of the Achaian and Macedonian churches (Rom.15.25-26). Paul had his premonitions that

i.   He may be apprehended by the Jews in Judea

ii. He was not sure that he will be accepted by the believers at Jerusalem (Rom.15.31). So, only God be willing he can make it to Rome (Rom. 15.32). (As he feared he was arrested and his wish was fulfilled, though differently in being taken as a prisoner to Rome around A.D. 62 and where he was executed by the Roman Government in around A.D. 64, prior to which, for two years he met the believers at his rented house (Acts 28.30). Fearing he may not make it, Paul puts forth the Gospel he preached, justification by faith, which includes all.

B.   The Question of the Last Two Chapters

There seems to be two versions in circulation: One with 15th and 16th chapters with it and the other without these two chapters. (These two chapters refer to greetings and names of people and places): Some manuscripts omit the opening salutation location words "in Ephesus" (Eph. 1.1) as Ephesians was used as a circular letter to be read by all churches. If that be the case, it was also possible that the omission of the name "Rome" suggests, that what was originally intended for Rome was later used as a circular letter for the benefit of the churches associated with Paul's ministry.

The practice of letters meant for one church were being read by nearby churches, as we notice in the case of the Colossians letter. In Col. 4.16 Paul himself mentions that it be given, after reading, to the near by Laodicean church and like wise the Colossian church to read the Laodicean church letter.

So, it is possible that the original Roman's epistle with full 16 chapters was later circulated to other churches to be read, removing the last two chapters where personal allusions, and their greetings and the occasion for writing this letter to the Romans occur. At least we know that chapter 15.1-13 continues the subject matter of the previous chapter 14, to be part of the epistle. The insertion of doxology of Rom. 16.25-27 at the end of chapter 14 could be for rounding off the circular purpose, of what was originally intended for the Roman church with the full 16 chapters.

The arguments of the people like Priscilla and Aquila were at Ephesus when I Corinthians was written and later again (II Tim. 4.19), Epenetus (Rom.16.5) as the first fruits of Asia and Phoebe, coming from Cenchrea

(Rom. 16.1) make some to argue that the last two chapters originally belonged to the letter written to the Ephesians. We have to note on the other side that the references to the 'household of Aristobulus' who was the 'younger grandson of Narcissus' (Rom.16.10-11) were the Christian slaves of Claudius, the Emperor's famous Freedmen slaves in Rome, while Aquila and Priscilla came there due to the edict of Claudius in A.D. 50, and possibly that they visited again at the time of writing this epistle. All this shows that the association with Rome is as much there, as the arguments of these last chapters with Ephesus. The suggestion that the letter originally meant for Ephesus, got mixed up with the letter to the Romans on the way, does not hold much ground. Of course, we do have a section in Rom. 5.1-11 with the number of first person plural 'we' used, while the next Rom. 5.12-21 where it does not occur even once, while 'everyone' occurs many times. This could be, that what Paul had written originally to some other church, was inserted here into the Roman letter. Such possibility we can see here, but not in the last two chapters which are an integral part of the epistle, though some versions like the two manuscripts of the Vulgate seem to leave out the last two chapters in their chapter record.

C. The Church at Rome

If Paul did not establish the church at Rome, then who did? Eusebius of Caesarea, and also Jerome maintain that Peter was its bishop for around 25 years. We have internal evidence to it in the first epistle of Peter (5.13), where he refers to Rome in the symbolic name of 'Babylon'.

Clement of Rome expresses in his writings, of his association with Rome as early as A.D. 95. Peter was at the Jerusalem Council in A.D. 50 and if he left for Rome after that, probably after the death of James (Acts 12.1ff), then his time at Rome from A.D. 42-67 is not tenable. Also, the silence of Acts 28th chapter and Romans 16th chapter shows that at the time of writing Romans, A.D. 57, or Paul's imprisonment in A.D. 62, Peter does not seem to be there at Rome.

Certainly Peter was associated with Rome and also met his martyrdom there, as the tradition firmly holds, during his last days, but how long and when, we are not definite, though A.D. 42-67 was given as the date in early tradition.

Emperor Claudius in A.D. 50 had promulgated an edict to evict the Jews from Rome for the riots caused due to the issue over one 'Christus' which could be the Latin version for Christ, 'Christus'. Acts. 28.22 gives the impression that the Christians were mainly Gentile converts and of humble origin like the slaves mentioned as 'households' of Narcissus and Aristobulus established by the Eastern Christians coming into the capital of the empire. The eastern names in Rom.16th chapter bear ample evidence: Priscilla and Aquila (Rom. 16.3), Epenetus (Rom.16.5) etc.

D.   The Roman Emperors (P.43)

I.   Julius Caesar : He rules from 14 AD. He changed the calender from Lunar to Solar. He shifted the beginning of the year from March to January. The former fifth month, Filitus, to the seventh month and named after him - July. He also added one more day to it making it 31 days.

II.   Augustus: He came next and like Caesar he wanted the month following July named after him as August, the eight month. Like Caesar he wanted it to be of 31 days duration. Thus February had to lose two days to make up for these two extra days. He was for emperor worship.

III. Tiberius: He ruled from 15-37 AD. The sea of Galilee was named after him as Tiberius sea (Jn 6:1).

IV   Caligula: He ruled from 38-41 AD. He was considered a madman. He asked the Jews to do emperor worship

V   Claudius: He ruled from 41 - 54 AD. He exmepted the Jews from Caeasr worship. All he wanted was that the Jews should pray for him in their synagougues. We find due to the clashes over the 'Christos' issue he asked the Jews and Christians to leave Rome. That was the reason we find Aquila and Priscilla returning to Athens, next to Corinth (Acts 18: 1-2) and finally to Ephesus of Asia Minor (Acts 18:20)

VI. Nero: He regined from 54-68 AD. He was an eccentric man. Rome was burnt and the Christians were blamed for it. So the Roman persecution got to its pitch. The Christians were thrown to the wild beasts in the Roman stadiums and burnt as torches in the garden of Nero. Peter was supposed to be curicfied upside down and Paul executed during his time along with many others.

VII Vespian: He ruled from 69-79 A.D. He did not insist on the emperor worship.

VIII Titus: He ruled from 79-81 A.D. He also did not insist on the Caesar worship.

IX. Domitian: He ruled from 81-96 AD. He was the one who put John as an exile to Patmos island close to Ephesus. He demanded that he be addressed as 'Lord and God'. Those who refused were persecuted or put to death.

X. Nerv: He came to power after Domitian in 96 A.D. John was released and he came to Emphesus, on the main-land of Asia Minor and there he died.

II. THE CONTENTS AND EXEGESIS OF ROMANS

A. An Outline of Romans

1.1-7	-	Address
1.8-15	-	Definition of the contents of 'Gospel' and introductory thanksgiving.
1.16-17	-	The *theme* of the Gospel (the Gospel is the power of God for salvation to every one who puts his faith).
1.18-4.25	-	Negative and positive proofs (of saving act in Christ). This makes possible justification by faith.
1.18-3.20	-	Negative proof.
3.21-4.25	-	Positive proof.
3.21-25	-	New righteousness of God by grace and through faith in Jesus Christ.
3.27-30	-	By God's revelation of faith all boasting denied.
4.1-25	-	The objection that the law abrogated was refuted by referring to Abraham, who was justified by faith.
5.1-8.39	-	The description of the reality of a Christian's new being. This new trend of thought commences after Rom.4.25(Dodd, Nydgren et. al)
5.1-11	-	With justification, salvation was made sure.

5.12-21	-	Christ, the second Adam brings life. Paul retorts against the charge that grace creates indifference to sin.
6.1-14	-	On the basis of baptism, the new life in principle is freedom From sin.
6.15-23	-	It is obedience and service.
7.1-6	-	It is freedom from the Law.
7.7-25	-	Law reveals sin and death, but in Christ they have no more power.
8.1-11	-	The believer controlled by the Spirit is free from sin and death.
8.12-17	-	The Spirit guarantees the certainty of salvation.
8.18-30	-	The hope of final salvation is made secure.
8.13-39	-	Paul gives thanks.
9-11 chapters	-	Paul discusses the topic of the unbelief of the Jews in the former times.
9.1-5	-	The rejection of the Jews is evident.
9.6-29	-	But God has not forgotten his promise to Israel.
9.30-10.21	-	Human guilt is the cause of the rejection.
11.1-32	-	The rejection of the Jews is temporary expedient.
11.33-36	-	A hymn for the conclusion of this thought.
12-16 chapters	-	Paul's practical advice.
12.1-2	-	Living Sacrifices.
12.3-13	-	Introduction and general exhortation for Christian relations.
12.14-21	-	Attitude towards the non-Christians.
13.1-37	-	Duties for the state.
13.8-10	-	Love of the neighbour is the highest duty.
13.11-14	-	In the face of the imminent end, Paul urges the believers to be earnest in their moral life.
14.1-15.6	-	The strong and the weak at the church at Rome.

14.13-15.6	-	Six exhortations for the strengthening of their faith.
15.7-13	-	exhortations with reference to the example of Christ.
15.14-21	-	Paul justifies his writing.
15.22-23	-	Paul refers to his travel plans and his visit to Rome.
16.1-2	-	Paul commends Phoebe.
16.3-16	-	Paul sends greetings to a number of friends.
16.17-20	-	Paul warns against false teachers.
16.21-24	-	Greeting from companions.
16.25-29	-	Doxology.

B.   The Contents and Exegesis of Romans

From the outline given above, we note that Paul deals with the content of 'the Gospel' he was preaching:

In Rom. 1.16-17 Paul refers to the gospel he was proclaiming. It offers salvation to every one (Jew and Gentile) who responds in faith. In this divine initiative, the righteousness of God was revealed

The reference to the *Jew* first could be that the Messiah was first promised to them (Rom.9.4) and Christ came as a man among the Jewish race though they did not acknowledge him(Jn.1.ff). and the Jews had the special privilege of being the first in God's promises as a chosen race (Rom.2.9-10).

i.   Rom.1.18-3.20:*The negative proof of God's saving act.*

ii.   Rom.3.21-4.25:*The positive proof of God's saving act.*

Paul was dividing *human history* into three categories:

a.   The *Gentiles* who are *without law*

b.   The *Jews with the law.*

c.   *Christians with Christ, fuller revelation.*

a. Those without the Law: The Gentiles were given in nature sufficient evidence to acknowledge God: (Ps.19; Is.40.12-31; Job.40ff. – "What can be known of God is plain to them"."God has shown it to them".

v.20 – "his invisible nature has been clearly perceived in the things that have been made".

The *negative proof* Paul discusses here is *'the wrath of God'* (Rom.1.18) or, *'God's judgment'* (Rom.2.2).

Paul tells that *the* Jews will be judged under the law, while the *Gentiles* according to the law revealed in nature (Rom.1.19-20). In Rom.2.15, Paul notes that the law was written in their hearts and their conscience bears witness to it, as to what is right and what is wrong. The conclusion was that the *Gentiles are without excuse*, even though they do not have the written law (Rom. 1.20b).

b. Rom.2.1-8: Paul refers to the *Jews who have the Law* and they too are *without excuse* (Rom. 2.1), for if they do what they blame others, then they too will come under the same judgment of God (Rom. 2.17-24). The Jew may be circumcised, yet by breaking the law is in the same condition, for it is an inward, not outward sign (Rom.2.25-29) that matters. So both the *Jews and the Gentiles* are under the indictment of God.

A Brief Note on the Wrath of God

i.   It does not refer to the malicious hatred of God's quality, but the negative reaction of God to man's sin (Cf. Is.20.27ff). This was the same shown towards Israel when they broke the covenant obligations (Is.9.8-12; Hos.5.10).

ii.   We also see here the reference made in eschatological context (Rom. 2.5): "On the day of wrath...God's judgment will be revealed".

This is similar to **'the day of the Lord'** referred by prophets like Amos(5.18), Zephaniah (1.14) etc., in the Old Testament. The wrath of God is opposed to the *righteousness* of God (Rom.1.17). The *'Dikaiosune'* in Greek refers to the basic nature of God. It is the quality of God as seen in his activity for man's salvation (Rom.3.21-22, 25-26;10.3).

Paul underlines the fact that God, is a Saviour God, but man by his rejection of God's will invites wrath upon himself, which is retributive, not in any way expressing the nature of God. It is like the *Chinese Proverb*: the sun is meant for sunshine but shadows fall. The shadows fall not because of the sun, but some object that comes in the way of the sunshine like a tree or mountain etc. so man and not God is responsible if the wrath or judgment that falls on him (eg., Matt. 25.31-46).

iii. **The positive proof of God's saving act in Christ Jesus,** Paul discusses in Rom.3.21-4.25.Rom. 3.21-26 is very important as it shows the core of the contents of Romans which is *justification by faith*. It is the new way shown by God in Jesus Christ, that through faith in Christ one is justified or counted righteous before God. In Rom. 3.21 Paul refers to this as the manifestation of *righteousness apart from the Law.*Paul *illustrates* this through the life of *Abraham*, Rom.4.13: "The promise to Abraham and his descendants… did not come through the law but through the righteousness of faith".

(Look up in the introduction to the following terms: referred in Rom. 3.24 and 25).

i.   'Justification', a law court metaphor.

ii.   'Redemption', a slave market metaphor,

iii. 'Expiation', a sacrificial term of O.T.

Chapter – 4

ABRAHAM'S LIFE OF FAITH

The origin of the nation Israel was traced back to the call of Abraham. It was given in Gen. 12.1-3. Here we find that Abraham belongs to the town of Ur of Mesopotamia. God called him with the promise that:

i.   He will become a great nation.

ii.   God will bless him.

iii.   Through him the nations of the whole world will be blessed.

Abraham had to leave his country, his people and go to a place God will lead him to. Abraham obeyed God and left. Heb. 11.8 says he left 'not knowing where he was going'. This means that he fully trusted that God will lead to the place he wished him to settle down. Later we know that it was Palestine. From Abraham came Isaac and from him Jacob and from Jacob the twelve sons, whose descendants became the twelve tribes to form the nation Israel.

Romans 4th Chapter deals with 3 topics, all dealing with the facts of faith:

i.   Works vs. Faith.

ii.   Circumcision vs. Faith.

iii.   The Law vs. Faith.

Section-1: In v.2 Paul asks the question "Was Abraham justified by 'works or by faith"?

In v.3 he quotes from Gen.15.6, which says ''and he believed the Lord, and he reckoned it to him as righteousness'. Earlier Abraham said to God in Gen. 15.2-3 that he had no offspring of his own and Eleazer, born among the servants of Abraham, now acting as the steward, will naturally become the heir. But God promised that it will be his son who will be born to him, he will be the heir. Abraham believed God's word though Sarah, his wife laughed, who so far was barren and now old.

In vs.4-5, Paul brings out the difference between 'gift' and 'wage'. Wage is that which is earned but 'gift' is that which is given freely, not earned. So Paul argues 'to one who does not work but trusts him who justifies the ungodly his faith is reckoned 'righteousness'. To substantiate this view he quotes from Ps. 32.1-2 in vs.7-8.

Section-2: Here Paul deals with 'circumcision' vs. 'faith' (vs.9-15). In v.9 Paul raises the question whether Abraham was justified by faith before or after circumcision? He refers in v.9 what he quoted in v.3 from Gen. 15.6, ie., Abraham's justification by faith. In Gen. 17.22-27, we find that Abraham and Ishmael and others in his household were circumcised. But before that incident of circumcision we note that in Gen. 15.6 Abraham was justified and it was by faith. In v.10 Paul raises the question 'Was Abraham's justification before or after his circumcision? We have seen it was 'before'. In that case Paul argues that the Jews' arguing or being proud that they are the descendents of Abraham or that Abraham was their father holds no validity. If by faith and not by circumcision Abraham was justified then he becomes the 'father of all' – both Jews and the Gentiles, those of faith justified like Abraham. The boasting of the Jews as seen in Matt, 3.9, Jn. 8.33,39 etc., has no basis. In v.11 Paul shows that the circumcision was only a sign and the Gentiles have also claim on Abraham as the father of all the faithful ones.

Section-3: Here the Mosaic law (of which the Jews boast of) was dealt with as against the 'faith' (vs.13-15). Paul argues that if one is justified by the law then 'faith' and 'promise' are null and void (v.14). The drawback of the Law was that it brings wrath and becomes the cause for the transgression (v.15). Vs. 16-17 deal with the fact that all should share in the 'heirship' promised to Abraham – not just to the followers of the Law, as Gen. 17.5 makes it clear where Abraham was made the father of many nations. In v.17 God was referred as the One who gives life to the dead, in addition to be the Creator out of nothing. We know that Abraham was 100 years old by now and Sarah was 90 years (Gen. 17.17). In v.19, refers in the context that being so old they were 'as good as dead' in terms of any hope of having children. But Abraham believed and hoped for a child based on the promise of God (v.20). So Isaac was born to them and this belief was considered as Abraham's righteousness (v.22).

V.24, in conclusion was the 'application' to the present readers of his letter to the Romans. All that was written in the scriptures about Abraham meant 'for our sake also'. Jesus who was put to death on our behalf and for our sins was raised for our justification (v.25). Do we believe in Jesus as our Saviour now? With this the 4th Chapter ends drawing from the life and faith of Abraham, the originator of the nation Israel and the father of all those who are justified by belief. The believers of the church thus fall in line of this great heritage of the patriarch Abraham of the Old Testament.

Chapter – 5

Rom. 5.1-8.39 deals with the *new life in Christ* for the believer.

5.1-11: We can notice here that Paul uses *first person plural* 'we' or 'our' over 15 times.

5.12-21: Not a single time 'we' occurs here; instead it has many 'one man' references. Is this a clue to the fact that originally 5.1-11 was intended for *some other letter*, but Paul must have felt that it fits in here and inserted here. There is such a possibility.

Justification Theme (Rom. 3.21-5.21):

a. **Rom. 3.21-31**   :   The *description* of Justification.

b. **Rom. 4.1-25**   :   The *illustration* of Justification (Abraham)

c. **Rom. 5.1-11**   :   The *benefits* of Justification.

d. **Rom. 5.12-21**   :   The *application* of Justification.

(Rom. 3.21-5.1-11 was covered in the book dealing with the Justification theme).

1. Let us look at Rom. 5.1-11 first, what the benefits are:

    5.1   :   *Peace* with God.

    5.2a   :   *Access* to God.

    5.2b   :   *Hope* in God.

    5.3-4   :   *Fruit* of tribulation.

    5.5a   :   *Love.*

    5.5b   :   *The Holy Spirit.*

    5.6-10   :   *Deliverance* from God's wrath.

    5.11   :   *Joy.*

2. **Rom. 5.12-21** : The *application* of Justification.

a. Rom.5.12-14   :   The headship of Adam.

b. Rom. 5.15-21   :   The headships of Adam and Christ contrasted.

Paul seems to justify his *novel method* of teaching about *Adam*. He tries to bring about parallelism which is antithetical *parallelism* between *Adam and Christ.Death* brought by *Adam* vs. *Life* brought by *Christ* (Rom. 5.15).

Rom. 5.15-17 where Paul shows what the surpassing quality of Christ has done, seen in the phrase '*Much more*'.

5.9   : *Much more* in terms of *Justification*.

5.10   : *Much more* in terms of *Reconciliation*.

5.15   : *Much more* in terms of the *Gift*.

5.17   : *Much more* in terms of the *Reign in life*.

5.20   : *Much more* in terms of the *abounding Grace*.

Rom. 5.12 needs some exegesis:

"Sin came into the world through one man and death through sin".

This was taken by the *Roman Catholic Church* in terms of '*inheritance of sin*' or sin as hereditary, i.e., the children inherit sin from the parents. In the time of *St. Augustine*, the doctrine of the *Original Sin* was developed. Later, the 16th Council of Orsage (A.D. 529) decreed in terms of the doctrine of Original Sin (i.e., sin is inherited from Adam).

When Pelagius, an English monk in Rome began to preach for renewal of the Roman Catholic Church, there he said:

"Man is capable *not* to sin".

Sensing that, it amounts that man can be his own Saviour and Christ becomes superfluous, St. Augustine opposed and just added to Pelagius' view the negative 'not'.'**Man is *not* capable not to sin'.**By this Augustine emphasized on the depravity of man and his sinful condition, based on his personal experience.

Martin Luther did not agree with this Roman Catholic doctrine. He recognized that the Justice of God is served only when there is an *individual responsibility*. So he showed that

Rom. 5.12 brands *all under sin* and death

"because all men sinned".

In the O.T. also we find prophets like Jeremiah and Ezekiel, who in the name of God spoke against the corporate punishment common in those days. Jer. 31.29-30 and Ezek. 18.4. Both have quoted the common proverb in Israel. "The fathers have eaten sour grapes and the children's teeth are set on edge".

Both of them repudiated such an unreasonable proverb as told by God. Both have told that "the soul that sins, it shall die", i.e., individual responsibility.

Though the propensity to sin is great in us, which accounts for the fallen world into which we have come, yet sin will not be counted on the basis of Adam's sin. The doctrine of Original Sin of Roman Catholic church deals with inheritance of sin, for which the children are baptized to cleanse them from the venial sins.

Martin Luther's point was taken up by the modern exegetes to say that **'every man is an Adam to his own soul'**. The justice of God is thus vindicated, i.e., God judges us for the sins we commit and not for what Adam did.

Two aspects from Rom. 5.12f we find:

a.   *Inheritance* of sin (interpreted by R.C.)

b.   *Universality* of sin (interpreted by Protestants) (Rom. 3.23).

Rom. 5.12-21: Paul tries to show that it is both

i.   *Uprightness* before God (Rom. 5.9)

('Status of gentleman' – Law court language)

ii.   *Freedom* and life before God (Rom. 5.18)

(Aquittal' – Court language).

Rom. 5.13-14 needs some exegesis:
The Rabbis divided the human history of 6,000 years into three periods and Paul was adapting it here.

i.   1st period from *Adam to Moses* – 2000 years.

ii.   2nd period from *Moses to the Messiah* – 2000years.

iii.   3rd period from christ to the pesent-2000years

i.   The *first period* was before the law was given. As sin cannot be counted when there was no law (Rom. 5.13). Paul got into a kind of anachronism. Only from the second period onwards sin can be counted, which is the transgression of the law. Inspite of that, Paul says that "sin was in the world before the law was given" (Rom.5.13).

This was like the Gentiles without the law, who in nature and in their conscience were given the law (Rom.2.1-20). On this basis, Paul puts all under sin including those from Adam to Moses (Rom.5.14).

The Two Adams – First Adam and Second Adam (Christ) (I Cor.15.45):

Paul contrasts the two Adams

Through Adam	**Through Christ**
a. Condemnation (Rom.5.16)	Justification
b. Many made sinners (Rom.5.1)	Many mader righteous
c. Sin abounded (Rom.5.15)	Grace much more abounded.
d. Sin reigned to death (Rom. 5.17)	Grace reigned through righteousness.

Paul puts this contrast aptly in I Cor. 15.45 of what Christ did.

"The first man Adam became a living being; the last Adam became a life-giving spirit".

As we have noted earlier, the first Adam brought death while the last Adam brought life to us.

Chapter – 6

Sixth chapter begins with the logical question.

Qn.: "Shall we continue in sin that grace may abound?"

Ans.: "No".

Rom. 6.6: "Our old self crucified with Christ".

6.3: "United with him in death like his".

If so, "we might no longer be enslaved to sin" (Rom.6.6b).

"We cannot yield our members to sin as instruments of wickedness" (Rom. 6.13).

The changed position is that we are now set free from sin.

Rom.6.17: "Slaves of righteousness" (Rom. 6.20).

Or

"Slaves of God" (Rom. 6.22).

Rom.6.1-8.39: deals with *Sanctification*.

The Christian is 'set apart' to God from sin (I Thess. 1.9).

Rom. 6.1-7.25: The *Sanctification* comes through union with *Christ*.

To Paul, baptism *symbolises* the redemptive work of Christ.

i.   The believer *dies* to sin with Christ on the cross.

ii.   The believer is *buried* with Christ when put under water.

iii. The believer is raised to the *newness of life* when he comes out of water, like Christ from the tomb (Rom.6.3-4).

(Refer to the book on the theme of Baptism).

Chapter – 7

This chapter deals with Paul's life under the law.

The *Mosaic Law* was *holy, just and good* (Rom.7.12). It was even spiritual (Rom.7.14).

   i.   The law was a *moral informer*: What is good and what is evil.

   ii.   The law informs what to do and what not to do.

But the problem Paul faced was that it gives you no power to put into action

In Rom. 7.18-19 Paul gives *this dilemma* under the law.

Paul cries out about his *wretched condition* (Rom. 7.24). Then he finally found in Christ, *who enabled him* what the law could not (Rom. 7.25).(Refer in the book to this theme on *Law*).

Some try to see in this, as that of a believer also, but basically Paul was contrasting the life under the law; how powerless it is, as against that of a follower of Christ.

Chapter – 8

Paul begins the 8th chapter in giving the answer (Rom.8.1-4) to the question raised in Rom.7.24: "Who will deliver me from this body of death?"

Rom. 8.1-17 : Shows how we *triumph* over sin in Christ.

Rom.8.5-13 : Those who follow the *flesh* vs. those who follow the *spirit.*

    i.   Minds set on *fleshly things,* vs. on things of the spirit.

    ii. Fleshly mind means *death* vs. spiritual means *life and peace.*

    iii. *Enmity* towards God vs. *pleasing* God.

Rom.8.14-30 : A believer because of the gift of the Spirit:

    i.   Child of God.

    ii. Born anew of God.

    iii. Given intimate presence of God.

Rom.8.12 : Where Paul gives us the *Trinitarian* reference to *God the Spirit,* the *Spirit of God* and the *Spirit of Christ.*

Rom. 8.18 : introduces the threefold testimony:

    i.   Rom.8.18 – the glory to be revealed.

    ii. Rom.8.23 – the revealing of the sons of God.

    iii. *the Spirit helps us in our weakness.*

Rom.8.19-23 : The creation is groaning for its redemption with us.

Gen.9.12-13 : Shows that with the sin of Adam, the creation or the world of matter was cursed.

Gen.9.12.13 : Refers to God's covenant not only with man (Noah) but with other creatures.

Rom.8.19 : Shows the *solidarity of human and sub-human world.*

Rom.8.21 : Though the ground was cursed, yet God gave the hope that the creation will share in man's redemption. The *Recapitulation* theory includes the *creation*. Paul speaks first here, which later *he develops* in the *Captivity letters*.

Rom.8.22 : The *Greek Philosophers* spoke of *vernal rebirth* comparing it with the *woman's travail*. Paul adopts this usage in showing creation in travail together with man. In today's *Ecology* emphasis, we find here that the *redemption* in Christ has *cosmic significance* as it will be *cosmic redemption*: human and sub-human, both.

Rom.8.14-17 : Sonship with God.

This is the first reference to the sonship theme in Romans plus *heirship*.

Rom.9.4 : Refers to *Israel* as the sons of God or *adopted*, being chosen of God (Ex.4.22; Is.1.2; Jer.31.9.11.1). Likewise, believers are the sons of God or adopted (Rom.8.23; Gal.4.5; Eph. 1.5 etc.).

Rom.8.17 : Paul goes beyond Gal.4.7, in referring to them as *heirs* also. As *Christ* in his agony in the garden of Gethsemane addressed God the Father as "Abba, Father", so too the believers address God, expressing their intimate relationship with God (Rom.8.15).

We are to be fellow-heirs with Christ, provided we first *suffer with him*.

Rom.8.28 : With God as the subject and "all things" as the object, it reads that "God makes all things work *for the good* of those who love him."

This is in the context of the purpose as stated in Rom.8.29: "*to be conformed to the image of his Son*".

John Calvin in his 'Christian Institute' holds the *sovereighty* fo God, i.e. everything that happens in the world does not happen without his will. God uses even evil to serve his purpose, yet he punishes the doers of the evil.

Rom. 8.29: the use of the term

    (i) foreknownledge

    (ii) predestination

The *foreknowledge* of God should not be seen that God condition our actions. No. He does not. We do so in our own free will.

The *predestination* should not be seen in a prospective sense but in a retrospective sense.

When a believer looks back, he ascribes to God all the credit, in saying "but for God ...", he would not have been able to do such and such a thing. Though in fact he worked for it very hard.

D.M Baillie in his book '*God was in Christ*' beautifually puts that a test of believer is seen in putting God first and himself next.

Both terms - 'foreknew' and 'predestined' are used by Paul to emphasise the interiority in the process of salvation.

Chapter–9

ISRAEL'S PAST

Rom.9.1-5: The rejection of the Jews was clear.

The *rejection of Christ by the Jews* was so great that Paul was willing to be accursed (Like Moses in the wilderness expressed for Israel, Ex.32.32: to wipe out his name from the Book of Life, if that helps for God to show favour to them), if that would help them accept Christ.

Rom.9.4-5 : Israel occupied a special position before God.

a. adopted into sonship with God (Ex.4.22).

b. the glory of God (Ex.13.21-22).

c. the Covenants with God:

    i. Abrahamic (Gen. 12.15) – nation.

    ii. Palestinian (Deut.30) – land.

    iii. Davidic (II Sam. 7.12-16) – kingship.

    iv. Aaron and Sons (Ex. 8.1ff.) – priesthood.

d. the Mosaic Law (Ex.19.5-6).

e. the promises:

    i. New Covenant (Jer. 31.31-40).

    ii. the Messiah (Deut.18.15f.).

f. the Patriarchs-men who feared God (Abraham, Isaac, Jacob etc.).

g. the advent of Christ according to flesh, a Jew (Gal.4.4).

Israel occupied such a privileged position before God which no other nation could boast.

Rom. 9.6-13 : The problem was that Israel spurned their privileges and turned against God.

As the promises of the covenants were not fulfilled, the *question* was raised: "How was God faithful in the face of such unfulfilled promises?"

The answer Paul gives is that Abraham's posterity are *not automatically* heirs to these divine promises.

Three Case Studies :   **1. Rom.9.7-6**: Isaac and Ishmael.

2. Rom.9.10-13: Jacob and Esau.

1. **Isaac and Ishmael:** Both were sons of Abraham but *Ishmael* was a child of flesh vs. *Isaac* who was a child of God's promise for which he was chosen by God.

2. **Jacob and Esau:** *Esau* was the eldest, as such he gets the birth right. But God chose *Jacob*, not on merit but by divine selection (Rom.9.11).

3. **Mosses and Pharaoh:** Paul quotes here, God's answer to Moses after the incident of the golden Calf in the wilderness journey (Ex.33.19).

God will show mercy on whom *he wills* and again in *Rom.9.18* he concludes alluding to it, adding also the hardening aspect of *Pharaoh's heart*.

Just as God's mercy was shown, so also Paul brings out that the hardening of Pharaoh's heart, which God used to save Israel. So Pharaoh also contributed to the announcement and exaltation of God's name in the world. In the O.T. the hardening of the heart of Pharaoh, though by himself (Ex.7.14,22 etc.), yet it was ascribed to God (Ex.4.21; 7.3;9.12 etc.).

Rom.9.19-29: Paul brings out the O.T. *illustration* of the *potter and clay* (Jer.18.1-11).

There is also an expression of *predestination* here. This has to be modified by *Rom.9.23* which speaks of those who have been chosen for a part in the history of salvation, who have been destined by God, which is not the exclusive privilege of Israel only, as Rom.9.24 indicates, both the *Jews* and *Gentiles*.

Rom.9.27-29: Paul quotes from prophet Isaiah on the idea of *Remnant* (Is.1.22-23).

Rom.11.2-6: Here also Paul brings out the fact of the remnant, alluding from the *life of Elijah* (I King.19.10-18).

In the 9th chapter, the reference was that God has not rejected his people and there are still some who follow him (Rom.11.2).

Rom.9.20-32: This last section of 9th chapter is the beginning of Paul's argument in the next chapter 10.

Quotes Is.28;16; 8.14-15:

In Paul's quotation, the 'Stone' stands for Christ. Though it was intended in the original as a help, yet by the negative attitude, this stone becomes a stumbling block. What Paul was trying to say, is that the reason for the unfaithfulness of Israel is in itself and not in God.

Chapter – 10

ISRAEL'S PRESENT WITH AN EXPRESSION OF SORROW, PAUL BEGINS THIS SECTION

Rom.10.1-11: The problem with Israel was that it had zeal for God but it was misguided. They were ignorant of God's salvation.

i.   They try to keep the law for righteousness

or

ii.   They try to establish their own righteousness

but

none is righteous to save themselves.

Paul's argument was, that if the righteousness could be gained by keeping the law, then what happens to the Gentiles who do not have the law?

Rom.10.5-13: Moses promised life to those who strived for righteousness(Lev.18.5).

Moses himself showed that the blessing of God comes through faith (Deut.30.1f). Israel missed this fact. They were ascending the heights or descending the depths to fulfill the law, while Paul says that Christ himself has done that, what need is there for any, except, to accept in faith the salvation offered by him.

Rom.10.9-10: Paul may be referring to the baptismal formula of the early Palestinian churches, of believing in the heart and making open confession by word.

This is faith-righteousness (Rom.10.11-12).

The Jews might have special privileges before God, but as far as salvation is concerned there is no distinction. It is for all, Jews and Gentiles. This shows that the Jews have no special offer of salvation from God.

Rom. 10.14-21: Here Paul shows that there is no faith about hearing, i.e knowledge should precede faith (Rom. 10.17). Paul also refers to the fact that the opportunity to hear the Gospal was first offered to Israel, but she did not take the advantage of it. So the fault his with Israel and not God.

Paul makes use of the reference to the goodness of the coming deliverance to those in Babylonian captivity through Cyrus, the Persian Emperor, announced to the Jews in Is.57.7, which is adapted for the proclamation of the Christian message now.

Rom.10.19-20: Paul takes the quotation from Is. 65.1and 2. V.1 refers to the nation and v.2 refers to the people in the Septuagint; the first verse, 'nation' reference, Paul applied to the Gentiles and the second to the 'people', he applied to Israel.

Paul quotes Deut.32.21 and Is. 65.1-2, the former refers to the Song of Moses where God tries to educate Israel and finally announcing that she will be humbled by the heathen. This Paul applies to the state of Israel being provoked by the Gentiles to put their faith in Christ.

Chapter – 11

ISRAEL'S GLORIOUS FUTURE

Israel's failure – only partial and temporary.

Israel's failure fits into the plan of God.

In Rom.9.27, Paul hinted that a 'remnant' of them will be saved. Now he takes it up and discusses further.

a.   **Rom. 11.1-10:** Israel's disobedience only partial.

b.   **Rom.11.11-24:** Israel's disobedience only temporary.

c.   **Rom.11.25-32:** The Jews included in God's plan of salvation.

d.   **Rom.11.35-36:** Paul bursts into a hymn to the wisdom of God.

Rom.11.1-10 : Israel's disobedience is partial.

Qn. : Does it mean God has rejected Israel for her unfaithfulness?

Or

For her rejection of the Gospel when the Gentiles accept it?

Ans. : 'By no means' says Paul with an indignant negative .

Rom. 11.2-5: We have noted that how Paul brings the reference to Elijah who was informed by God, that 7000 are there who did not bow their knees to Baal (I King 19.10-18).

The 'Remnant' idea is that all Israel did not reject the Gospel. There are some who accepted, so Paul is not the only one like Elijah. Of course, the majority of Israel did not accept Christ, which was an occasion of sorrow for Paul (Rom. 9.1-2).

Rom. 11.8: Paul quotes from Deut. 29.4 (adds Is. 29.10, Ps. 69.22f). This was where Moses speaks to Israel that inspite of all the plagues sent against Pharaoh, they have never appreciated its significance. Paul adds 'to this day' 'a spirit of stupor' has taken over Israel. But to Paul it is not final.

Rom.11.11-24: Israel's disobedience is only *temporary*. Paul admits Israel stumbled over Christ, yet not fallen down completely.

Israel's stumbling in the province of God helped the Gentiles to come to Christ. From Acts 13.45ff.; 18.6f., etc., we find that when the Jews rejected the Gospel, the evangelists turned to the Gentiles, who believed it.

Rom. 11.12: (also v.15) Paul asks if the stumbling of Israel turned into a blessing to the Gentiles, what will their acceptance be?

Rom.11.3ff.: Paul addresses the Gentiles and cautions against any boasting over Israel.

Christ according to the flesh expressed solidarity *with* the Jews. *Paul*, though chief apostle to the Gentiles, yet he was a *part* of the *Jewish* community.

Rom.11.15: Paul brings out two analogies

i.　*dough* in a whole lump.

ii.　*root and branches* of a tree.

If the dough or root is *holy*, so too the rest of the lump or the branches respectively must be holy. If the first portion of the meal offered at the temple is holy, then the whole lump acquires legal status of purity (Numb. 15.18-21).

Rom. 11.15: Paul hopes the coming in of Gentiles will make the Jews jealous and draw them to Christ.

The reference to "life from the dead" could be to the Jews themselves of their passage, from death to life and need not refer to the end time resurrection.

Rom. 11.17-24: The grafting in horticulture illustration was used here.

Israel compared to an old worn Olive tree.

Gentiles to the young wild Olive branch.

Some maintain that in actual practice, it is the good branch that is grafted to the wild tree.

The above could be the ancient practice.Israel was the branch of the good Olive tree which was broken. So the Gentiles got an opportunity to be grafted in its place.

Rom. 11.18: Paul was not saying that Israel was broken off so that the Gentiles could be grafted in, rather it was an opportunity for the Gentiles.It is God's grace for which the Gentiles should be thankful, and not think that it was due to any merit.

Rom. 11.22: Paul talks of the i) kindness and ii) severity of God.

If the Gentiles do not fulfill the conditions of God's gracious action, then they too will face the severity of God. If God did not spare the natural branches (Israel), it will not be difficult for God to chop off the grafted branches (Gentiles) (Rom. 11.21).

Rom. 11.23: God has power to graft the Jews again, by faith in Christ into the parent stock of Abraham.

Rom. 11.25-32: The Jews included in God's plan of Salvation.

Paul reverts to what he said earlier in Rom. 11.1-12 about Israel's failure, **partial.**The Gentiles have to be careful not to despise the Jews.Paul discloses the secret plan of God: That is, that when the fullness of the Gentiles come in, the conversion of the Jews will take place. Paul sees a connection between the conversion of the Gentiles and the conversion of the Jews.

Paul quotes O.T. now in favour (earlier against) Is. 59.20f. (though Is. 27.9 added not much in context). This above quotation deals with spiritual destiny of Israel as per the covenants.

Rom. 11.28:   a. Enemies of God – for rejection of the Gospel.

b. beloved of God – as per God's election or choice.

The election of Israel is irrevocable, the claim which the Gentiles do not have.

Rom.11.31: Just as Jew's disobedience led to divine mercy for the Gentiles.Likewise the mercy shown to the Gentiles will be used for Israel.

Rom.11.32: God confined all men, Jews and Gentiles to disobedience so as to show his mercy and what kind of God he is.

Rom.11.33-36: Paul shows his admiration for divine plans for the salvation of Jews and Gentiles.

Chapter – 12

Rom.12.1-25: Practical Advice.

Rom.12.1-13.14: Believer's life in society based on humility and love.

Rom.12.14-21: The verb 'offer' indicates that what is dedicated is more than helping others. It is used in the sacrificial context of animals killed at the temple.

The only difference is that Paul wants, that it will be a living offer of a believer's life guided by reason.

The advice not to be conformed with the world corroborating with what he referred to as a transient one, I Cor. 7.31. Paul must be using the same world views of the Rabbis: "The world" vs. "the world to come".

These two world views have Christ as the meeting point (I Cor. 10.11).

On this basis, that though believers live in this world, yet they should not be conformed to its value-judgments.

"Be transformed", the Greek word "Morphe" from which comes **metamorphosis** in the English language which denotes the internal change.

Take the illustration of the caterpillar, how it weaves a cocoon which soon will be metamorphosed into a beautiful butterfly.

Paul emphasizes that it is through the work of the Holy Spirit and involves also the human mind ("nous" in Greek).

Rom. 12.3:Life in the society based on humility and love. Paul's advice was that each believer should measure himself or herself according to the standard of the object of his faith, which is Jesus Christ himself.

In this comparison, each one knows his limitations which keeps him humble indeed.

Each was given a faith which puts him in the right place to function in the body of Christ.

Rom.12.5: Paul brings in one of the metaphors of the Church here, which is the Body of Christ.

i.   The body of Christ (I Cor. 12.12-30 – given in detail).

ii. The building (temple) (I Cor. 6.19; II Cor. 6.16 etc.).

iii. The bride (Eph. 5.21-23; II Cor. 11.2; Eph. 2.21).

In these three metaphors (the three B's we can say) used by Paul for the church, we find that both the **physical body** and the **building** carries the emphasis of many parts or members, but are expressed in one being or building - the unity emphasis.

Rom. 12.5-6: Here Paul is not talking of the body of Christ but '**one** body' in Christ (from 12.5). In the next verse, he shows that how the believers should realize the social character of their God-given gifts when they use them.

Rom.12.9: Paul advises the relationship of believers within the body of Christ. It should be 'Philadelphia' in Greek terms or 'Brotherly love' (Philia- love; adelphos-brother). This is distinguished from the wider service in the society at large.

Rom. 12. 11: The basis for all Christian service or conduct in the society should be in terms of "Serving the Lord"

Rom.12.13: The believers at Rome should also look to the needs of other believers like the 'saints' at Jerusalem church.

Rom.12.14-21: Extending love to all, including enemies.

v.14 sounds similar to the words of Christ: "Bless your persecutors" (Matt. 5.44).

v.16: 'to have the same or mutual esteem for one another and to associate with the 'lowly', if masculine gender '**people**', or if neuter then it means 'to give ourselves to **lowly tasks**'.

v.17: "Repay no one evil for evil" echoes the words of Christ in the Sermon on the Mount (Matt. 5.43-44), and the words "aim at what is honourable" seems to be Paul's adaptation of Proverbs 3.4.

v.19: "Do not take revenge" – for this, Paul gives two reasons:

i.   non-retaliation of evil of enemies.

ii. Leave the retribution to God (Paul quotes Deut. 32.35a in support). This could be the final judgment. Paul's advice already was "don't repay evil and live in peace with all" (Vs.17-18).

v.20: Paul, making Prov. 25.21-22 as his own, advises to give drink and feed the enemy when hungry, which will be like **burning coals** on his head, meaning burning pangs of shame (coal symbolizes so).

v.21: The core of Paul's advice to the believers was that they should pursue only good and with good only they should conquer evil.

Chapter – 13

Practical advice (Continued).

A. Rom.13.1-7: duties to the state.

B. Rom.13.8-10: loving the neighbour, the highest duty.

C. Rom. 13.11-14: to be earnest in moral life.

A. Rom.13.1-7: Duties to the State

Paul's advice about the believer's relation to the state seems to be taken over from the practice at the synagogue, where prayers used to be offered for the state officials (I Tim. 2.1ff. etc.).The believer has to submit to the state authority recognizing it as being instituted by God.

This passage has given rise to the theory of Divine Right of Kings in England etc. Samuel Rutherford, the 17th Century Scottish Puritan, faught against this view in his work 'Le Rex'. In the book of Revelation, we find Rome (symbolically referred) to as 'Babylon' was opposed. The reason seems to be that by then the Emperor worship was forced on the Christians.But at the time of the writing of Romans in A.D. 57 there was no such persecution from Rome and also, Paul being a Roman citizen was favourable to paying taxes to Rome.

We find from the book of Acts, Luke takes pains to show the Christian loyalty to the state against the Jewish slander of the Christians as the enemies of the state (Acts 18.12ff; 21.7ff; 23.29. etc.).Paul may be following the same attitude what Christ showed towards the state, though he held that the children are free, in Mk. 12.17 (pay to Caesar what is Caesar's).

The Dissenting Christians were at the beginning persecuted by the British monarchy. Their cry was for 'freedom of Conscience', and that the monarch has no right over this, the matters concerned about the individual's soul. Paul's advice would not be of much help here, though in general, under normal conditions it would be so.

B. Rom. 13.8-10: Loving the neighbour: One of the N.T. scholars observed four motifs in the ethical demand:

i.   The eschatological motif.

ii.   The holiness motif.

iii. The fellowship motif.

iv. The personal motif.

v.8: "Love is the fulfillment of the law".

v.10: The Christian virtues (Phil. 4.8f) should be seen as demand of love. The neighbours' need should goad us into action in love.

Under the fellowship motif, we find that the demand of *love* should occupy a high place. At the end, the love commandment replaces all others.

C. Rom. 13.11-14: To be earnest in moral life.

Vs.12-14: The use of the phrase, "cast off" the works of darkness or "put on" Christ, show that Paul was thinking in the analogy of putting on clothes.

The use of "night far gone" or "as in the day" – refers to the hope of the imminent end or the soon coming of Christ.

Here Paul is using the eschatological motif for the ethical demand

Chapters 14 and 15

Here Paul is dealing with the question of eating meat offered to the idols, similar to what he discussed in 8-10 chapters in his first epistle to the Corinthians.

Rom.14: The man who is weak in faith is the topic of consideration here.

The issue was that extra meat that was offered in sacrifice to the idols used to be sold in the market. The Christians used to purchase and eat that. This disregards the conscience of weaker brother.

Rom.14.1-15.6: The strong and the weak of the church at Rome.

Rom. 14.1-4: Paul was not siding with anyone.

i   The one who eats (also vs.10-12), and

ii. The one who abstains. He was advising that, let not any one pass judgment on the others; Leave it to him and God.

Rom. 14.5-6a: Paul brings in here the observance of the days also.

Rom. 14.6b-9: Each one whether he eats or abstains; it is for the honour of the Lord as he gives thanks for it.

Rom. 14.13-23: Nothing is unclean in itself according to Paul (v.14). But by eating meat offered to idols, one puts a stumbling block or hindrance in the way of another (vs.13,21).

Paul's advice is 'to walk in love' (v.15). One should not cause ruin of one for whom Christ died (v.15).One should pursue for "what makes for peace" and for "mutual upbuilding" (v.19).

i.   In the 1st Corinthians, Paul deals with the fact that though the idols are no gods, yet he believes that demons exist (Deut. 32.17), so that one enters into fellowship with demons, if so, one cannot again join at the table of the Lord (I Cor. 10.28-29).

Surprisingly here, Paul does not quote the decisions of the Jerusalem Council on this matter (Acts 15.20, 29; Acts 12.25).

This issue also falls under the Fellowship motif.

Rom. 15.1-6: The strong have a responsibility to please his neighbour, not just himself but for the other's edification.The example of Christ was brought out, who did not please himself but bore the reproaches of others (v.3).The exhortation was that the believers at Rome

i.   should live in harmony with one another

ii.   and in accord with Jesus Christ (v.5).

Rom. 15.7-13: The example of Christ who became a servant.

i.   to the circumcised to confirm to their promises.

ii.   to the Gentiles that they might glorify God for his mercy (vs. 8-9).

Rom. 15.14-33: Paul's ministry, and the reasons for not visiting Rome so far and now has travel plans.

As the apostle to the Gentiles, Paul tells that he took the liberty to write to the Roman Christians even boldly (15.1). Paul did not visit the church at Rome as his motto was not to enter into another man's field, but to go where Christ was not named (vs. 20,22).Now he desires to visit Rome as he plans to go to Spain and Rome falls in his path. So he wishes to halt on his way en route (vs.24,28).This trip he will take after completing the job of taking the contribution of Macedonian and Achaian churches to the saints at Jerusalem (vs. 25-28).

Rom. 15.30-33: i.Paul seeks their prayers so that he may be delivered from the Jewish opponents at Jerusalem. He has a fear that the Jews there may harm him. This may be his premonison that they may not accept him

ii.   his services to the saints at Jerusalem be accepted.

<h1 align="center">Chapter –16[*]</h1>

COMMENTARY

S. 1-2:

Phoebe was of Cenchrea, which was a Port of Corinth. She was a Deaconess of the church at Cenchrea. She must be going to Rome and Paul must be using the opportunity to send his letter to the Romans through what we call 'a hand letter,' as she will be personally handing over to the church there.

Some Churches which are not in favour of women in Church office do not favour of calling her as a Deaconess. What Paul was asking the Church at Rome, not supposed to be founded by Paul, to look after her well, to make her feel at home with the Church leaders there, as she was willing helper to many, even to Paul himself.

S. 3-16:

In his greeting Paul mentions some of the Christians at Rome:

I.   Priscilla and Aquila (Rom. 16:3). This couple was referred to as returning from Rome when Emperor Claudius ordered all Jews to leave Rome. Claudius ruled from 41-54 AD. The reason seems to be

---

[*] N.B.: We have already dealt with the contents of this chapter in the introduction, of the occasion for writing, the question of unity of the last two chapters etc.

that there were disturbances over the issue of "Christos" or Christ between them and the Christians. They belonged to Pontus. Paul met them at Corinth of Greece. We find that they helped Apollo from Alenxdra of Egypt when he came preaching chiefly about repentance, they expounded to him about the Christian faith at Ephesus of Asia Minor (Acts 18:20-26.). We find that in Acts 18:26 it was Priscilla, the wife, who was mentioned first in vs. 2. Paul mentions the house church at Rome at their place (Rom . 16.5) this shows they were also active in leading the congregation at Rome.

II. *Epaenetus* (Rom. 16.5) was said to be the first convert from Asia corroborated by 1 Cor . 16:15.

III. Aristabulus's family (vs. 10), he might be the grandson of king Herod. We have the information that Caesar's household was reached with the gospel when Paul was at Rome as a prisoner (Phil. 4:22).

IV Paul's Kinsmen (vs. 7&11), Andronicus and Junias, also fellow prisoners and senior to Paul and of note among the Apostles, Herodian, et al. These could be the Jews like Paul as against the others.

V. Rufus (vs. 13) we have the reference to his father who made to carry The cross of Christ (Mk. 15:21). He was Simon the Cyrenian. Alexander was the brother of Rufus. Probably these were Blacks.

VI. Some of them not familiar or known to us they are:

     i.   Mary, laboured much among them (vs.6).

     ii.   Amplietus, Paul refers to him as his beloved in the Lord (vs.8).

S. 17-20:

Already Paul gave his greetings naming many of the members of the Church at Rome. This should have been followed by closing with the usual saying of the Grace. Paul must have remembered which he felt important to write as an appeal (i) the one about those who cause divisions in the Church, thereby disturb peace in the church. (ii) Those who put hindrances to spiritual growth. It is the man whose lifestyle and whose negative attitude is evil influence on the faith of the believers.

One of the N.T. Scholars aptly puts this kind of Church members as "a man who speaks well but who acts ill". I would say the above two characteristics and progressive membership of Church.

S. 21-23:

(a) Here Paul refers to greetings for his fellow workers like Timothy, Lucius, Jason (of Antioch Church, probably Acts 17;5-9), including Paul's kinsmen Sosipater (of Beroca, who brought Church's offering, Acts; 20-4)

(b) The writer of this letter Tertitus personally offers his greetings

(c) Gaius (who was baptized by Paul, I Cor. 1-14) and his brother Quartus send their greetings.

S. 25-27:

In closing grace Paul refers to what he called as the uniting of the Jews and the Gentiles, as a mystery of Christ now made known in Christ (Eph 3:3-6).

2
I Corinthians

PAULINE AUTHORSHIP

Acts 18.1-17: St. Paul at Corinth. 2nd Mission Journey

Acts 16.6-10: from Macedonia to Athens and Corinth.

wrote from Ephesus, date – 55 A.D.

Corinth: Vanity Fair (Tax on ships goods sold – bazaar of Asia)

1. Destroyed by Rome in 146 B.C. (by Lucius Mummius, the Roman General).

2. Rebuilt by Julius Caesar, and Augustus Caesar – in 46 B.C. as a colony of Rome

3. Trade between East and West – Trade route. Pulled ships from East to North – 4 miles – through Isthmus bay (By this way saved 202 miles).. The Isthmus games famous next to Olympic games only.

4. Chenchria – Eastern port (Lechaeum – western port) (Roman letter from this port (Rom. 16.1)

5. Romans, Greeks and Jews settled here. Corinthian on stage referred to of low morals (drunkards, reckless, riotous living) (I Cor. 6.9-10).

6. Clement – 47 A.D. and Marcion – 140 A.D. – from here.

MAIN DIVISIONS

1. 1-4 Chapters – party strife at Corinth

2. 5th Chapter – the Incestuous man.

3. a. 6.1-11 – the scandal of Christians using pagan courts.

    b. 6.12-20 – Liberty not license to strife.

4. 7th Chapter – problem about marriage

5.   8-11 Chapters – eating meats offered to idols

6.   12-14 Chapters – spiritual gifts

7.   15th Chapter – the Resurrection of the dead

8.   16th Chapter – Items of business, personal affairs and salutations.

I.   CORINTHIAN LETTER

I Cor.16.21 – The closing greetings (Paul's own hand writing) (Col. 4.18)

Rom. 16.22 – like Tertius writing the letter to Romans (probably Timothy also)

Acts 18.1ff – Priscilla and Aquila left Rome and came to Corinth

v.2 – on Emperor Cladius' order

v.3 – They were Tent-makers. Paul joined in that trade.

"Tent-making" ministry refers now to "self-supporting" ministry.

The Progress of the Corinthian Correspondence

1   The previous letter (" I wrote to you" I Cor.5.9)(II Cor. 6.14-7.1)

2   i)   The arrival of Chloe's people

ii)   Stephanos, Fortunatus, and Achaicus (I Cor.16.17f)

3   The 1st Corintheans (letter) was written in reply and sent through Timothy (I Cor. 4.17).

4   The situation becomes worse and Paul makes a personal visit to Corinth (II Cor. 12.14ff). This was a complete failure that it almost breaks his heart.

5   There he writes a "Severe letter" dispatched with Titus (most probablycontained in II Cor. 10-13 chapters).

a. II Cor. 2.4 – Paul says "wrote out of much affliction".

b. II Cor. 7.8 – Paul says "even if I made you sorry".

Unable to wait for an answer, Paul sets out to meet Titus (II Cor.7.6,13).

Paul meets Titus in Macedonia. He learns from him that all is well.

Most probably from Macedonia (Philippi town) writes the "Letter of Reconciliation" (II Cor. 1-9 Chapters).

a   The previous letter – II Cor. 6.14-7.1

b   The Severe letter – II Cor. 10-13 chapters.

c   The Reconciliation letter – II Cor. 1-9 chapters

Chapter - 1

COMMENTARY

v.1 – 'Apostle' adds "by the will of God" (Eph.1.1)

Gal. 1.1 adds "not from man or through man"

Reference Background (I Cor. 9.1-2):

1) The Corinthians seemed to question Paul about using for self the Title 'Apostle', as he was not one of the 12 chosen by Christ.

   <u>Illustration</u>: Now-a-days – churches use such title as dignity for they don't have Bishop's title usage.

2) Sosthenus, ruler of the Synogogue(Acts 10:17) and Crispus, ruler of the Synogogue (Acts 18.8)

   So too many Corinthians were baptized and 4 leaders groups formed at Corinthian church.

1 **APOLLOS:** He arrived at Ephesus. He was from Alexandria of Egypt. He was the Baptist's disciple.

   Acts 18.1-2: Aquila and Priscilla took him and instructed him

   Acts 18.2-4ff : At Ephesus in the Christian faith.

   Acts 18.27ff: Apollos wanted to go to Greece (Achaia).

   Acts 18.27 : The Christians at Ephesus wrote to the Christians at Corinth to receive him.

   Acts 18.28 : Apollos convinced the Jews there that Jesus is the expected Messiah.

2 **PETER :** He never visited, yet the Judaizers group at Jerusalem held him as their leader.

   Gal. 2.7: For to Peter and John, the responsibility of the Jewish converts was given to them.

Gal. 2.7 –Peter himself with (Barnabas) joined a separate mess of the Jews at Antioch, of which St. Paul was not happy.

3.   **St. PAUL,** as he preached and won many of the members of the church at Corinth, they held him as their leader (Acts 19.1-10).

II Cor. 10.10 – Paul's personality – weak they said. (II Pet. 3.15-16 – though his letters weighty said Peter)

Acts 18.2 – Acquila and his wife Priscilla came from Rome (as emperor Claudius asked all Jews to leave Rome).

Acts 18.3 – They were tent-makers; so Paul joined them

I Cor. 9.13 – Paul preached to those at Corinth free of charge.

4.   **CHRIST** – As the Founder of Christian church, some wished to follow Christ only

Matt. 16.18 – Christ referred to the church as 'My Church', so there were 4 parties in the church at Corinth of Apollos, Peter, Paul and Christ. Of course Paul questioned even to name him as the head of one of the parties. Paul asked them:

I Cor. 1.13 – " Is Christ divided?" or "was Paul crucified for you?" or "Were you baptized in Paul's name?"

v.14 – Paul says "I baptized none of you, except Crispus and Gaius".

v.15 – (i.e., not in Paul's name baptized)

v.16-- In fact Paul says he baptized also Stephanas.

v.17– Paul says "Christ sent him not to baptize but to preach". This statement is not negating baptism,but emphasizing the mission task of winning souls.

I Cor.1.18 – 2.5 – Cross foolishness to the world but it is God's power and wisdom.

Paul says in human rhetoric (like Apollo's).

I Cor. 2.1-13; 3.18 – He says, Human wisdom nothing compared with Divine Wisdom.

I Cor. 2.7;3.19 –Divine wisdom (SOPHIA-(Gk.) vs. human knowledge (GNOSIS- Gk.)(3.20; 8.1, 7).

THE CROSS

1. **The Jews** – sought signs (Jn.4.48),which in a way becomes a stumbling block to them.

2. **The Greeks** – sought human wisdom which is "cleverness" (v.19).

Illustration: Danish Theologian Soren Kierkegaard : He held – "Man cannot reach God in his own cleverness, as human knowledge is limited. It's only by "a leap of faith" can bridge the gap between man's knowledge and God.

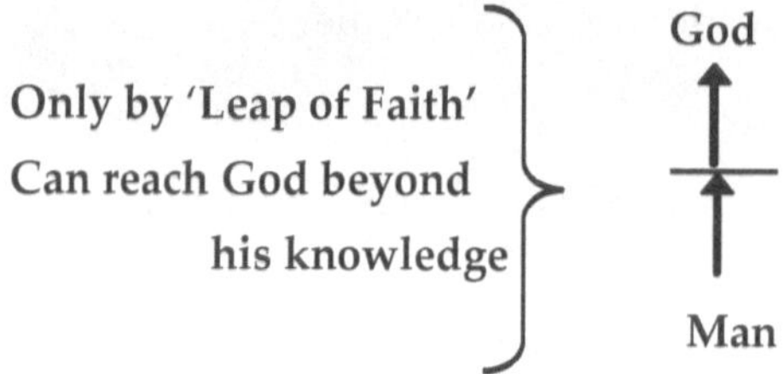

Only by 'Leap of Faith'
Can reach God beyond
his knowledge

his Knowledge to reach God
is very limited.

1. The Greeks argued in human knowledge (=cleverness); To Paul its mere silliness (I Cor. 1.19).

Is.29.14 – "The wisdom of the wise men shall perish; the discernment of them will be hid".

The Greeks argued that if God can feel (like the Cross – suffering) then some one can influence him. So a suffering person can not be God. Only an 'APATHIA' (Gk.)= "non-feeling one," can be God.

The argument of Paul is that the Divine wisdom

a.   in the Jewish wisdom literature   semi-personified.

b.   in the Christian faith seen   embodied in Christ.

I Cor.1.23 – Some Jews might have cancelled the doctrine of the "crucified Messiah".

v.25 – the **"weakness of God** is **stronger than man"**.

Illustration: Chang Naga warriors of Nagaland, in the gospel preaching when heard of the crucifixion, left saying "It is for women" not warriors like them,as Jesus seen as a feeble Person.

v.26-31 – "Christ for us" – 4 things

a.   Wisdom (SOPHIA (Gk.)) – v.30

b.   Righteousness (DIKIASUNE (Gk.) – right relationship with God.

c.   Consecration in Christ's presence – life what it ought to be.

d.   Deliverance (APOLUTROSIS (Gk.) – Christ delivers.

Illustration: Acts 4.13 – Apostles illustrated as uneducated commoners – no boasting indeed.

v.30 – Holiness {HAGIOS (Gk.)} – By his death Christ Justifies us.

Chapter-2

1. **v.2** – Paul says he is determined to preach Christ – crucified.

2. The world has enough Teachers:

    a. The Jewish

    b. The Greek wise men   set them aside

    c. The ancient philosophers.

3. What the world needs now is a Redeemer.

vs 1-5 – The 1st visit remembered

    i.   Paul's simplicity.

    ii.   his fear

"His heart beats fast to preach", yes the result: lives changed – by the power of the Holy Spirit.

vs. 6-16 – like a herald announced – the basic facts of Christianity.

    i.   The Kerygma – Christian Doctrine

    ii. The Didache –The explanation of the Kerygma

God's spirit shows what Christian wisdom is. It is "like is known by the like" principle.

v.16; (and Phil.2.5)– Paul says "we have the mind of Christ".

Eph. 3.9-10 – "The hidden mystery of God's plans now made known'.

Illustration:

a.   Pythagoras divided students into:

    a.   'Babes' = junior students

    b.   TELEIOS' (Gk.) = Mature students (Col..1.28; I Cor.2.6)

b.   Jews – i) Proselytes = "Spiritual babes"

St. Paul here is not making like caste distinctions but showing different stages of maturity in faith.

Conclusion

1. The Jews would not have put Jesus to death if they had known the "True hidden wisdom" (2.7-8; Rom. 8.27).

2. The hidden wisdom enables the mature believers to know that Christ has won victory over all the hostile powers (Rom. 8.27).

Chapter - 3

---

vs.1-17 – Further denunciation of the party strife.

vs. 1-10:

v.1 – Jealousy and strife still prevalent. These are signs of being of 'Flesh' i.e., carnal people.

v.4 – "I belong to ", Paul says "you are merely men".

v.5 – Apollos or Paul = are servants of God, through whom you believed.

v.9 – You are God's fellow-workers.

Corinthians   a. God's Field,   Two metaphors of
                   b. God's Building   the church.

A. God's Garden – a. Paul – planted

                 b. Apollos –watered

                 c. God – gave the increase

Illustration: The rich land lord (Lk.12.15-21) – called 'Fool'– Why?

Lk.12.18-19 – 6 times reference to 'I'–No reference

i. to God Or ii.to the neighbours

"The Test of a true Believer = puts God – First; self (man) next.

"God was in Christ" – Book by D.M. Baillie, emphasizes this point.

Illustration:

Anantapur farmers – After all field work done, no rain sent by God, or pests Spoiled,etc. Result – No crop.

B. God's Building (v.10) – foundation – Paul

Structure – others – each share how one builds on it (v.10).

v.11 – Jesus – Foundation

v.12– Builds with gold, silver, precious stones, wood, hey, straw.

v.13 – The judgment Day will Test – costly or cheap work.

II Pet. 3.7 – It will be tested by 'Fire' on the last day.

I Cor. 6.19 – the metaphor of building.

vs. 16-18 – Refers to the Holy Temple at Jerusalem (I Cor. 6.18).

Not to 'HEIRON' (Gk.) the courts but to NAOS (Gk.) =Temple (inner) holy building.

St. Paul refers to 'immorality'= sin with the body. (I Cor. 5ᵗʰ Chapter refers to such case in the Corinthian church).

vs.18-23 – 'Fool' – 'anti-philosopher' term.

v.19 – Quotes Job 5.13 v.18 – Paul's advice "Become Fool for Christ"

v.20 – quotes Ps.94.11 (by rejecting philosophy). Zeno says "all things belong to those who are wise".

Chapter- 4

vs. No Christian leader can come between Christ and the believer.

St. Paul says he will be if necessary judged by Christ alone, not by any converts or himself. No real ground for convert's self-esteem.

Lk.16.2f –Christ chose some as ministers and some as stewards. In a steward reliability expected (not originality).

On the judgment day, God will reveal everything with the status of the doomed Gladiator, the hypothetical spiritual wealth of the converts contrasted. The converts at ease in Zion while the Apostle (Paul) fighting for his life.

vs.14.21 –A Paternal appeal (father and child relation).

vs.15– St. Paul's mood changes from severity to affection. He will spare them out of love and not of weakness. Other apostles like tutors taking children to school.

Illustration: Jenny Pal an M.Div student at Calcutta Bible College refered to me as 'Father' at convocation. Dr. Thomas, the Principal asked if he can be at least as Adopted Father. As a new convert ,I had to counsel her and pray with her often.

Acts 19.21-22 – Paul written a letter to Timothy to come, follow by land, while Paul by sea reaches Corinth.None should think Paul was afraid to come in person. With rod or in love he will come, dependent on the converts' response.

v.16– "Be imitators of me" (St. Paul). (I Cor. 11.1; I Thes.1.6)

v.19 – Paul says he will find out, not the talk of the arrogant people but their power.

5.1-14.40 – 6 Issues discussed.

1.	5.1- 13	–	Incest case Moral lapses.
	6.12-20	–	Prostitution
2.	6.1-11	–	law suits between Christians.
3.	7.1-40	–	Problems of Marriage discussed.
4.	8 and 10 chapters	–	The eating of meats offered to idols.
5.	9.1-27	–	The right of the Apostle for support.
6.	11.2-14-40	–	The question of worship.

Chapter -5

vs. 1-13 – The Corinthian Christians tolerated a member living with his step-mother.

It is seen an offence, not found even among the pagans (v.1).

St. Paul was shocked at this sin. a. Roman law-prohibited it.

b. Jewish law also prohibited it (Lev.18.8).

v.2 – 'PANTHEIR (Gk.) = mourning for the dead

Anselm (Later Arch Bishop of Canterbury, England) – SIN – serious (crucified Christ) – it's against God (Gen. 39.9 – Joseph at the insistence of Photiphar's wife to be in bed with her, he told her it's not only deceiving the master but sin before God

v.3 – a. St. Paul wants him to be excommunicated.

b. In spirit, already Paul did it.

c. Paul unhappy over the complacency of the church members.

d. The members claim spiritual gifts but fail to realize, "A little infection affects the whole body".

v.6 – "A little leaven, leavens the whole lump". (**Prov.** – "A small leak, will sink a whole ship")

A strict Jew searches the whole house and casts out the leaven food item if any, before the Paschal rites,as no leaven allowed before it begins (Deut. 6.1-3,6) – Christ our Pascal lamb.

Pagans, newly brought into the Christian faith, find it difficult to give up unclean pagan practices. Only when they are serious – they give them up.

Illustration

Dr. Venkatramanan (A scientist of RRL, Jorhat) at a get together of Brahman friends he raised the need for widow marriages among their community. But they were all silent. Then he stated "we are all (scientists), educated and qualified, but have not evolved out of our religious prejudices".

II Cor. 6.14-7.1 – Not to associate with sinners.

v.9 – It was misunderstood. So Paul clarifies. He says "It refers only to those within the church".

This was the only passage of Paul to show that Christ died when the Pascal lambs were killed (Jn. 19.7, 14-16).

Telugu proverbs

a. "Konga swargamuku vellina,

   Nattalni vedukutadi"

Eng: The stark even if it goes to heaven,it will look for shells(or) crustaceans to eat.

b. "Rameswaramku vellina,

   naa sani nannu vadalaledu".

Eng: Even if I go to the Temple town Rameswaram, my ill luck does not leave me.

Chapter-6

Christians Going to the Pagan Law-suits:

(Some feel it is possible that the incestuous member was planning to sue Paul before the court)

Paul insists that Christians must settle their own disputes.

Paul points out –   a. that saints would judge the world.

b. They even judge the Angels.(Dal.7.22; E 1.38; Rev. 20.4; Wisdom 3.8).

Paul's argument was, "if so, Christians can easily judge one another in secular matters".

If necessary, let a Christian accept wrong or be defrauded. So let Christian wise men be the judges, says Paul.

vs.12-20 –   a. Liberty is not license (free from Jewish law).

b. It destroys unity in Christ.

v.12 – Paul taught "All things are lawful". This does not mean licentiousness'. If so, it will be "spiritual ruin".

Body is not evil, so it should not be used for prostitution, i.e., evil.Body should be for the Lord.

a.   The Lord himself gives up for us (in the Lord's Supper).The body will be raised up, at the Resurrection as God did to Christ. No point to pursue rigorous   asceticism to control the body.

b.   There is no anti-thesis between flesh and spirit and between Incarnation and Resurrection.

Chapter -7

MARRIAGE, DIVORCE AND MIXED MARRIAGES

vs.1-7 – Marriage in general.

vs.8-9 – The unmarried (specially the widows).

vs.10-11 – to the Married.

vs.12-16 – The mixed marriages.

vs.17-24 – Whatever state called remain as you are.

v.25 – St. Paul's opinion.

vs.26-31 – About the virgins.

vs.29-31 –   a.   Those with wives

            b.   Those who mourn

            c.   Those who rejoice.

            d.   Those who buy

            e.   Those who deal with the world.

Some Rabbis unmarried; yet celibacy is not the ideal.

vs.5-6 – If no self control, better marry – but only a Monogamous marriage.

vs.7-8 – "To remain single, as I am" (Paul –widower or unmarried ?).

In the context of the immanence of the 2nd coming of Christ, celibacy advocated by Paul.

Illustration:

Widow remarriages – 'Water' cinema shooting at Mumbai, to show the plight of the widows (now of West Bengal; 'Sati' before) at Juhu beach, Sivasena smashed screen sets,not wanting the outside world get a bad opinion about Indians.

v.9 – wife should not leave the husband. In case she separates, let her remain single or reconciled to her husband.

v.10 – The husband should not divorce his wife.

vs.12-16 – **Mixed Marriages** – From now on St. Paul's Advice.

If one gets converted to Christian faith, stay out, for children's sake and hope, the other also becomes Christian. Paul was against tampering with domestic relationships.

I Pet. 4.15 – or else (as Peter shows here) commit your life to God and He takes care. (Dalai Lama = Ocean of Wisdom).

Paul deals here with supreme practical wisdom.

v.15 – If the Pagan does not convert, he or she can remarry, as she is not bound to him.

v.28 – If you marry you do not sin.

vs.25,36,38 – Don't make an unnatural thing of religion.

v.32 – Unmarried pleases God.

v.34 – Married her / his interests are divided.

vs.39-40 – Second marriages for widows and widowers. Wife bound to her husband as long as he lives.

Paul advices to remain single.

COMMENTARY

Marriage, Divorce and Mixed Marriages

1. Christ's Teaching:Matt. 5.32; 19.9　　　Divorce forbidden

　　　　　　　　　　Mk.10.9;　　　　by Christ except in cases of
　　　　　　　　　　Lk.16.18　　　　adultery

2.　St. Paul's own teaching – v.12

　　　i.　Unmarried and widows – v.8,9.

　　　ii.　Married – vs. 10-11.

　　　iii. Believers and unbelievers – v.12. – Not the Lord's teaching.

vs.17-24 ; vs.17,20,24 – Whatever state called remain there; only serve God faithfully in that state – married or unmarried – in view of the 2nd coming of Christ.

a.   **v.18** – Circumcised or uncircumcised.

b.   **v.20** – What counts is, obedience to God's commandments

c.   **v.21** – as slave when called remain so, never mind the slave condition. But if one can get freedom – avail it.

d.   **v.22** – As free-man called – then you are slave of the Lord.

e.   **v.23** – bought with a price of Christ; don't become a slave of man.

Ref. I Pet. 1.18 – bought with the blood of Christ.

vs. 26-38 – Advice to Virgins

a.   Parents give daughters in marriage – its right.

b.   Engaged already – to a Christian.

In view of the above state. – **Qn:**. Should they be married or not?

Paul's Advice:

a.   better keep the tradition and marry them, specially if the boy insists on marrying her

Paul's advice seems to some not helpful – as if marriage is second best.

vs.25, 36, 38 (I Cor.14.34) – vows for prayer etc., don't make an unnatural thing of religion

vs.29-31 – a. Those with wives forget them.

b.   Those who mourn as though not;

c.   Those rejoicing – not so.

d.   Those who buy goods – not buying.

e.   Those who deal with the world, as though not.

vs. 32-35 – **Qn**. Roman Catholic celibacy. Why?

Ans. To give undivided devotion to the Lord.

Vs.39-40 – Second marriage – for widows and widowers.

Paul's advice: They better remain single.

Qn. Is he in favour of ascetism?

Chapter 8

Eating Meats Offered to Idols

'Left over meat' offered as sacrifices to idols seem to be sold in the markets. This eating disregards the conscience of the weaker brother.

Paul says :

1. The Believers may say God is one. The pagan gods are not real. He says   such knowledge is not enough. Love must settle the issue

2. Some in the recent past were idol-worshippers. To them the idol is real.

3. So the stronger (old believers) should not destroy the faith of the weaker – new brothers for whom Christ died.

4. Paul does not quote the Jerusalem Council's decision (Acts 15.28; 21.25; 25.20,29).

    a.   To abstain from what has been sacrificed to idols.

    b.   To abstain from blood and what is strangled

    c.   To abstain from unchastity.

Chapter 9

Paul's Apostleship – Issue

vs.1-18 – Series of short Rhetorical questions.

Paul asserts his freedom and apostleship.

The Corinthians seem to have questioned his Apostleship.

v.2 – Paul says in the church there is the seal of his apostleship.

v.4 – a. If he wished he could have supplies of food and drink from them.

b. He could have his wife accompany him like

i.   Christ's brothers

ii. Other apostles.

iii. Cephas etc.

Both Paul and Barnabas waived their rights.

vs.15-18 – Paul's work of evangelism not a career of amassing wealth.

But i. an opportunity

and ii. a privilege to serve others.

Illustration

Jeevan Babu (Youth Secretary of NCCI; His Book: "Positive Approach to Christian Politics") in this book points out that at the start of the ministry many Christian workers work for "the Kingdom of God" (Mk. 1.14-15). Once bank account gets bigger – slowly shifts to his own kingdom, forgetting the Kingdom of God.

v.16 – Paul says "woe to me if I preach not the gospel (free)." "Necessity is laid on me".

v.17 – If out of my will I preach, I will have reward.

Paul gives examples:

"The labourer is

worthy of his life" (v.14)

1. A soldier (v.7)

2. A farmer (gardner)

3. Oxen

4. Track runner (v.24)

5. An Athlete (v.25)–a crown of leaves

   (Isthmus games practice – self control)

6. A Boxer (v.26) "blows in the air"? No.

The African proverb – "If you chase two rats you don't catch either one".

(Kingdom of God or of your kingdom or ambition?).

For the Gospel's sake identified with different people and races

1.   Jews   – v.20
2.   Gentiles   – v.21
3.   Weak   – v.22

v.17-18 – a. Necessity laid on him to preach the Gospel

b. Free will service gets the reward

c. He was commissioned by Christ (Acts 9.15; 26.15-17)

d. I make myself slave to all

e. I serve under the law and outside of the law, but under the law of Christ.

v.22 –   f. Became weak to reach the weak

Conclusion: "I became all things to all men".

Mk.10.42-44 – Jesus gave new standards

"who ever wants to be great must be servant of all."

Illustration: Leadership and Ambition

In Shakespeare to "Cromwell, I charge thee, fling away ambition, by that sin fell the angels; how can a man, then the image of the Maker's hope to profit by?

Mk.8.31;9.31;10.33 –3 passion sayings of Christ :i.e,Christ will suffer,crucified at the end.

3 times ambitions by the disciples at each passion saying by Christ.

1st – Peter rebukes Christ (Mk.8.32)

2nd – who is greatest discussion (Mk.9.33-34)

3rd – James and John special request for good positions with Christ in his Kingdom. (Mk.10.35-40).

v.25 – Paul must have been present at the Isthmusian Games, near Corinth, at which he might have seen the Victor wearing a leaf crown, palm in hand, offer thanks to the goddess of Good fortune. But soon that crown gets withered.

In contrast for the Christians – It is the unfading crown (I Pet. 5.6; Rev.2.10).

v.27 – For the prize, the sportsperson practices (To put his body in condition, or else lose at the end). So Paul says "I may be a cast away", if not prepared for the Lord's ministry.

Chapter 10

vs.1-13 – St. Paul returns to the topic of eating meats offered to idols.

The church is the heir of O.T. Scriptures.

To Paul – Church is the "True Israel of God".

To Paul even Baptism and the Lord's Supper are no guarantee of victory to the Christian.

1. **Baptism** – refers to Exodus story – based on Ps.105.39 and Ex.15.21.

    i. 'Cloud – A type of Baptism.

    ii. 'Sea' – A type of baptismal waters. (Ex. 14.1ff).

2. **Eucharist** – The Hebrews shared in the wilderness 'Manna' and 'water from the Rock' – a type of Eucharist (Num.20.8-11; Ex.17.6).

The Rabbis held that the Rock moved with the Hebrews.

Num.21.16-18 – The song of the well (with angelic force behind it) = supernatural power   and wisdom.

St. Paul went further to say "It is Christ himself source of the Living Water".

This reference to O.T; Paul uses here is not so much for Types but for warnings

Even if a Christian has access to Christ, the source of Power and Wisdom, yet he may fall.

Vs.6-13 – Warnings from the O.T.

a. Just as the Hebrews lusted for flesh-pots and died (Numb.11.4, 33 ff). or to idolatry.

b. As the Hebrews danced and reviled before the golden calf for impurity; (Ex.32.6,19).

c.   As the Hebrews died of Fornication – 23,000 (Numb.25.9) or for testing God's mercy.

d.   As the Hebrews died of serpent bite (Numb.21.6) for murmuring and grumbling.

e.   As the Hebrews died being struck by the destroying angel. (Numb.16.45-50).

As per St. Paul, these warnings were written for Christians at the end time.

Though these temptations allowed by God within man's capacity, yet no Christian should be too complacent that he can stand.

v.13 – Paul tells that Divine help is always there in our Temptations.

v.14-22 – Idol sacrifices   – Christian should shun idolatry.

In the Lord's Supper – we have communion with Christ through the bread and the cup.

Illustration: Those who ate sacrificial meal, are partakers of Jewish altar.

1st Objection: One may object saying that the pagan gods are no gods. True, says Paul, yet holds that demons exist. So to offer sacrifices is to enter into fellowship with them.

Partaking of the Lord's Table and of the Demons Table – So a Christian cannot partake of the Lord's Table and that of the demon's table.

2nd Objection: You may say 'I am strong'.

Qn.1.   Are you stronger than God? Asks Paul.

2.   Do you provoke God to jealousy? (by siding with Demons)

I Cor.10.23-11.1; 6.12 – Arguments picks up here.

"All things are lawful but all things are not helpful" (I Cor.6.12).

Here Paul was concerned with the actions of the Strong Christians and its effects on the other believers.

1.   If one is called for a meal by a heathen, one should eat meat if set before you without any questions.

2.   But his attention was drawn to the fact that meat comes from pagan sacrifices, a Christian should abstain, so that the other believers can not say "He has no conscience (in such eating)"

3. Yet another man's conscience is not the yard stick.for one's conscience.

4. If thanks given for food, a believer can eat it.

5. Every thing – eating and drinking – must be done for God's glory. (v.31). without offending the Jews, Gentiles, or Christians

Illustration: C.H. Spurgeon once was found smoking.

Qn. Is it for the glory of God? asked a believer of Spurgeon's Baptist Church in England as that great preacher preached to do all things for the glory of god.

Result – He stopped.

Paul earned the right to say – "Imitate me, as I imitate Christ".(I Cor. 11:1)

Chapter 11

vs.2-13 - Christian Women in Worship at Corinth. Women without covering heads with veil, praying.

Paul gives his opinion based on the customs of the ancient East. Paul's reasons, however weak, (v.13f) but fitting to the times. Some women while praying or at worship – not covering their head.

v.17ff – Some one may have written to Paul of this, so Paul gives his answer.

In replying to that particular question Paul gives his opinion about women as a whole.

v.3 – Paul shows the descending order of headship.

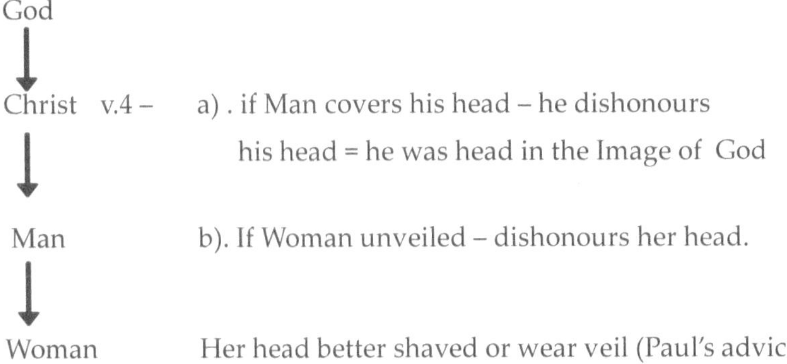

God

Christ   v.4 –   a) . if Man covers his head – he dishonours

his head = he was head in the Image of God

Man   b). If Woman unveiled – dishonours her head.

Woman   Her head better shaved or wear veil (Paul's advice)

v.6 – If she does not wish to cut her hair or shaved – better wear veil,

v.7 – as she is "the glory of man."

1. vs.8-12; O.T. – Woman (=Eve) made from Man (=Adam)

    i.   Gen.2.7,21-22 – 1st Adam, next – Eve – 'J' ('Jehovah' = for God) source

    ii. Gen.1.27 – Man and woman = equal, in God's image ('P=Priestly source) – Paul does not quote this priestly source.

2.   v.14 – Nature – long hair – woman's pride; for man – degrading.

3.   Long hair – for covering – to protect from the lust of evil angels (Gen.6.1-4).

Objection: No distinction as male and female in Christ.

Ans. – Unveiled woman liable to disturb other worshippers.

Illustration: 1st Missionaries to Mizoram (N.E.India) earlier:

a.   Men's seating arranged facing the side wall

b.   Women's seating – facing the pulpit.

Basel Mission Church (Mangalore) earlier;

a.   Women in the church hall seated.

b.   Men – on the balcony above seated.

These above illustrations at the beginning of the Missionaries work in those fields. Now it is changed.

Illustration: In Saudi Arabia an Indian Doctor visited by his wife from India for holidays. He met her at Rhyad airport and put on her the Burka he brought; as a woman she has to wear so.

Paul's reasons, however weak for now, happen to be suitable to that time at Corinth.

The Lord's Supper and its Misuse (I Cor. 11.17-22)

The Background:

a.   The converts seem to have forgotten the original Religious meaning of the Lord's Supper.

b.   They seem to be more concerned with the social aspect.

The social side: The rich did not care for the poor.

Acts 3.46 – The Jerusalem church in the beginning

a.   "breaking bread in their homes,

b.   they partook of food with glad and generous hearts." i.e., the Lord's Supper eaten with their common pooled food – 'AGAPE' meals (The Gospel writers dropped the agape meal reference when they wrote of the Lord's Supper) .

The Lord's Supper account in I Corinthian letter was of primitive church tradition, as it was penned before even the Gospels were written (St. .Mark's the earliest – 68 A.D. or so, while I Corinthian letter was written in 55 A.D. – 13 years before the writing of the 1st Gospel).

vs. 23-26

a.   Paul reminds of the original solemnity of the Lord's Supper.

b.   He received from the Lord most probably through the Antioch church tradition.

The words of the Lord's Supper – (in the present tense) a)"This is my body" – for bread. b) "This is my blood" – for the cup (wine).

1.   R.C. Church holds – **Transubstantiation** view-The substance of the bread and and wine changes at the priest's prayer.

2.   Luther held – **Consubstantiation**' Theory-The presence of the Resurrected christ in the bread and wine.

3.   Zwingli (Reformer from Zurich, Switzerland) held – Memorial Theory – "Do this in remembrance of me" (**v.25** of I Corinthians,11th chapter.)- This based on the tradition earlier, as gospels were written later (after 68 A.D.) than Paul's epistles (before 64 A.D.).

Ex.13.9 – O.T. Covenant at Mt.Sinai.

I Cor.11.25 – New Covenant in Christ's blood. We find here

1.   The church is the Body of Christ.

2.   Spiritually united; there should be no factions (v.18).

3.   Represented before the Table of the Lord.

4.   The Memorial aspect of its observance.

5.   The New covenant, as prophesied by Jeremiah.(31.31)

6.   It replaces the Old Covenant (Ex.24.8)

7.   It is covenanted in the blood of Christ (v.25).

8.   It is to be repeated ("as often as you eat it")(v.26).

9.   To remind the IInd coming of Christ (v.26).

10. To eat unworthily, makes one guilty of the body and blood of Christ (v.27).

11. Invites Divine judgement upon such one (v.27).

12th and 14th Chapters – Spiritual Gifts: St. Paul was asked about his opinion about the question of speaking in Tongues. This he takes up again in the 14th chapter.

Chapter - 12

The Gift of Tongues Issue

4 types or levels of speaking in Tongues

1.   Inarticulate sounds

2.   Articulate sounds resembling words

3.   Coined with words and phrases.

4.   Utterance of phrases in foreign languages.

Tongues = "GLOSALOLIA" (Gk.) –   a. 'LALIO' = to speak

b. 'GLOSA' = tongue

vs.1-3 – through the Holy Spirit one speaks "Jesus is Lord" (v.3)

St. Paul says those speaking in Tongues should be tested. If the professes curses, "Jesus is Anathema", then he is not of God's spirit. i.e., some of them might be inspired by the pagan deities like the Scythian goddess.

vs.4-11 – as Tongues is one of the many gifts, Paul considers others also.

a.   These gifts are not offices of the church but are functions – These are called "Charismatic" ministries.

'CHARIS' (Gk.) = Grace = so these are Grace gifts.

b.   **v.11** – The Holy Spirit gifts "as He wills", not any body can claim or request for a particular gift – so "Grace gifts" based on the Holy Spirit's grace, the Holy Spirit being the donor.

c.   These being charismatic, they are different from official ministries appointed by the church to serve that church or its Mission like Pastors, Deacons, etc.

d.   **v.11** shows – the Holy Spirit is a person (= He wills)

e.   These spiritual gifts are not given for personal benefit, but for the well-being of the church as a whole. (Icor.14.3-4, 12).

vs.12-26 – The metaphor of the Body elaborated (I Cor. 12.27) (Rom.12.6-8; ICor. 13.14)

Metaphors of the church–   a.   The church as a Body (ICor.12.27)

b.   The church as a Building (ICor.3.9).

These metaphors show–   a.   One Body but many members.

b.   One structure but of many materials.

Important: i.   This shows unity in diversity.

ii. a.   All members should function to co-ordinate with others

b. A member however humble is needed.

Gifts –   for the building up of the church (ICor.14.12).

–   for the common good (ICor.12.7).

–   for the edification of the church (ICor.14.4).

–   a.   for upbuilding.

b.   for encouragement

c.   for consolation – (ICor.14.3).

v.28 – Various ministries–   1.   Apostles,

2.   Prophets,

3.   Teachers,

4.   Workers of miracles,

5.   Healers,

6.   Helpers (Deacons),

7.   Administrators,

8.   Speakers in Tongues

9.   Interpretation of Tongues: in number all in all

It seems Evangelists and pastors missed, which we find mentioned in Eph.4.11.

Additions to the officers of the church (4 nos.), the others

a.   Miracle workers,

b.   Healers,

c.   Speaking in Tongues,

d.   Interpretation(of Tongues) are charismatic ministries.

Chapter - 13

A Hymn of Love

5 kinds of Love

1. Philia (Gk.)– Filial love (Philadelphia) (Rom.10.10)= brotherly love.

2. Eros (Gk.) – Sensual love.

3. Agape (Gk.) – Divine love.

4. Charitas (Latin) – Loving the good.

5. Cupiditas (Latin) – Loving the evil (or) bad.

Note: 'Charity' (from 'Charitas') used in A.V. Bible, as it is the opposite of 'Cupiditas', the love of the bad (as per St. Augustine). But Martin Luther, the Reformer, preferred 'Agape' as it is the 'sacrificial love' shown on the Cross in the life of Christ. So in the Revision 'Charitas' as 'Charity' in English was replaced by the word 'Love'.

1. Without the gift of the self-giving love Christian sacrifices are valuless.

    It will be like the resonating of the pagan worship – gongs, symbols, empty wind bags.

2. Even gifts of preaching, i) knowledge, ii) understanding the divine secrets, iii) even faith without Agape (=love) those are useless.

3. **Characteristics of Love ('Agape')**

    a. Patient = long suffering with people.

        and Kind = sweet to all, kindly disposed.

    b. Not jealous – not envious of other's prosperity.

        and not boastful – inflated with self-importance.

    c. Not arrogant – proud (some big person's fall often to his arrogance) or rude – behaving rudely – no kindness.

    d. Does not insist his own way – his rights claim

e.   Not irritable – flaring up in temper

nor resentful – brooding over wrong.

f.   Does not rejoice in wrong but rejoices in the right.

v.6 – bears all things; believes all things; hopes all things; endures all things.

Positive Traits i.e.,= Forgiving, hopeful and trusting.

1.   Without the gift of the self-giving love, any Christian sacrifice is valueless – like gongs or symbols resonating at pagan worship. These are just empty bags.

2.   a.   Even preaching, understanding divine secrets,

b.   Even faith that moves mountains, without Agape is useless.

Vs. 4-7: The characteristics of 'Agape' (=love).

a.   'Makarothumein" (Gk.) = longsuffering

b.   Kind disposition to all.

Not covets or grudges – not self-seeking rage or bitterness, not braggart or inflated self-importance

c.   Agape (=love) does not brood over wrong

i.   not for injustice but truth.; always forgiving, trusting, hopeful and patient.

ii.   Agape is indestructible. Prophecy, Tongues, knowledge – all will perish, not Agape.

Illustration: A metal mirror gives dim reflection. In this life we see God's truth like that. Faith, Hope, Agape remain in the New Age.

Chapter-14

PROPHECY AND SPEAKING IN TONGUES

Main Divisions

vs.1-19 – a. Agape love to be sought.

b. Among the spirit-gifts, prophecy to be desired.

vs.20-25 -Christians should use brains like adults (as Infants to Vice only).

vs. 26-40 - rules for worship.

vs.1-19 – Prophecy vs Tongues

vs. 1-2 a. Paul says he himself exercised this gift of Tongues more than others

vs.3-5 b. but wanted to limit Tongues in preference to prophecy (=N.T. it is chiefly preaching).

v.32   c. The prophets have their gift in control.

d. They presented it with intelligence. Above all, to Paul, 'Agape' love to be sought

e. Any one speaking in Tongues, speaks with God (=unintelligible to men).

v.3, 12 f. any one prophesying builds up the church.

g. If Tongues interpreted edifies the church so it's alright like flute, harp and bugle.

vs. 7-8 – h. i. just as a musical instrument played for a recongnisable tune is good, if not useless.

ii. Just as a bugle unless sounds clearly, it cannot summon soldiers for battle.

iii. Like wise an unknown tongue, does no good to the church.

If converts come to church and anxious for spiritual things, they seek such gifts that bring blessings.

St Paul holds that both spirit and understanding have their place in singing and praying, Paul says that if a new convert comes to the church and if a blessing given in an unknown tongue, how can he say 'Amen".

v.16 – If a Thanksgiving (may be the Eucharist form prayer) may be excellent, but if unknown tongue, how the other members can be edified. Paul though speaks in tongues more than others, yet he prefers few words with understanding.

v.20-25 – Paul advises – Christians should use minds intellectually like adults, not like children. Yes, you can be like children with regard to vice.

Vs.22-23 – a.   Tongues impresses unbelievers by its phenomenon,

b.   Prophecy impresses the believers.

V.23 – Unbelievers can hear Tongues in the church and may call them as "mad".

v.26-40 – **Rules for Worship.**
v.26 – All are anxious to show their gifts in public; but all should be done to build up the church.

v.27-2 or3 – atmost, one can speak in tongues, by turns, and with one interpreting them.

v.28 – If no Interpreter, he should keep silence and speak to God.

v.29 – 2 or 3 prophets can prophesy by turns. Others should exercise discernment.

v.31 – but he should be silent if any one has a revelation.

v.32 – the prophetic gift can be kept under control by the prophets.

Finally Paul advises the Corinthian church to keep order in the worship service and peace.

vs.34-36 – Women's place in the worship service.

Paul says if a woman wishes to join in a discussion of a prophecy or a sermon, they should do so at home with their husbands.

The commentators feel this injunction of Paul does not mean prohibiting them to prophecy. It refers to the women to cover their heads and be silent.

v.35 – the remark of Paul "It is shameful for women to speak in the church" refers more to women's subjection to men, as the custom of the society then.

Acts 18.26f – Paul did not prohibit women from private impartation of God's word (eg., Priscilla).

Conclusion

While Tongues are not to be prohibited Prophecy has to be more desirable.

Chapter - 15

The Resurrection Faith

Introduction

v.20 – The faith of the Christian rest on the Resurrection of Christ.

Questions were asked by the Corinthian Christians about the nature of the Resurrection; i.e., the state of the resurrected body.

a. To the Pharisees, human body re-animated. Man's risen state will be in heaven or on New earth. It is not the earthly body though its continuation.

b. The Greeks thought of the immortality of the soul (like the Hindus)=the body (soma(Gk.) the tomb (=sema (Gk.) of the soul.

II Cor.5.10 : It will be a spiritual body, to give account of deeds done in the earthly life before the Judgment seat of God. It preserves its continuity and its identity. The basis is Christ's resurrection. Christ appeared to the disciples with a risen body.

v.17 – Without Resurrection, Christian faith is futile. The life-giving power of the spirit in the present time is a guarantee of a future bliss.

vs. 1-11 – The appearance of the risen Christ.

a. to Peter (Lk. 24.34)

b. to the Twelve.

c. To more than 500 (in Galilee)

    St.Paul says many of whom were alive then.

d. To James, (the brother of Jesus) (Jn.7.5).

e. Last of all to Paul himself (Acts 9.4-6).

v.9 – Paul felt unworthy to call himself an Apostle as he persecuted the church.

(Not like other apostles, yet his labours more and as good as other Apostles).

vs. 12-19:

Paul forestalls any possible argument.

Because of Christ's Resurrection our Resurrection is possible.

Paul argues, if Christ did not rise, Christian preaching futile and Christian faith in vain.

v.19 – if in this life only hope, Christians of all men, most pitiable.

vs. 20-28 :

In fact Resurrection faith is certain;

Eye-witnesses had seen his power.

Resurrection by stages– 1st stage – Christ's

                          Next stage – those who believe in him.

                          Last stage – when Christ hands over the power to the Father.

vs. 29-34 – I.   Why Christians baptized for the dead?

               II.   Why Paul takes the risks in his life?

               III. Why the struggles with beasts at Ephesus?

               IV. Why Paul dies daily if Christ has not risen?

The implications are that Christ rose from death.

vs. 35-49 – The Nature of the risen Body.

a.   The seed if it dies sprouts into a plant. The one who denies God admits this fact.

b.   The plant body will not be exactly like the seed.

    God gives to each plant an appropriate body.

So Paul argues, just as different kinds of body of man, beast, birds etc., so too earthly and heavenly bodies.

The Anti-Thesis shown

1.   Dishonour – glory.

2.   Weakness – power.

3.   Natural – spiritual.

I Cor. 15.45 (Analogy) – Ist Adam vs. IInd Adam.(Rom.5.12-21; II Cor. 4.6

Vs. 50-53 – Transformation to the risen life.

The argument of v.42 picked up.

Paul believed "Parousia" will take place in Paul's time.

Qn. What happens to those alive?

Ans. I Thes.4.13-17 – When the trumpet sounds those on earth will be transformed. They put on the Heavenly body. The dead would be raised incorruptible.

Chapter 16

This is the concluding chapter of the I Corinthians letter.

Vs.1-4: It has 24 total verses and the main concern shown here is the collection (this term used for religious purpose) to be raised .no definite demand was made but up to the believers' decision.

The point to note is why some of the members at Jerusalem so poor as for the other churches to come to their aid?

We read of raising money by Paul, in Rom. 15.26; II Cor. 1 ff. Acts 24.17.

We can note a few

v.2 :a) to be collected on the 1st day of the week, when the believers gather. This was based on the Resurrection day of Christ.

v.3: b) Not to collect after Paul arrives, but before and keep with them.

v.4: c) Paul does not wish to touch it but their own selected emissaries can carry it and give it to the mother church.

d) Not mentioned how much but left to each believer to decide for himself or herself. But as God prospered each.

e) As Gentiles got the Gospel from the Jews, so this is an expression of the Gentile converts their gratitude to the Jewish believers at Jerusalem.

f) It was also to express unity, with believers of the mother church their solidarity.

Vs.5-9: Paul's plans were uncertain as he plans to pass through Macedonia but that he may stay the whole winter with them. He wants to let the Corinthian Christians know he desires to visit them.

Vs 10-12: In Acts Paul spoke of sending Timothy and in Acts 19.22 Erastus accompanies Timothy.

Paul refers that Timothy be "without fear" among them, this shows Timothy being young must be of timid disposition.

v.11: In view of the task Timothy was carrying on, that he should not be despised by the others at Corinth

V.12: Paul refers to Apollo, the Alexandrian forceful preacher, who was instructed by Priscilla and Aquila when he visited Ephesus, into the fuller truth of the saving work in Christ Jesus (Acts 18.24-28).

Vs.13.14: In this brief exhortation, Paul was in a series of imperatives , points to a better way to them.

Vs.13:Paul exhorts the Corinthian believers

a)   To stand firm in their faith- refers to stability in faith.

b)   To be courageous and be strong in faith.

c)   Let every activity of their love be motivated by love.

Vs.15-18 : Paul refers to Stephanas the 1st convert in Asia and his household, how they have helped the servants of Christ in terms of the hospitality.

d)   Paul adds to subject themselves to such servants of Christ.

e)   V.17 Three believers Fortunatus, Achaicus along with Stephenas have kept company with Paul and thus in a way though Paul visited Corinthians yet these above believers made it up with him. These must have worked after the needs of Paul in their absence.

f)   Vs. 19.20 Paul refers to the greetings of those who gave company to him.

g)   The church in the house of Pricilla and Aquila at Ephesus including probably other churches of Asia too send greetings to the believers at Corinth . In turn Paul asks the Corinthians to greet one another in their name.

h)   Vs.21.23 For 2nd coming of Christ the churches were waiting for and Paul calls on a curse to those who oppose this faith. Grace and love Paul sends in closing.

3
II Corinthians

We note that Paul was at Corinth in the 2nd Missionary journey (A.D. 49-52) by sea to Athens and by land to Corinth (Acts 18.1-28). Also he visited Corinth in the 3rd Missionary journey (A.D. 53-57) by land from Thessalonica to Corinth (Acts 18.22 ff).

From the Corinthian correspondence we find,

a. the 1st Corinthians written after some news from Corinth, including a letter from the Corinthian church (I Cor. 7.1). It was sent through Timothy (I Cor.4.17).

b. Paul pays a personal visit (I Cor. 12.14) as the situation at Corinth becomes worse. Paul writes a letter (II Cor. 10-13 chapters). It was a "severe one" and sent through Titus.

c. Paul goes from Troas and meets Titus at Macedonia (II Cor.7.3). He learns that all was well at Corinth.

d. From Philippi of Macedonia probably writes a letter of Reconciliation (II Cor. 1-9 chapters).

INTRODUCTION

Corinth was referred as "the Vanity Fair of Asia".

a. It was destroyed by Romans in 146 B.C.

b. It was rebuilt by Julius Caesar (and Augustus) by 46 B.C. as a Roman colony.

c. Isthmus river there gave the name for Isthmus games, second in importance to the Olympic games.

d. The Eastern port Cenchreae connected to the western port, Lecheum. It saved over 200 K.M. round voyage by sea.

Illustration : As I travelled from Athens to Corinth, I noticed the bus crossing this great deep rock cut across from East to West. It is said that 2000 Jews brought from Babylon worked for this work and more added later.

e.   The goods from the boats used for sale at Corinth by the sailors. Thus the name of Corinth as "the Vanity Fair of Asia".

f.   Romans, Greeks, Jews etc., were settled here.

g.   On the Acropolis mountain was the Temple of Aphroditus, the goddess of love, with around 1000 prostitutes catering to the visitors.

h.   Thus the moral standards were low there, so that to call any one as "Corinthian" means a person of low morals.

i.   On the stage a drunkard, riotus and reckless living, is referred as "a Corinthian".

To such a situation of Corinth, St. Paul with his companions like Silas, Timothy, Titus et. al. visited Corinth and won converts and established a church there.

MAIN DIVISIONS

1.1 – 2.16	:	St. Paul's experience of the church situation.
2.17 – 7.16	:	St. Paul's ministry – the Reconciliation and confidence.
8.1 – 9.15	:	Offering for the poor at Jerusalem .
10.1 – 13.14	:	Paul's credentials of his Apostleship.

COMMENTARY

1.1-2	:	Greetings
1.3-7	:	Suffering for Christ
1.8-11	:	Paul's deliverance
1.12-2.17	:	The reason for the change of Paul's plans to visit Corinth

Chapter – 1

1.1-2: Greetings from Paul, in the manner of Jewish or Aaronic blessings – 'grace' and 'peace' conveyed. Sosthenes (I Cor. 1.1) and Timothy are just fellow-workers but Paul an 'Apostle' of Jesus Christ, as He commissioned him when he met him in his vision on the road to Damascus (Acts 9.1-19). In Gal. 1.1 he writes as an Apostle "by the will of God", i.e., not of any man's appointment. In that way Paul asserts his divine authority to his ministry.

vs.3-7–vs. 3 & 4 – God's character a. A Father of mercies (Ps. 86.15)

b. God of all comfort.

vs.5-6 – The sufferings of Christ, if we too share, then we are enabled to comfort those who suffer. Paul refers to his trials as sharing in the sufferings of Christ.

St. Paul indeed told of the trials he would undergo, as he fulfils the given post of an Apostle to the Gentiles (Acts 9.16; Col. 1.24).

Believers too undergo sufferings being united with Christ (II Cor. 4.10).

v.6:a. Paul feels personally his sufferings and comfort in Christ benefit the Corinthian believers as he serves them.

v.7:b. The believers too can benefit from such experience in Christ.

The Greek: "KOINONIA" refers to not only the "fellowship" but also in "sharing" of joy and pain with one another.

vs.8-9 : Paul looks back of his experience in Asia Minor where when he lost all hope, a sudden turn of events led to his deliverance. This he felt almost from death to life i.e., the Resurrection (II Cor. 11.23-27; Eph. 1.19f.).

vs.10-11: He requests Corinthian believers to uphold him in prayer as it was almost "fighting with beasts" at Ephesus like gladiators used to do in the Roman amphitheaters (Acts 19.23-41). Though Paul was not directly involved, yet there was a plot and a mob violence then. This we find by

Demetrius, a silversmith, engaged in making Artemis images, Paul's preaching went against their livelihood.

1.12 – 2.17: The change of venue in Paul's ministry.

vs.12-18: There was trouble in the assembly at Corinth. One member seems to have fallen in sin and turned as an opponent to Paul (2.5-11). Paul thought over and changed his planned visit (1.23). Paul wrote a sharp letter and that erred member seems to have repented and Paul thus willing to forgive him.

[In **II Cor. 2.12-17** we find reference to Paul's ministry after the Ephesian riots (Acts 19.23ff; Acts 20.1ff)].

vs.12-14: Paul refers to his conduct at Corinth as irreproachable and not of dubious nature as to speak one thing and mean another. Paul even refers to the final judgment when both Paul and the Corinthian Christians realize how each helped the other.

vs.15-16: Paul had plans to visit Macedonia, after which he felt he could go up to Corinth also (I Cor. 16.5). When he got unfavourable reports of Corinthian Christians, he changed his mind and left just for Macedonia only.

v.17: Paul's adversaries referred to him here as unprincipled, one who vacillates.

vs.18-20: Paul holds that his life has been consistent as much as God is faithful. The Gospel Paul preached, including his companions Silvanus and Timothy, was always positive, 'yes' to the Corinthian believers.

All the promises of God find their 'Yes' in His Son, Jesus, for the glory of God, the closing 'Amen' of the Hebrew term as well the Greek 'Yes' give the endorsement of satisfaction in Christ (Rom. 11.36).

vs.21-22: God whom Paul holds as the One who in Christ called as an Apostle, with his fellow-workers commissioned, with his seal and the pouring of the Holy Spirit as a sign (=Gaurantee).

vs.23-24: The changed plan, as stated at the outset, was to avoid 'another painful visit' (2.1) and here adds "for he would have come with a rod" (I Cor. 4.21) but to spare the Corinthian believers, Paul did not visit them. Paul's concern was always "for their joy" (Phil. 1.25) and for them "to stand firm in their faith" (v.24).

Chapter-2

vs.1-17: The change of Paul's plan to visit (Contd.).

Paul already made "a painful visit"in this situation of Corinth (II Cor.12.14; 13.2).

v.1: So Paul decided not to make another painful visit.

vs.2-4: To make another such visit will make the Corinthian Christians further sorrow. He has already written "a severe letter" (II Cor.10-13 Chapters) sent through Titus earlier. So Paul decided not to go then. So that when he visits next time he will have joy and together rejoice with them. The previous letter he wrote, Paul says, not only with much "anguish" but with much "tears".

Illustration.: A new England Puritan pastor called the congregation "to weep" for their unsaved lives, and added "if you do not, then I have to weep for you".

St. Paul was a true minister of his congregation at Corinth to shed tears for them.

vs.6-8: St. Paul now states the offending member alone did not make Paul grieve but the whole assembly there.

From Titus, he learned that immoral person was disciplined by the majority.

v.7: Paul says he should have been restored now, showing 'forgiveness' and 'comfort' to him.

v.8: Not to be overwhelmed by too much sorrow, Paul advices the church to reaffirm "their love" to him.

vs.9-11: Paul sees this advice to the Corinthian church as "a test of their obedience to his authority".

In this Paul also sees the unity of the church with his decision in absence. In Christ this action was taken by them and by Paul in unision, and reminds them "the presence of Christ" also in this regard can be seen.

v.11: Negatively this community action keeps Satan away , for Paul says "we all know his, Satan's (evil) designs".

'Satan' of Persian origin term for the 'devil' in Hebrew language (11.14; 12.7).

vs.12-13: St. Paul recalls that after "the severe letter" he dispatched through Titus, he visited Troas as an opportunity came to take the Gospel there.

But Paul says that he was restless about the outcome of 'the severe letter" he sent through Titus. So he left for Macedonia (probably to the believers at Philippi town of Macedonia), where he must have met Titus with Corinthians.(Eusebius says Titus became Bishop of Crete).

vs.14-17: Paul now breaks out in praise of God. In the scene of a victorious Roman General leading the captives and booty parading through the streets of Rome in triumph over the enemies. Paul sees in this way the victory of God at Corinth (Col. 2.15).

He also sees the **Gospel knowledge** spreading **like the fragrance** by the incense bearers who joined the triumphal procession of the above scene. The aroma sweet to the victors but death to the doomed. Paul asks at the end that who is able to proclaim the Gospel with such great awesome consequences?

Negatively Paul sees the pillars of God's word at Corinth, for selfish gain in business terms.

v.16: "from death to death....and life to life" seems Semitic expression of emphasis.

Paul and his fellow-workers were men of sincerity with pure motives, commissioned by God.

Paul's Evangelistic Campaigns: 3.1–7.16

3.1-18	–	Old vs New ministries.
4.1-15	–	Man's weakness vs God's manifestations.
4.16-5.10	–	Human weakness vs Divine strength.
5.11-6.10	–	Reconciling task of the church.
6.11-7.1	–	To keep aloof from unspiritual
7.2-16	–	Paul's assurance to the Corinthian Christians.

Chapter – 3

3.1-18 – Old and New Ministries

vs.1-3:

v.1 – letters of recommendation to the Corinthian Christians.

v.2 – Our letter of recommendation to the Corinthian Christians.

v.3 –A letter written by Christ.

    a. These letters delivered by Paul and his colleagues.

    b. These letters written not with ink, but the Spirit of the Living God.

v.3 –c. These letters written not on tablets of stone (reference to the Decalogue given to Moses on Mt. Sinai – Ex.24.12).

v.2 –d. **These letters** written **on your hearts**. (a reference to the New Covenant, Jer.31.33).

Three things we notice here:

1. The Jewish opponents (The Judaizers) managed to get letters of recommendation when they visited Corinth, to discredit Paul's ministry.

2. The Sinai 'Decalogue' (The Ten Commandments) of O.T. were given on stone Tablets. But now in Christ **God's will** given **in their hearts.**

3. This refers in effect the New Covenant in Christ (Mk.14.24) replaces the Old Covenant under Moses.

All this does not mean Paul was negating the Law of Moses, but rather sees in Christ as its fulfillment (Rom.10.4;Gal.4.4).The Law was our Custodian until Christ came(Gal. 3.24).

Paul raised the question, "What is the Gospel?" If the answer is "justified by faith", then why return to a different Gospel? (i.e., as insisted by the Judaizers to observe the Law and follow circumcision).

Paul was also saying the believers at Corinth are the living witness, "to be read by all men" (v.2) i.e., their transformed lives testify to it (II Cor. 5.17).

v.4-6: v.4 –   a. "Our confidence" (v.4) here Paul says "through Christ' about his appointment as 'Apostle' by God himself.

vs.5-6 –   b. 'Competent' (verb) and 'Competence' (noun) of Paul and his colleagues in the ministry is not of himself but "of God".

Two things to note here

v.5 – i. the competence of Paul (and colleagues) are from God.

v.6 – ii. the competence of Paul (and colleagues) to be ministers of the New Covenant.

vs.7-11: The old dispensation vs the New Dispensation.

The splendour (or the glory) of the old dispensation {='DOXA' (Gk.)}

v.7: a. The Hebrews could not look at Moses' face (Ex. 34.29-35) (it shone as he was with God for 40 days on Mt. Sinai).

v.9: b. The Old Dispensation was of condemnation, of lesser splendour.

v.8: a. The New Dispensation must be of greater splendour.

v.9: b. The New Dispensation of righteousness must far exceed in splendour.

vs.10-11:a. It disqualifies any splendour of the Old Covenant, (as the moon fades away when Sun rises).

    b. for the splendour of the New Dispensation is permanent; far surpasses that of the Old.

Note: The 'glory' (DOXA (Gk.) actually refers to the 'worth' of a person. With reference to God's glory, seen in the exercise of God's sovereign power in creation history.

The glory of Jesus seen in his ministry (and in his miracles) in his saving activity of mankind.

vs.12-14: The Gospel (preached by Paul).

  a. It does not pass away.

  b. It does not have anything to hide.

The veil over Moses' face refers

    a.   to the fading radiance of the Old Covenant.

    b.   to the impermanence of the Old Dispensation.

The greater dispensation of the New (Heb. 8.13).

Paul's mission is to show the greater dispensation to follow Christ and his Gospel.

The old dispensation (Covenant) intelligible through Christ as he fulfills it (Rom.10.3f).

vs.15-16: The 'veil' over the Old Covenant – its removal in Christ.

It means the righteousness or justification of a sinner is possible only in the coming of Christ (epistles of Romans and Galatians deal with this fully).

Vs.17-18: The conclusion of this chapter 3 is that in Christ, who is the Spirit, there we get freedom.

    a.   freedom to behold the glory of the Lord

    b.   and to be transformed into the likeness of Christ

    c.   from one degree of glory to another.

    d.   as it is the work of the Spirit.

Chapter – 4

---

vs.1-15: Man's weakness and God's glory

v.2: Some who are engaged in the evangelistic ministry seem to follow unfair ways:

    1. Disgraceful ways   2. Underhanded ways

    3. Practice cunning ways   4. Tamper with God's Word

a. 'Cunning' (or deceit) ['PANOURGIA'(Gk.)] is what was referred about Satan deceiving Eve in the garden of Eden.

b. 'Tampering' of God's word is chiefly a reference to the Judaizers, who insist it applies chiefly to the 'Torah' (The Old Testament), though includes the Christian revelation. They seem to misapply it (II Cor.2.17) or even pass over relevant Texts (ICor.14.21 etc.).

In contrast St. Paul's presentation of the Gospel was a statement of plain truth appealing all listeners' conscience.

v.3: Paul recognizes the Word of God of the Gospel at times do not bear fruit, but the blame has to fall on the hearers like the bad soil, i.e., not the seed or the Gospel proclaimed (eg., Matt. 13.18-23).

v.4: It is 'the god of this world' = Satan (Isa.14.14), who "blinded" i.e., misled the hearers to reject the proclaimed Gospel.

Actually it is   a.   the light of the Gospel.

               b.   the glory of the Christ.

               c.   the true image of the invisible God (Col. 1.15).

v.5: The Gospel: a. not about ourselves the preachers = your servants

               b. but Jesus Christ = the 'KURIOS' (Gk.) = Lord = his sake.

v.6: In the Old Testament, the Prophets when they prophesied they prefixed to it saying "Thus says the Lord," i.e., **the content** of **preaching** should be **'God's word'** not of the preacher's own words.

Reference to Genesis 1st chapter to God's creation referred here:

Old Testament: Gen.1.3 – God first brought light.

New Testament time: That light comes in person in Christ Jesus (Heb. 1.2f).

vs.7-12: v.7 – The Believers likened to "the earthen vessels" (Is. 64.8). But the content of these vessels is the light of Christ.

The messengers of the Gospel may be frail, but the Gospel message is magnificent power of God.

vs.8-9: To manifest the life of Jesus in their bodies, the evangelists had to undergo many trials, like

a.   afflicted in every way – but not crushed;

b.   perplexed – but not driven to despair;

c.   persecuted – but not forsaken.

d.   struck down – but not destroyed.

v.10: The death of Jesus always carried in the body so as to manifest the life of Jesus in the life of the preachers. It was in a sense sharing the earthly experience of his Master, Jesus.

v.12: The **conclusion** here is that the Corinthians may reap the benefit of what Paul was passing through. This is the paradox.

vs.13-15:v.13-Paul quotes here Ps.116.10 as an appropriate reference,to express his faith.

v.14: Even if he dies, yet the hope is there, based on the resurrection of Christ, the believers will rise again (I Cor.15.20ff).

So death does not separate him from Corinthians or Jesus Christ.

v.15: More and more learn from Paul's life the work of Christ, it naturally has to lead to the way of Thanksgiving to God, leading to his glorification (Rom.1.21; Ps.50.23).

v.16-18: In conclusion Paul says "I do not lose heart".

Qn.: Why?

The answer is as follows:

Ans.: The present experience – in reality.

a. The outer nature wasting away – but the inner nature is renewed every day.

b. There is a slight momentary affliction – but it is preparing them to an eternal Glory beyond all comparison.

The reason for this hope is,

a. We look not to the things that are seen – but to the things that are unseen.

b. The things that are seen are transient – but the things that are unseen are eternal.

This above, in a sense, is the crux of the faith and hope of St.Paul.

Chapter – 5

vs.1-10: The Heavenly Renewal

a.vs.1-5: Earthly dwelling vs Heavenly dwelling.

| **v1:** Impermanent or the transitory nature of the earthly life, like a 'Tent' pitched for a short time. This is the Greek idea of 'body'. | a. It is referred as **a.** building
b. a house – not made with hands
c. eternal one in the Heaven. |

vs.2-4: a.   Here we groan.

b.   long for Heavenly one, to be no more naked.

c.   We sigh with anxiety, to be further clothed

d.   this is mortal life.

v.4: "This sigh of Anxiety" is with regard to the delay in the second coming of Christ, in the 1st Century.

I Thes. 4.13 shows some believers died before Christ's coming

But v.5 shows there is the "Guarantee" of the Holy Spirit for the future hope of the believers.

v.5: The Hope for the Heavenly home is based on the guarantee of the Holy Spirit.

The word "Guarantee" is a business term, referring to the 1st deposit for Spirit's guarantee for future full blessings of redemption in Christ.

vs.6-10: v.6 – While the believers not obtained the Heavenly hope "to be with the Lord forever"; in a sense "we are in the physical perishable body now in the world".

v.8: On this above understanding the believers should live "of good courage" or not to lose our hope of the hereafter, i.e., Heavenly abode.

v.9: In either case, of "here" or "here-after", a believer should have the aim "to please the Lord", i.e., obedient to his will always.

v.10: The final day of Judgment where Christ sits to judge all for the life they led – good or evil deeds. Revelation 20.11-15 shows this related to the second coming of Christ. This should not be seen in the negative terms for "punishment" only, but also for "rewards". Here in addition to the "Book of Deeds" is also shown "The Book of Life" where the believers are already booked for their place with Christ in Heaven.

vs.11-15: There seems to be some doubt about the credentials of Paul and his ministry by the believers at Corinth. So Paul gives his reply to that here.

v.11:   1. "What we are, known to God"

2. "It should also be known to you (="your conscience").

3. Paul says:

a. "we are not commending ourselves to you again."

b. "but giving occasion to Corinthian Christians to be proud of Paul and his colleagues."

c. So the Corinthian Christians can answer others who pride themselves and who doubt the credentials of Paul and his colleagues".

v.13: Paul argues that he is not in the ministry

i.   for his own benefit, but

ii.   for Divine service and Corinthians' Spiritual benefit.

v.14: The love of Christ for Paul as a sinner controls all his actions. Christ died for sinners, in their place.

vs.18-21: The theme of Reconciliation.

v.18: God is both the Reconciler a. who initiated it,

b. who is the goal of it.

v.19: Though men committed sin, which is against God, yet God takes the first step – to set aside this estrangement of man.

That means, the "Divine wrath" brought about by man's sin, God puts away now in Christ's death for man's sin.

So the Gospel is the preaching of the Reconciliation. It is the Divine Gift offered now freely to man's salvation.

v.20: The Christian ministers therefore become the Ambassadors to this above ministry of Reconciliation.

v.21: To be therefore "justified" or "made righteous" ("DIKIOSUNE (Gk.) is in Rom. 3.26, refers not only to the believers but also shows that God by this act shows his righteousness in accepting those who have faith in Christ and his redeeming work for sinners.

Chapter – 6

---

vs.1-3: The presentation of the Gospel and its reception:

a. **Salvation** work is entirely the work of Christ and it is "**divine grace**". (Is.49.8).

b. But to human beings it is given the responsibility to receive it.

But men are misled by some false Apostles in saying that in addition

1. to the saving work of Christ

2. they should add to it on their own something more (II Cor. 2.17; 11.4).

Here we find Paul was urging the people to accept the Gospel as

1. it is the time of salvation decreed by God showing His Grace to men (Is.61.2).

2. Paul says, as such it is for people to respond, **not to miss** this time of God-given **salvation** in Christ.

v.3: Paul still adds **3)** let no one who listens to the Gospel reject it with any excuse of fault with the preachers.

vs.4-7: Paul says that a great endurance is needed for those in the Christian ministry: **9 trials** listed here, which are **classified into 3** categories by one of the N.T. scholars.

The First Group

I. a. Afflictions: Physical, mental and spiritual pressures.

    b. Hardships – physical.

    c. Calamities – in different situations.

II. There are **second group** of difficult situations created by the people.

    a. Beatings (11.24)

    b. Imprisonments (Acts 16.23etc.,)

    c. Uprisings or tumults (Acts 13.55; 14.5).

III. The third group of hardships are for the sake of the Gospel spreading and the resulting establishment of the Christian fellowships.

    a.   Physical and mental hardships in labours.

    b.   Sleepless or restless nights (Acts 20.31).

    c.   Hungry, at times starving. etc.

We in return can see the spiritual qualities of Paul, which enabled him to endure these above hardships.

1. Holy life with single-minded purpose in the ministry.
2. Holding to the Truth of the Gospel – the knowledge.
3. Forbearance in terms of not easily provoked to fight.
4. With kindness (forbearance associated) (Gal. 2.22; I Cor. 13.4).
5. The gift or quality of Christian life aided by the Holy Spirit.
6. The righteousness resulting quality of life.

vs.8-10:Paul's enemies in the ministry;

    a.   as "unknown" or "he is not worth noticing" (yet "well known" in truth).

    b.   as "dying" i.e., "he is finished", (yet "keep on serving") (Acts 14.19).

    c.   as one "punished" (yet "always rejoicing in the Lord") (Rom. 8.3f.; Phil. 4.4).

    d.   As "poor"yet   i."making many rich in divine knowledge" (Eph.3.14; Phil. 3.7f).

                      ii. "Possessing everything" (I Cor. 3.2ff; Rom. 8.17 etc).

6.11-7.1: To Keep away from Unspiritual life.

a.   Here Paul writes to the Corinthian Christians of the church there to keep away from the immoral member in the church.

b.   He clarifies, on the other hand, he does not mean from such ones in the world.

vs.11-12: Paul writes   a. "our heart is wide".

                          b. "you are not restricted by us".

Paul wrote regarding the immoral man not to associate with him (I Cor. 5.9).

But in I Cor. 5.10 Paul writes to clarify that this injection does not apply to those of the world.

v.13: Thus he writes "widen your hearts" on this issue.

Here Paul speaks as "to children", as he wishes to deal with them intimately as he trusts them and expects loving response from them.

vs.14-16: Paul deals here with the Corinthian Christians, referring to the uncommonness between the "believers" and "the others of this world".

In vs.14-16, in a series of antitheses Paul shows to the believers that nothing is common between them, so as not to mismatch with them (Lev. 19.19; Deut. 22.10).

1.   Righteousness vs Iniquity.

2.   Light vs Darkness.

3.   **v.15a:** Climaxes with Christ vs Belial.

In conclusion **vs.15b: 4.** what has Believer in common with the Unbeliever.

v.16:5. What accord the Temple of God with idols? In this last contrast St. Paul refers to the Believers, as the Temple of the Living God.

Here the O.T. references seem intended for support (Ex. 25.8; 29.45; Lev.26.12 etc.)

The **question** asked seem to be "What relationship Christians have with idols?

Ans.: God promised to dwell with his people, it involves separation from old relations.

vs.17: Paul quotes here Is.52.11.

vs18: Paul quotes here Hos.1.10; Is.43.6.

In **vs.14-16** for example

1.   Though a Christian cannot marry an unbeliever (I Cor. 7.39), yet Paul concedes for a mixed marriage (I Cor. 7.12f).

2.   Though Paul vetoes heathen sacrifices, as immorality often associated with their worship, yet eating of the meat he shows no objection, except

for the "new converts" whose weak conscience not to offend (I Cor. 7.12ff).

The Conclusion: 7.1: Paul calls on the Corinthian Christians to cleanse from all defilement of body and spirit.

This is in relation to a. the fear of God.

     b. the perfection of holiness (God being holy demands holiness – (Matt. 5.48).

The church referred as the Holy Bride of Christ (II Cor.11.2). As such the believers (church) have to cleanse themselves from every defilement of body and spirit.

vs.2-16: St. Paul's confidence in the Corinthian believers.

In 6.11 Paul told them "Our mouth is open to you and our heart is wide open".

Ill.: The medical science shows,one out of a lakh people has the heart on the right side. It is termed as "DEXTROKARDIA". How many hearts (out of a lakh) cheerful for the Good News of Saviour.

v.4: Qn.: Why Paul was cheerful about the Corinthians now?

Ans.: v.5: At Troas port he got opening for the Gospel. Though he was engaged in the Gospel ministry, yet he was restless (2.13).

Before this he sent Titus to Corinth. He took the 'Severe letter' of Paul to Corinth. He delayed to return. So Paul left Troas and went to Macedonia, across the Agean sea. There he met Titus, returning from Corinth. He brought the comforting news that all is well at the Corinthian church (II Cor. 1.3-4).

vs.6-7: a.   Titus was first comforted there at Corinth.

b.   Paul was next comforted by that news that all is well there.

v.5 refers a.   'we were afflicted at every turn'.

b.   'so that our body had no rest"

c.   'They had fighting without,

d.   and 'fear within'.

v.6: Paul was now relieved and feels this turn of events as that of "God, who was first comforted us at Corinth".

vs.8-9: Paul felt sorry to hurt Corinthian Christians but in one way he was happy as it has the salient feature of bringing them to repentance.

v.10: A distinction was made between

i.   the godly grief – it leads to repentance.

ii. the worldly grief, on the other hand, makes them remorse. (Ill.: Judas Iscariot).

Paul notes in the second category grief (worldly one), there is no place for

| | 1. | hope, | 2. | grace | 3. | forgiveness. |

It produces   1.   despair   2.   suicidal state   3.   death.

v.11: Paul says that in all this matter the Corinthians proved guiltless.

v.12: It made the Corinthians to set their house in order, so it is necessary to punish the one who did wrong.

Ill.: Now-a-days some of the city churches do not seem to enforce the "Excommunication" though as a disciplinary act of the church as an institution. In the small towns and villages probably it is still in practice as it is a close knit local community, yet the danger of the disciplined one joining a different denomination or starting a new denominational church is there these days in India.

v.13: The result is   a.   Paul and his colleagues were comforted.

b.   Titus' mind has been set at rest now.

c.   Paul and his colleagues rejoiced at the joy of Titus himself.

In effect it means, Paul's satisfaction at the success of Titus' errand for which Titus himself was happy.

vs.14-16:

v.14 –   a. Paul's expectation of the Corinthian reaction proved right.

v.15–   b. Titus seemed to love the Corinthians (during his stay he felt so).

Paul says to them "his heart goes out all the more to you".

v.16: Like a proud father, whose children not disappointed his expectations of them, he has confidence in the Corinthian Christians.

N.B.: After this Paul was able to launch on the delicate task of calling for their offerings for the Jerusalem poor Christian members (8-9 Chapters).

8.1-9.15: For the poor believers at Jerusalem church, the Corinthian Christians' 'love-offering'.

a. **8.1-24:** The Collection.

b. **9.1-15:** The basis for this monetary offering.

(Ref.: Acts 11.27-29; Gal. 2.10; Rom.15.25-29).

This was seen as a responsibility of the Gentile Christians for the poor members of the mother church at Jerusalem.

8 and 9 chapters deal with this topic of church collections.

Chapter – 8

vs.1-2: To encourage the Corinthian Christians St.Paul places before them the fine example of the Macedonian church giving.

a.   In spite of their extreme poverty, and

b.   In severe test affliction they demonstrated the Grace of God by their generous giving.

In contrast Paul shows the state of the Corinthian church was not in that plight (v.14).

vs.3-4: Further the Macedonians gave

a.   of their own free-will.

b.   and even begging Paul to arrange for sending it.

v.5: This surprised Paul.

The reason seems to be a. "They gave themselves to the Lord first".

b. Next they gave themselves"to us"says Paul.

Paul sees in this the philosophy or lessons for others in giving. There is no negative thinking here as seen in an American preacher's saying on giving.

1.   **Ill.:** "Give according to your salary, lest God make your salary according to your giving" (Peter Marshall , US Congress Chaplain).

2.   **Ill.:** Oswald J. Smith, the pastor of the Peoples' Church at Toronto, Canada, authored a book on Missions. We all know the Mission bodies collect funds for sending missionaries to the unevangelised areas of the world. Oswald Smith cites an illustration about an Atheist questioning the missionary ventures. He asked a believer "What will any one does if he is saved to go to Heaven?" (for which funds are collected).

The believer (answered): We will meet God there.

Next: Thank Christ for salvation.

Next: Thank the Mission Board for sending missionaries.

Next: Thank the missionaries for the Gospel.

Next: Thank those who contributed money and for their sacrifices.

Next: The Pastor, the church elders to support missionary works, and so on, so much so, at the end the Atheist finding no answer left silently.

Of course here in the 8th chapter (II Corinthians) it is chiefly referring to collections to help the needy at Jerusalem church.

I am taking this opportunity to address those questioning church collections for Mission.

Here we find the lessons Paul seems to convey to the Corinthians:

1. Spontaneity   2. thoroughness

3. Christian spirit   4. confidence in Paul.

v.6: Titus seems already started collecting (I Cor.16.1f). from the Corinthian church (to add to the Macedonian gift).

v.17: He has to return to Corinth to complete this collection.

v.19: He was appointed to join Paul to carry the collection to Jerusalem.

v.7: The Corinthians' lauded here for their Christian qualities.

They excel in everything (II Cor.8:4-7). This may refer to their spiritual gifts(I Cor. 12-14 chapters):

a.   Faith

b.   Utterance and knowledge (I Cor. 12.8-10).

c.   Earnestness

d.   Love (for Paul and colleagues).

v.8: The Macedonians also demonstrated – their generosity i. in love and ii. in Christ.

Imp.: The "Have-nots" help seen here.

v.9: Illustration from the life of Christ.

Though he was rich he became poor.

Jesus was sharing the Father's glory,

Yet by his "incarnation" he became poor in limiting his self to human life (Phil. 2.7f).

v.10: Paul's advice to the Corinthians to complete what they had started in giving a year ago.

vs.11-13: Paul asks them to give from what they have and not to get into debt. Probably they had promised more than they are able to redeem themselves now.

Ill.: Oswald J. Smith, the pastor of the Peoples' Church in Toronto, Canada.

He refers to his first experience of "faith-promise giving", at a small church, he started to minister. It was January, the Mission Convention for the church there. The ushers were distributing envelopes for promise for the whole year. Mr. Smith got only $25 a week, he has a wife and daughter to look after and no bank account. He thought he will not give anything. But in his heart he felt God telling him that how much he trusts that God can give him that year. Finally he put on the envelope $50. To his surprise he paid all by the end of the year and he doubled year by year till he started to give thousands to the Missions. He called it a **"Faith-promise giving"**.

vs.14-15 (Ref. Ex. 16.13-21): This is a reference to "Manna" given by God to the Hebrews during their wilderness journey of 40 years. They should gather for each day of each family's need. Each had enough – not more (spoiled by next day) or not less for those who could not gather enough (Ex. 16.18).

The Early church at Jerusalem practiced "limited Communism", those with prosperity sold and gave to the church. So those poor widows, disciples etc., could continue serving in the church (Later though they gave it up) (Acts 2.44f).

The giving principle here was – "EQUALITY".

Paul says here, later, in case Corinthian church in straits financially then Jerusalem church should come forward to help Corinthian church.

vs.16-17: Titus, on his own, collecting from the Corinthian church as we have seen.

Here the reference to him as "Famous preacher" shows Titus was good for both – preaching and fund raising.

It is often felt good preachers or religious persons in general are often blamed for mis-handling the finances.

Titus' life should be seen as a good example of the opposite of above opinion. We should rather say that a good preacher or church worker should be also a good steward of church finances.

vs.20-21: v.20-Paul affirms in this regard that he and his associates wish to be blameless.

v.21: Paul affirms in this regard that he and his associates wish to be blameless not only in God's sight but also in the human sight – in both.

In selecting Titus as one of the group on this mission shows his blameless life before God and the church people.

vs.22-23: Titus qualified on both sides and certified by Paul also, two messengers to join, seems to be selected by the Corinthian church.

v.24: Finally Paul calls on them as all is settled who will carry the collection, now to give proof :

i.   to show your love,

ii. of your boasting of the integrity of the selected carriers of the collection, i.e., to give generously when they come for collections.

Chapter – 9

---

vs.1-15: The Philosophy or **Principles of Giving**.

vs.1-2: Paul sure of the readiness of the Corinthians of Achia (=Greece) boasts before the Macedonians.

a. Ready since last year (few months before).

b. Your zeal stirred up others to give.

v.3: Paul says he was sending few brothers, so that his boasting may not become futile.

v.4: Paul was accompanied by some brethren from Macedonia (Rom. 15.2). Paul was concerned that by chance the Achians (it was the Roman province from Isthmus river to Corinth) not ready, the result will be that Paul will be humiliated (As per Acts 18.11 – Paul stayed for 1 ½ years at Corinth).

v.5: For this Paul was sending some brethren ahead before Paul reached Corinth himself later. So he asks the Corinthian church leaders to arrange this gift in advance.

Ill.: When I visited a town called Kakinada, in South India, Andhra Pradesh state, some kind of collections by some organization of the town's people was going on. In this connection I came across a chalk writing on the roads as follows:

"Not as an exaction, but as a willing gift".

v.6: The principle underlying the giving, Paul gives as follows:

a. He who sows bountifully

will also reap bountifully" (Prov.11.24f; 19.17)

b. "He who sows sparingly will also reap sparingly" (Gal. 6.7-10 – applied to spiritual harvest Matt. 6.14 – applied to forgiveness).

v.7: Paul adds   a.   give not under compulsion, not reluctantly but as one made up his mind" (on his own) and adds   b. "God loves a cheerful giver" (Prov. 22.8 = Mk. 12.41) genuine gift exhilarates)

v.8: In return   a.   God-provides you in abundance

b.   so you always have enough of every thing (Phil. 4.11; 4.19; I Tim. 6.6).

vs.9-10: Scriptural support taken in these verses – Ps. 112.9

Is. 55.10

Hos. 10.12.

Phil. 4.19: For every good work in God's service, He provides both spiritually and materially.

v.10: A sowing God is the giving God, as seed potential is under God .

Righteousness = Right action, here refers to give liberally.

vs.11-12: "Giving is an enriching experience.

Paul refused to take anything for self (11.7-9).

a.   Their generosity meets the physical needs of the saints.

b.   It also physically overflows – for many thanksgivings.

In essence – it is fellowship sharing.

Qn.: Why Paul refused to take anything for himself?

"Liturgia" was the public service for which the wealthy Athenian citizens paid for. It also meets the needs of the saints. Spiritually it overflows in thanksgiving to God.

v.13: The result is that the Gentile Converts demonstrate their Christian profession to the Jewish converts and this way express their unity with them.

vs.14-15: This results in their "KOINONIA" = fellowship with the Jews, by the Gentiles. This Paul terms as "The surpassing Grace of God in you".

v.15: Paul finally closes in saying "Thanks be to God for his inexpressable gift".

As he says in Rom.8.22 – "Human language is inadequate to describe the full extent of either the gift or its consequences".

Ill.: It seems the Christian of the Mormon church of Utah state of USA as a rule fast one day in a month, so that the proceeds of that given or used by the church to help the poor among them.

10.1-13.14: St. Paul's Apostolic Authority

a. 10.1-18: St.Paul's credentials

b. 11.1-33: Misrepresentions answered.

c. 12.1-13: Paul's experiences of his glory and of his weaknesses.

d. 12.14-13.4: The imminent 3rd visit.

e. 13.5-14: His final charge and word of cheer.

Chapter – 10

vs.1-18: Paul's certificates or credentials shift from 1st person plural = 'we' to singular = 'I'.

v.1-2: He says like
1. "When I am away from you I am bold to you".
2. "I, who am, humble when facing you.
3. "I entreat you with a. the meekness and
   b. the gentleness of Christ
4. If necessary now I will show boldness in speaking severely of some at Corinth.

vs.3-4: Paul says: The Christians in the world

i. have to live with its troubles.

ii. have to live in the flesh with its frailties

Paul says
1. The real battle is Spiritual (i.e., not physical).
2. We cannot destroy the stronghold of Evil of
   a. the society or of
   b. the individual.

v.5: By using
a. one's intellect or
b. one's will or
c. one's pride or
d. one's self-sufficiency.

v.6: To accept the Gospel seems too humbling an experience.

St. Paul feels
a. the majority will accept the Gospel.
b. a remnant will reject (who will get divine punishment).

v.7: Paul feels under attack of
a. not his faith
but b. his authority given by Christ.

v.8: He says 1. his boasting: a.   not self-centered

                   but   b.   magnifying what God has done (in his life).

Paul's credentials: The lives of Christians of Corinth.

vs.9-11: The charge against Paul:

I.   While present: a.   Physical – his bodily frame or presence – weak and ineffective.

                         b.   His speech – in speaking not very fluent.

II.   In absence: a.   his letters – frightens or terrorizes his opponents.

                         b.   his letters – some hold they were just put on show.

     Of course   a.   physically he may have a weak frame of body but

                         b.   he was hard   i. when there is a wrong to set right.

                                            ii. or a great principle to fight for.

v.12: Paul says that any comparison of any believer to make is not between one another but with Christ, who is the unchanging external one.

vs.13-18: The above topic enlarged here.

v.13: Paul says   a. we will not boast beyond limit.

                     b. we will keep to the limits God has set for us.

Paul's ministry has limits:

v.14: 1. He was the Apostle to the Gentiles (Gal. 2.9).

v.14:2. That in reaching Corinth first Paul says, he was not going beyond the limits set by God.

v.15:3. Not entering into other men's labour (That's how he planned to reach Spain when the time came, leaving the ministry at Asia Minor (Rom. 15.20).

Chapter – 11

vs.1-33: Paul's replies to the misrepresentations.

v.2: As Paul established the Corinthian church (I Cor.4.15), he now proceeds to the stage of a father, who gives in marriage his daughter.

There are many **metaphors** used for the **church**, but the prominent ones are the so called **3 'B's** or the three starting with the letter – B. They are as follows:

1. The Building	The first two refer to the fact of "unity in diversity".
2. The Body	a. Many kinds of material but one structure – 1st one.
	b. Many members but one organism – 2nd one.

3. The Bride :

The **third one**, the bride, this metaphor **refers to holiness** or purity, as such, Paul refers to the church as pure bride (Eph. 3.25; Rev. 19.7), Christ being referred as the Bridegroom (Mk. 2.29). In the book of Revelation, the 2nd coming of Christ at the end time is associated with the time **Christ receiving the church** as his bride (Rev. 19.7).

v.3: The Corinthian church's loyalty to Christ seems to be under question. The reference to Eve, the 1st woman and wife of Adam, was deceived by Satan, so too now the Corinthian church's 1st loyalty to Christ seems to be under question.

v.4: 3 disturbing references made here, suggesting the questioning of their undivided devotion to Christ:

1. Another Jesus	This will be:
2. Different Spirit	a. to be led astray in your thoughts.
3. Different Gospel	b. so as not of sincere and pure devotion to Christ.

This will be like repeating the falling into sin by the first parents by the cunning deception of Satan in the garden of Eden.

The different Jesus or Gospel seems to refer to Gnosticism who preach Jesus is just human and a sort of demi-God.

vs.5-6: To these preachers, whom he refers as 'superlative Apostles', Paul says

1.   he is never inferior to them
2.   specially in the knowledge of the person of Christ.

Paul in effect is saying:

1.   They are intruders (II Cor. 3.1).
2.   They make self-commendation (II Cor. 10.12).
3.   Hebrews (11.28) but mercenary minded (12.13-18).
4.   They plan to lure Corinthians to Mosaic laws' bondage (11.15).

v.7: Paul reminds the Corinthian Christians that

1.   He abased himself in presenting the Gospel to them.
2.   And he did not take any payment for that from them.

vs. 8-9: By Tent-making (along with Aquilla and Priscilla) Paul earned money for his Gospel work (Acts 18.1-4).

1.   So without pay, Paul says, he preached and served the Corinthians.
2.   He got support from other churches like the Philippians of Macedonia (V.10;Phil. 4.15,18).

v.8: "Robbed" is for "pillaging" or "support" = ration money are said to be military terms, which the conquerors take from the others. It refers to support from other churches for Corinthian Gospel work.

So no one from Corinth could accuse him as their 'Exploiter'.

vs.10-12: "Not to take any help from the Corinthians" was Paul's decision.

It was 1. to express his genuine love for Corinthians and

2. to disprove those who claim to serve similar to Paul, but they accept help.

vs.13-15: Paul now tries to prove that these so called

1.   super-Apostles are Satan's Agents.

2.   Though disguise themselves as Angels from the kingdom of light.

3.   They disguise themselves as servants of righteousness.

     These above classified ministers Paul seems to recongise as

4.   The Judaizers whose main teaching was salvation by works (opposed to 'by faith in Christ')

5.   Paul says "their 'End' only reveals truly who they are".

vs.16-19: Paul was embarrassed to speak in that way as he did.

v.17: 1. Not Christ, but Paul wishes to challenge his opponents on their own standards.

v.18: 2. On the basis of their antecedents of birth, race etc.,

v.19: 3. Paul wants the Corinthians to rise up to this standard.

v.20: 4. Their bullying treatment of the Corinthians to submit to the regulations of the Jewish legal system.

v.21: 5. Paul was a failure at Corinth if judged by the super-Apostles' standards.

          a. Tyranny   b. Greed   c. falsity

          d. arrogance e. violence.

v.22: The above False-Apostles were boasting that they were pure Hebrews.

From Paul's side he recounts his antecedents though his birth was outside Palestine, i.e., Tarsus, yet he was "impeccable as a Hebrew".

But as a servant of Christ, Paul says he abhors these Hebrew symbols of paltry vanity, what glorified earlier.

v.23: Where Christ's ministry is concerned, Paul says he is beyond their horizon.

Paul lists few of his labours (in vs.23-28), chiefly in the book of Acts 16.23-25, Already at Philippi his imprisonment took place.

1.   3 imprisonments: a) at Jerusalem b) Caesarea c) Rome (Near death (1.9; I Cor. 15.31).

2.   3 times beaten 40 lashes, less one = 39 lashes (Acts 14.15; 16.22); vs 24-25 – once stoned.

Only few examples of his sufferings mentioned (he was also at the mercy of the Jews and Gentiles who attacked him from time to time. He was ship wrecked – 3 times; 24 hours adrift at sea.)

This portrays tough character and great courage.

v.28: The daily pressures of the care of the churches, his anxiety for all the churches

St. Paul looks back to his experiences.

v.30: If he has to boast, he will of his weaknesses only.

vs.32-33: Lastly he remembers how he was dropped in a basket from the fort at Damascus, when they tried to kill him.

Chapter – 12

St. Paul's experiences of his glory and wseakness

v.1f: If Paul had to boast, he says, he has nothing to gain by it. He has visions and revelations of the Lord.

v.5: Paul does not wish to boast of himself.

He seems to have seen some one in his visions who went up to third Heaven, 14 years ago.

We know that after conversion he went up to Jerusalem after 14 years to visit the Apostles (Gal. 2.1). This was about 40-42 A.D.

This vision seems to be some years after his Damascus experience (II Cor.11.32-33).

The Jewish expression for the immediate presence of God for Paul it was the most sublime experience indeed.

The word 'Paradise' was a Persian loan-word for the Jewish usage in Hebrew. Literally it refers to "a park".

In the Septuagint (LXX), (the Greek translation of the Old Testament,) this above term 'Paradise' (= Park) was applied to the Garden of Eden.

In the New Testament, this term was used in Rev. 2.7, for regaining the place lost in Eden.

Paul here states that he does not wish to reveal what he has seen and heard in his vision here.

vs.5-6: Of such visions of glory Paul does not wish to boast but only of his weaknesses.

So he calls on the Corinthians to accept him as he is, not as a special one for his glorious visions.

vs.7-8: To keep Paul humble, he tells here, that 'a thorn' was given to him in his flesh.

N.T. scholars think it must be 'malaria' fever prevalent in these regions. Once one is effected, it constantly reoccurs.

v.9: It seems 3 times Paul prayed to God for its removal but God's answer was "My grace is sufficient for you".

Observation: Is there a single servant of Christ, who can not profit to some thorn in the flesh – physical or psychological – which after many prayers, allowed by God, to keep him/ her humble.

Human weakness and Divine grace – go hand in hand.

v.10: Even troubles made Paul strong in faith.

v.11: Of 1 ½ years stay at Corinth, the so called Mission center of Paul for Greece, Paul refuted the allegations of the super-Apostles.

v.12: The signs of True-Apostle are seen by all:

   a.   in evangelistic programme, and

   b.   in the resultant church-planting.

v.13: The only exception what Paul did to them was, he did not burden them for financial assistance. Paul supported himself from his earnings of the Tent-making work he was engaged in.

vs.14-13.4: The Immanence of the 3rd visit.

v.14: Paul's motto of not taking any monetary help from the Corinthians, seems to have been

vs.14 & 16: a. misunderstood, or | by some Corinthians
          b. misrepresented

So Paul was determined to set right these allegations against him.

Paul argues in the analogy of parents and children, where he like a parent supports himself and not by the Corinthian Christians, the other way round.

He is their spiritual father, in this regard he supports them.

v.15: As Paul was loved less in this respect, he makes a hurtful response.

v.16: Some held that Paul was crafty he will take the money collected by his agents.

vs.17-18: Paul challenges the Corinthians to show:

How he was benefited from Titus' first visit?

In 8.16-24: a. safeguards made regarding the collections raised to be sent to the   poor at Jerusalem.

b. Neither Paul nor Titus gave any scope for suspicion.

They were trusted by the Corinthian Christians beyond doubt.

v.19: St. Paul's consistent effort was for the upbuilding of the Corinthians as the body of Christ.

Not to be misunderstood, Paul uses some terms here like

1. "in the sight of God"

2. "speaking in Christ"

3. Address them as "beloved".

v.20: In coming to a conclusion, Paul speaks out of meeting Corinthians in his next visit, face to face

1. 'to find you not what I wish" – from Paul's side

2. "you may find me, not what you wish" – from Corinthians' side.

The reference to his visit here is the Third time.

1st visit – in founding the church

2nd visit – the painful visit (II Cor. 2.1;7.12)

Here Paul makes it clear his consistent purpose was

1. for their up building –   (Positive)

2. it involves elimination of evil Characteristics – (Negative).

The Negative habits to eliminate are –

a. quarreling   e.   slander

b. jealousy   f.   gossip

c. anger   g.   conceit

d. selfishness   h.   disorder

v.21: Paul at the end shows concern for the possible unrepentant immoral members in the church there. In seeing them, his reaction to them, Paul expresses here.

With regard to those sinful (i.e., immoral) members in the church Paul shows

a.   These have sinned before.

b.   They have not repented yet.

Paul says 1.   God may humble me before you

              2.   I have to mourn over the sinful.

Chapter – 13

---

vs.1-3: The imminence of 3rd visit (Contd.)

v.1: As we have noted Paul made 2 visits already.

This is the 3rd visit he hoped to visit any charge against any one needs to be sustained by more than single witness, i.e., two or more as per the Deutronomic code – Dt.19.15 (cf. Jn. Matt)

a.   One is the immoral man (II Cor. 12.21).

b.   The other is Paul himself put in the dock " as noted earlier with regard to his self-support etc. (II Cor. 10.4).

v.2f: With regard to himself Paul already cautioned them that when he visits he "will not spare" them.

v.4: In **v.3** Paul says "Christ was speaking in him"

In **v.4** he says as Christ, who was crucified, (i.e., expression of weakness) Christ now deals with "the power of God" in Paul and his colleagues, being with the resurrected Lord is understood.

vs.5-14: Paul's final charge which includes "a word of rejoicing".

vs.5-7: So far the Corinthian Christians finding fault with Paul, now Paul turns this on the Corinthians "first to examine themselves".

Here Paul refers to the final test   a. on Paul's side for their charges against him.

b. on their side – Paul says his prayers that they "do no wrong" and "do what is right" (v.7).

v.10: All this Paul says that "In his visit he may not be severe; in the authority (he will exercise), which Christ has given him".

Of course it is "not to tear down" (Negative),

but "for building up" (Positive).

v.11: The concluding Appeal:

1. Mend your ways

2. Heed my appeal

3. Agree with one another

4. Live in peace.

Then the "love and peace" of God will be with them.

v.12-13: All the believers ("saints") greet them. They too to greet one another as a sign of Christian brotherhood with a "holy kiss".

v.14: Paul concludes this with the benediction.

4
Galatians

DIVISIONS

The Epistle to the Galatians can be divided as follows:

1. The testimony of Paul about his apostolic authority. Chapters 1-2

2. Contrast between Law & Grace.; Chapters 3-4

3. The life of the believer- not under Law but Grace. Chapters 5-6

First Section : Chapters 1-2

Paul independent of the apostles before him shows how he became as apostle and traces down his experience.The gospel he preached is acknowledged by James,Peter and John. The Judaizers made Peter a prominent leader but Paul,when he visited Antioch, rebuked him when he did wrong.

Second Section : Chapters 3-4

This section defends the truth of the Gospel. The Holy Spirit leads in the truth : Contrast between law and grace – not ordinances of the law but faith justifies a man – why the law was given – when faith came it was the end for law. Those in faith are no longer under the tutor. In those who are in faith dwells the Holy Spirit who makes them the sons of God.

Third Section : Chapters 5-6

A believer is justified by faith – should walk by faith. Under grace and not by law. It is a walk in the Spirit and manifestation of the fruits of the Spirit.

INTRODUCTION

The term refers to the inhabitants of the Roman province of the Galatia – may not be by race similar to the Gauls-so, may refer to the inhabitants of cities like Antioch (Pisdia) , Derbe,Lystra, and Iconium (in the Iconium valley : People spoke that language in addition to Greek which was the official language) , which Paul visited in the first missionary journey in 48 A.D (ref: Acts 13:24,14:28;16:1-5)

Date

Galatians epistle is dated as 48 A.D and is the first writing of Paul. On his second Missionary journey Paul passed through Galatia (ref: Acts 16:6) – may be around 50 A.D

But no account of his work was given.

This comes after the Jerusalem Council decision regarding the Gentile converts' observance of the law of Moses. But Paul mentions no such councils in the epistle to the Galatians.

- Gal. 1: 18-2:1 Paul refers to two visits to Jerusalem.
- Acts shows 5 **visits of Paul to Jerusalem** as follows :

1.   Acts 9:26-30 After his conversion.
2.   Acts 11: 27-30,12:25 brings offerings from Antioch with Barnabas.
3.   Acts 15:1-3 To refer the Judaizers' demand on issue of Gentile converts from Antioch.
4.   Acts 18:22 After the second Missionary journey.
5.   Acts 21:15-23,33 The final visit when Paul was arrested.

The Galatians is said to be the most passionate letter. Paul felt his Gentile converts in a great crisis losing the central doctrine of their faith. The main topics covered in " The Galatians".

1.   The purpose of God for the Gentiles
2.   The relationship between the Jewish & Gentile converts.

The Judaizers

1.   The judaizers demanded that the gentile converts be circumcised.
2.   They also demanded that they should observe the law of Moses.

The belief of the Jewish converts to Christian Faith about the purpose of God for Israel

1.   All nations are to believe that God had a purpose for them also.
2.   The purpose of God is fulfilled if they accepted the Law and Judaism.

3. Jerusalem is the centre for all to come and receive the Law of God (ref: Zech 8:20-23)

4. Jesus is the Messiah of the Jews first and then the Messiah of the Gentiles also if they became followers of Judaism.

So, the question which rises here is – ' Is faith sufficient for salvation or something else is also needed '?

The Attitude of the Jewish Christians:

1. In Jesus the New Covenant has come, the old moved (ref: Acts 7)

2. God has special place for Israel, so at least some part of the Law is to be kept and circumcision of the Old Covenant.

Jerusalem Council's Decision (Acts 15:19-20)

The Gentiles need not follow the Law but since the church is made up of both the Jews and the Gentiles, the Gentiles must accept the food laws of the Jews at common meals.

The fundamentalists however insisted that the Gentile converts keep the whole law. (Acts 15:5). James kept it as Jewish converts' group and was so respected by outside Jews also.

So, Paul raises the question, 'what is the Gospel'? If the answer is 'Justified by faith', then why revert to a different Gospel, which talks of observing the Law and follow circumcision'?

Chapter-1

COMMENTARY

V.1-5 : Paul's commission direct from Jesus Christ, though at Antioch they laid hands on him and commissioned him, he was already a missionary. Paul and Barnabas-The Holy Spirit commissioned them at Antioch.

V.6-9 : The truth of the Gospel is threatened. Paul rebukes the Galatians for moving away so soon to a different kind of the gospel. On false teachers-Let God be judge upon them – for creating confusion. "Even if an angel preaches a different gospel – let God judge him."

V.10-24 : How Paul became an Apostle: Paul did not receive the gospel from men but from Christ Himself – Paul tells a bit of his life story – God has a different purpose for him- to proclaim gospel to the Gentiles. Paul did not refer this matter to human authority – The apostles serving before him were his seniors- yet his authority is the same as those before him. Paul began his ministry in Damascus-great commotion-so he slipped to Arabia-and then back to Damascus-three years thereafter he visited Jerusalem – he was with Peter for 15 days and he met James. There was agitation against him – so he was sent back to Tarsus.(Acts 9:30)

Acts 11:20-26 : Barnabas was sent to Antioch. Barnabas came and picked him up from Tarsus to serve at Antioch – The Jewish Christians at Jerusalem heard that " THE PERSECUTOR NOW PREACHES THE GOSPEL".

Chapter -2

Vs.1-10 : Paul visits Jerusalem after 14 years (since he was converted) with Barnabas from Antioch.Titus went along. Barnabas went on behalf of Antiochian church, – Paul told about the gospel he preached to the Gentiles. Some questioned his right to preach and admit to church by baptism directly. If their point of view is accepted Paul's work would be left undone. They should accept it as a part of the work of Christ.

Trouble started with Titus' case – Titus was a Greek speaking Gentile. He became a Christian directly without first becoming a Jewish proselyte. He was never circumcised like Jewish Christians. Paul and Barnabas went up to the temple at prayer time but Titus could not as he was not a Jew, not circumcised. At Jerusalem they kept Jewish food laws-but kept Christian fellowship. Jewish converts joined; later this became known and the Jews came to spy on Paul.

A question was raised as to whether Titus should be circumcised . If this was agreed to, it would be the end of Paul's mission. Jesus who gave commission to Peter to preach to the Jews also gave commission to Paul to preach to the Gentiles accompanied by signs and wonders. The third pillar of the Jerusalem church extended their hand of fellowship. They agreed to the division of labour and to help the poor saints of the Jerusalem church.

Vs.11-16 : The truth of the Gospel is threatened. Barnabas and Paul went back to Antioch. Peter visited Antioch and had separate meals for the Jews and Gentiles. Paul rebuked him, since though one in faith with Gentiles he had separate eating with the 'party of James'. Barnabas also joined them. Then there was 'One Lord' but 'Two table fellowships'; they have broken the visible unity of the church; the Gospel was at stake. Paul was the only Jewish Christian with the Gentile converts. Paul was a better Jew than Peter,who was a Galilian Jew. James kept the whole law and was respected by the other Jews. Though Jews, Peter and Paul followed Christ. They knew that one cannot keep the law and that the law only condemns, through Christ God accepts them as righteous.

Vs.17-21 : The meaning of new life in Christ opponents take back the law-Men fall into sin. Paul's experience is that Law promoted Son's death-Paul defines faith as the belief that the Son of God died for one's sin or in other words Paul said 'The Son of God died for me'.So Paul died for sin and has a new life in Christ (Gal 2:20).

Chapter -3

Vs. 1-5 : The experience of the **Galatians**: Paul wonders if Galatians had **taken leave of their senses**. He asks them whether the coming of the Holy Spirit on them was through the works of the law or by hearing the Gospel. He also asks them as to which is superior, the spirit or flesh.

Vs 6-14 : First testimonies from the scripture, Abraham believed God and was counted righteous. Abraham believed in God's promise of a son at most unlikely time.i.e; in his old age.

God called Abraham a friend (Is 41:8) – Jews are the children of Abraham. There are two ways to be Abraham's children

i. by being physical descendents of Abraham

ii. by faith- like Abraham's faith which is possible for the Gentiles

To the Jews if they are already the sons of Abraham what more can circumcision give them? In Genesis God promises Abraham "in thee all Gentiles be blessed"-Abraham believed and was blessed, so too all gentiles who believe will be blessed. Opponents asked "is there no blessing for observing the law?"

Answer to this is : The law brings a curse – two principles

1. deeds bring no blessings   2.   trust brings blessings

Faith is related to promise – Law is related to command – breaking a single law brings death – Christ acted on man's behalf and set us free.

"Jesus is Cursed"-to this : Jesus hung on the cross not because he sinned but for our sake.

Vs. 15-18: Illustration of making a will-a will unchangeable; much more the divine contract (i.e; the will) the promise to Abraham and to his offspring (singular),which is fulfilled in Christ only. Later the promise and the Law : The answer to the question- "Did the law annul the promise?" No-the inheritance is based on promise on that basis Israel became Heirs.

Vs. 19-22 : Functions of the Law : 1. It is simply a parenthesis between the promise and the coming of the seed. 2. Law was given to educate the conscience of people. 3. To reveal the nature of sin. Law was given by Angels to Moses. The promise came to Abraham directly- hence no mediator, whereas in the case of the law, it came to Moses from God through the angels and from Moses to the people; through the promise is given righteousness and life. Through the law is given sin and death.

Vs. 23-29 : Slaves and Sons – until Jesus came there could be no faith. So for **the time between promise and Christ**, people were under **a tutor,the law**. But just like when one grows up, the tutor is dispensed, the law was dispensed with when Jesus came so, in faith people accepted Christ and are no longer under the control of law. Galatian Christians became sons of God in Christ and baptized when full grown. By this the Gentiles share in the promises made to Abraham, the ancestor of the Jews by flesh. In Christ all are one into one New Man.

Chapter - 4

Vs.1-7 : Our knowledge of being sons of God – illustrations from life:

An orphan boy is an heir to his father's property yet he cannot touch the property while he is young. In this respect he is no better than a slave. He is under a slave tutor whom he has to obey. Likewise, till Christ came we were under domination of nature i.e; Sun, Moon, Stars..etc. and we offered rituals to them, yet when Christ came he set us free from these and now we are Sons of God. The question '**how do we know that we are Sons of God**?' is answered as follows: When God sent the Holy Spirit into our hearts, we pray as 'Abba' meaning 'Father' like Christ.(Mk. 14:36). The slave can never use this. Only sons can use this address. If we are Sons, then we are Heirs as promised to Abraham.

Vs. 8-11: Contrast the present status with the past. The past was the state of slavery subject to pagan gods. With the return to slavery and subject to worthless elements of nature again there is no means to prove their state of libety in Christ. False teachers instructed them to observe holy days, sacred seasons etc. All Paul's labour seems to be in vain.

Vs. 12-20 : Paul's personal feelings.: During his first visit Paul was sick. He says to the Galatians – 'You could have thought it as a curse of God' and so thought of Paul as not a messenger of God. But the Galatians thought of Paul as an angel of God or even like Christ. In those days the Galatians would have eagerly given him their eyes. New teachers eagerly seek them only to separate them from their fellowship with other believers like a mother in birth pangs they were born like children into the kingdom of God. Now also, Paul has some pangs for Christ to fully form in them.

Vs. 4:21-5:1 : Interpretation of the Law – Galatians agreed to obey the law as taught by some. Old Testament talks of two covenants which runs right though the Old Testament   a) Old Covenant at Sinai b) New Covenant prophesied by Jeremiah –first one is the covenant of the law and bondage. Second one is the covenant of promise and liberty. The two sons of Abraham represent two generations –Ishmael, born of the bond woman Hagar, representing the physical generation – Isaac born of Sarah according to promise as she was too old to bear children. The two women represent the two covenants-

a.   Hagar represents the first covenant –Hagar is a slave woman hence her son inherits the status of a slave.

b.   Sarah represents the second covenant-her son is the son of promise, Sarah being a free woman.

The first covenant was given at Mt. Sinai situated in Arabia of the country of Ishmael. The first covenant has there for a relationship of a servant to God. So old Israel and its temple at Jerusalem of the first covenant, another Jerusalem from above which is by the act of God Himself, shares the relationship of a Son of God.

Paul asks – To which covenant the Galatians belong ' the answer to this is "The second covenant-like Isaac, wonderfully born in Christ – From the beginning hostility existd between the two covenants. The Jews were against the followers of Christ. The inheritance belongs to Isaac only, as too to Christians –quotes : Gen.21:10-13. Cast out the slave woman and her son, who cannot be joint heir- So, Christians' inheritance or citizenship in New Jerusalem – Christ set us free, so stand fast in that freedom.

Chapter - 5

Vs. 2-6: The issue of circumcision – New teachers say it is needed. Galatians have to choose between Christ and the law " If the law is chosen then circumcision has to be practiced and the whole law is to be observed , this would in turn lead to acceptance for salvation by work of law – that would further mean that those who practice circumcision do not belong to the new covenant under Christ.

If Christ is chosen – it implies the fact that one is under the new covenant under Christ. One is then led by the Holy Spirit and then to salvation by Faith. If one has the second what will circumcision add? In Christ there is no distinction between a Jew and a Gentile-there is only one door for all, which is Christ – there is only one faith to open that door to enter God's kingdom. It makes one a new man – love the basis of this new life.

Vs. 7-12 : Urgent warning and appeal – Don't say circumcision is a minor addition to faith – To illustrate this point Paul says a small portion pervades the whole lump, similarly a false doctrine corrupts faith. New Teachers say Paul himself shows the need for circumcision. Paul says he never said the Gentiles be circumcised. If so why he should suffer persecution. In the light of the cross of Jesus one can judge faith in Jesus as one who was crucified for Jews explain it away – To Paul, the Cross is the central theme of the Gospel.

Vs. 13-15 : The nature of Christian freedom – some say Paul's teaching as 'Believe and you can do whatever you like' – Freedom is more difficult to exercise as followers of Christ. Freedom is to realize that one can give reign to ones lower nature.Christ took the form of slave for love's sake. The law for all to live together in fellowship is 'Love thy neighbour as thyself'-(Ref. Lev.19:18). Galatian Christians are quarrelsome people – like wild beasts biting each other- unless they let love change them nothing will change them and no one will be left in the church.

Vs. 16-18 : Life in the spirit – The above lines may be discouraging to the Galatians.

Vs. 19-24 : Flesh Vs Spirit – Christians live in two worlds – this world and the heavenly kingdom of God. – Each has its principles. In the flesh principle everything is contrary to God's will; In the Spirit principle one is free from the domain of the law.

They have to choose by which principle to be guided of – If one wishes to follow the flesh principle-

i.   It destroys all true relationship-Man's relationship to himself is destroyed.

ii.   Man's relationship with God is destroyed

iii. Hate replaces Love

iv.   Ambition replaces Service – so evil nature dominates

v.   One becomes incapable of healthy enjoyment and so turns to drugs etc;

On the other hand if one allows the Holy Spirit to take control of his life –

i.   One's nature is transformed to the likeness of Jesus

ii.   That reproduces the qualities of Christ i.e; Love, Joy, Peace, longsuffering, Kindness, generiosity, faithfulness, meekness and self control.

Vs. 5:25-6:1 : Walking in the spirit, not only guides in inner experience, but it turns into a guide in every relationship in life.

Chapter - 6

Vs. 2-5 : The Law of Christ – Each one wants to be first – this is contrary to the example of Christ. Each must become servant and take the load of others – thus the burden is lightened and one fulfills the law of Christ. Christ sets us free so as to serve him and not to be on command of one's life. If one thinks good of one self, then he is deceiving himself – stop comparing with one another and feel superior, rather in the light of standards Christ laid down. If satisfied keep to oneself – between oneself and God. One must do one's responsibilities laid down by God as no one else can do it.

Vs. 6-10 : The Right Use of Money – some of you appointed as teachers to teach God's words – so this teacher has no time to earn money or his livelihood – so others have to support them – when some are blessed it has to be shared with others. One must take care not to be deceived, there are two worlds, that of the flesh and that of the Spirit. One reaps what he sows in which field. 1). One may reap food harvest from lower world at the end it perishes – the owner also perishes with it. 2). In the other field which is that of the Spirit , if one sows in terms of service to Christ, which includes his wealth, his harvest will never perish. It will be everlasting life itself though invisible now, one should not get discouraged and continue to serve, at the end one finds his rewards laid up for eternity. So far Paul spoke of responsibilities in the fellowship of believers, but it extends to those fellowship outside for whom also Christ died. One should not let any opportunity to slip by.

Vs. 11-17 : Summary in Paul's own hand : It was Paul's custom to pen the last paragraph with his own hand – to the question 'who are these who want you to get circumcised?' Paul answers – These are more interested in the flesh than the Spirit. Their real aim is to avoid persecution – yet these do not accept the full demands of the law; they pick such laws that suit them; they wish to celebrate their triumph in making you submit to their demand i.e; circumcision – Paul has one occasion for triumph – the

Cross of Christ, which set him free from the dominion of sin. It is to live in Christ and the new creation. In this new creation , Jew or Gentile does not matter. Those who accept Christ are New Israel brought into being by God's new covenant. Paul has no hard feelings to these new teachers – they only hindered his ministry – they should stop troubling him. When Paul said he was crucified with Christ, his body has the marks of the sufferings – this testifies he is Christ's Apostle.

Vs18:Final Greetings

REFERENCE BOOKS:
1. Paul to the Galatians   - by Stephen Neil
2. In the Annotated Bible   - by A.C.Gaebelein
3. Letters to the Galatians & Ephesians - by William Barclay

5
Ephesians

INTRODUCTION

It is one of the 4 prison epistles (Other epistles – Philippians, Colossians, Philemon). Paul wrote from Rome – 60-61 A.D.

(1. John Bunion – Pilgrim's Progress; Jawaharlal Nehru – The Discovery of India; Letters to Indira" published by Dr. Mallik etc, written from prison).

THE CHURCH AT EPHESUS

A.D.: Established during the 2nd Mission Journey. Its composition: Acts 19th Chapter

a.   **vs. 1-6:** John the Baptist's Disciples – 12 of them.

b.   **vs. 8-9:** Jews (from the Synagogue – 3 months)

c.   **vs. 9b – 10:** Greeks (at Tyrannus Hall – 2 Years).

Ephesus – Asia Minor Mission station of Paul.

Acts 20-31 – 3 years Paul ministered from here.

Some MSS of Ephesian letters do not have name Ephesus of the church, sent.

Probably it was a circular letter and most probably distributed to churches by Tychicus (Col. 4.7-8).

It's no ordinary letter (i.e., pastoral) sent to a specific church. Eph.1.1 refers to 'at Ephesus' was lacking in many MSS (Except.Eph.6.21-22 at the end).

Though a tract ("Sermon") than a pastoral epistle, the author has specific needs in mind – It speaks to the readers in 2nd person 'you' (Eph. 4.17-18).

MAIN SUBJECT

Style: It is influenced by possible Liturgical and Hymnic speech. He marvels at 'the Grace of God' which he brought into being a United Body = the church in which the Jews and Gentiles find a place, Eph. 2.11-22. It's nothing less than the Body of Christ (1.23; 3.6; 4.4; 5.30).

Illustration: Siva Sena attacked the Rally of Samaj Wadi Party of Mulayam Singh. The next day's paper shows the Biharis with latties in procession against it (The Hindu, 4th and 5th Feb., 2008). No unity.

One New Man in whom a New Humanity has been created by God through Christ's Reconciling work on the Cross (2.16).

There are marks of Early Catholicism.

1. apostles as closed group (2.20; 3.5; 4.11).
2. The Gentiles taken their place in the unity of the church.
3. A matter of concern- the fading expectation of the soon coming of Christ (4.13-16).
4. This letter has many points of similarity with Colossians (Eph. 6.21-22 = Col. 4.7-8). It seems both Ephesians and Colossians letters being carried by the same messenger, must be of the same time of writing.
5. Ephesians was the last letter in the group of Imprisonment Letters.

MAIN OUTLINES

1. **1.1-14**: Introduction.
2. **1.15-3.21**: The Church's life in Christ.
3. **4.1-6.9**: The Church's life in the society.
4. **6.10-14**: Conclusion.

Chapter - 1

Details: St. Paul follows the pattern of the 1st Cen. Letter writing :

a.   Begins with his name.

b.   Greets the Christians as 'Saints'.

c.   Invokes the twin blessings of peace and Grace (I Thes. 1.1).

Apostleship – gets authoritative exercises – God-given authority

> a.   Not self-derived
> b.   Not conferred by
>   others

Tracing to
Christ
(Acts. 9.1-9; 26.15-18)

Paul begins with, like the Jewish eulogy prayer. With 6 sections of the description in Chapter 1 of God and His Blessings.

vs. a) 1.3b- 4   b) 2.5-6 c) 3.7-8   d) 4 .9-10 e) 5. 11-12 f) 6. 13-14.
The Blessings for the believers seen in the

a.   Father's actions

b.   what we received in His Son.

1.3-14: The purpose of God: a. in Eternity and

b. in Time.

Vs. 3b – 1. Blessed us 2. Chose us 3. **v.4** – 'before the foundation of the world'. Eg., Gal. 1.15 – Paul chosen in his mother's womb.

Trinity: a.   Father: Who chooses his people.

b.   Son: Who redeems at the cost of his death.

c.   Holy Spirit: Who makes real the Eternal purposes.

v.5: destined us as sons.

v.6.7b.: His gracious will.

v.7: redemption and forgiveness.

v.9: make known the mystery of His will.

v.10: He has plan to unite all things in Christ.

v.11: His purpose.

v.12: destined and appointed to live for His glory.

v.13: sealed with the Holy Spirit.

v.14: The guarantee of our inheritance.

1.15 -23 : The Christian's life in Christ

vs.15-16: Paul prays for them.

v.15: Your faith and your love.

v.16: without ceasing prays for Christians at Ephesus (ref: Rom.1.9; Phil.4.6; I Thes.5.17-18).

Illustration: Qn. Do you pray for Carey Centre or any Christian organisation or servants of God?

v.17: Wisdom {Sophia (Gk.)}= Divine wise of Knowledge {Gnosis (Gk.)} } Often God's children not having much worldly knowledge.

Illustration: Sagacity: Not to give your word unless sure.

Integrity: To keep your Word.

v.18: The eyes of your hearts enlightened.

    a.   the hope of your calling.

    b.   the saints glorious Inheritance.

v.19:   c.   The immeasurable greatness of His power.

    d.   The mighty God's acts(-the Resurrection victory over Sin and death-Rom.6.3-4).

v.20: The enthronement of the Resurrected Lord.

v.21: 1. This Age; 2. The Age to come (future).

v.22: Christ head over "all things" in the church (all Spirit forces, Eph. 2.2).

v.23: The Christ – Christ's body (1.23; 3.6; 4.4; 5.30)

Christian Gospel: The Gospel of Cosmic redemption and reconciliation (Rom.8.22-23). Christ Lord of all cosmic forces human and subhuman.

Illustration: As dog lovers in England dog tombs common (Rev. 22.15 though e.c No dogs allowed in Heaven).

Chapter - 2

2.1-10 – The Christ's History – Past, present and future.

v.1 a. Those outside Christ – their plight= Divine wrath (Rom. 1.18; 2.5,24-26).

Illustration:　　　　Sun = God; spiritual Death – caused by SIN

Chinese Proverb: As we cannot blame the sun for shade; it's the tree responsible for it. So too we cannot say God's personal anger on us. Rather like the tree that obstructed sun's rays so too our sin only brings our plight= Divine wrath.

v.2: Walked according to worldly standards. The prince of the power of air works for disobedience.

v.3: for carnal sin.

v.4: with great love god loved us out of mercy. (Rom. 5.8 – Christ loving the unlovely.)

Lk. 19.10 – Christ came (unlike the Hindu avatars for destruction of the wicked)to seek and save sinners.

v.5: a.　made us alive with Christ (Rom. 6.3).

v.6: b.　raised us up with him . Illustration: Baptismal Formula

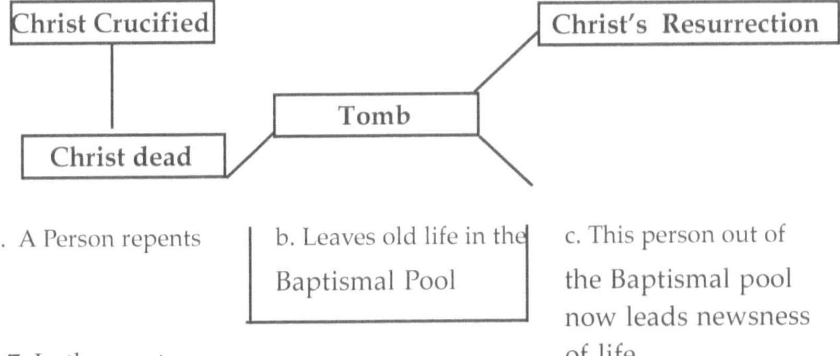

v.7: In the age to come

v.8: a.   By grace – God's side vs. Not of works (of man) (Gal. 2.16).

b.   By Faith – Man's side

v.8: Summary of God's work

a.   Past:-originates in the grace and the saving love of God.

b.   resent:- enters human experience by one's faith.

c.   Future:- entirely of God's doing

Martin Luther: 1. 'Sola Gratia' - freely offered gift {Dorin (Gk.)} of God

2.'sola fida' by faith only (Rom. 6.23)

v.12: Gentiles: in the past   a. (separated No hope without God) Godless.

b. aliens

c. strangers

v.13: a.   Once- far off

b.   Now – brought near through the blood of Christ

a.   Sinai covenant – blood of animals

b.   New Testament – Covenant – blood of Christ (Mk. 14.24).

v.14:- The dividing wall of Hostility.

Illustration:1.   Berlin wall – broken now.

2. Mother Teresa – Calcutta – poor feeding – 'Kichidi' food.

Once a Bengali gentleman complained about Kichidi. He said Bengalese eat by courses.

Mother Teresa replied – difficult to feed that way 9000 each day.

Then asked her "Mother do you eat this 'Kichidi'? She replied – Yes' every evening. "

Then he said "Mother, then I will also eat."

Mother Teresa observed "the middle wall between Donar and the poor broken". She remarked: "Only then the ministry successful".

This is the way Christ identified with the sinners (Phil. 2.6-8).

v.15: created a man. a New Man.

Illustration:P.Chenchiah of Chennai (of Rethinking Christianity) (Rom. 12.2 -3). Christ creates in one self- a New Man.

Rom. 13.12 cast off old   Dont be conformed   vs.   Be transformed

    13.14 – put on (new)   (old life)   (new life)

v.18: Both groups have now access in one spirit to the Father. .

v.19: No longer strangers and sojourners

--->but now – Fellow Citizens.

with   saints

Household with saints of God.

v.20: a. apostles and prophets - = Foundation

    b. Christ – Corner stone.

v.21: grows into a Holy Temple.

'Neos' (Gk.) = Holy place. (II Pet. 2.5– living stones (=Believers).

Chapter - 3

St. Paul's Apostleship and Prayer for the Church

vs.1-2,8: Apostle to the Gentiles

vs.4-5: The Divine mystery – made known.

   (**v.9** – hidden for ages) – fulfilled now.

II Pet. 3.15-16:- Peter finds it hard to understand Paul's writings.

vs. 6-8: Privileges to the Gentiles

a.   fellow heirs.

b.   Members of the same body.

c.   Partakers of the promises in Christ.

v.8: Paul says "I am least of the saints to preach to the Gentiles (except through the grace of God).

Acts 1.8: The Disciples (+ Apostles) witness in

a.   Jerusalem (Jews) – (1)

b.   Judea {region – (2)}

c.   Samaria (Mixed race)(3)(Jews+Gentiles)=5 Heathen races brought by Tiglathpileser (Assyrian king). (II Kings 17.24)

Matt. 28.19-20: The Great Commission to take the Gospel to the end of the earth – to all races.

v.10: To the principalities and powers in the Heavenly places.

These are the hostile angelic powers (Eph. 2.2).

a.   held at wonder.

b.   Sounded their death knell.

God in Christ – for Cosmic Redemption.

The Mystery revealed: 1. To unify all things in Christ.

2. Jews and Gentiles to worship as one body (Eph.2.11-22).

v.12: This St. Paul calls as Eternal purpose revealed in Christ.

v.13: Not to loose heart (for Roman prison he was put in). Paul says he was suffering so, for this ministry.

vs. 14-19: Personal prayer (for churches in the world).

Trinity: v.14   –   The Father.

v.17   –   Jesus, the Son.

v.16   –   The Holy Spirit.

v.16: The inner man of the Ephesians too he strengthened in the Spirit.

v.17:   a.   Rooted   –   A. The Tree symbolism

b.   Grounded   –   B. The Building symbolism

A.   The deeper the roots, the greater the strength.

(The Acacia tree of Sinai in the trip we were told by the Swiss guide, has roots up to 150 ft. deep while digging the Suez canal. That's why it was found in that alluvial desert of Paran where hardly anything grows except Acacia. For this Moses was asked by God to make furniture of Acacia wood for the Tabernacle in the wilderness journey of the Hebrews (Exo.26.26; 27.1 etc.).

B.   While visiting New York, climbed the Empire State Building – 104 stories, the Tallest building in the world then in the mid 20th century. (Now the Twin towers of Malasia tallest building). It's strength was shown by the guide after 8 stories in the ground – a huge solid rock facing the Atlantic sea shore.

Both in terms of Love Paul speaks here.

In **Col. 2.6-7** – the same in terms of Faith.

In Assamese (Translation) : **I Cor. 14.1** : "Tumi premok khedi juva"

(=You)(=to love)(=chase after).

It is literally:You chase after Love.

vs.18-19: God's Redemptive plan of Christ's.

Its length, breadth, depth and height shown in quadratic dimension.

To comprehend such divine love surpasses all our knowledge.

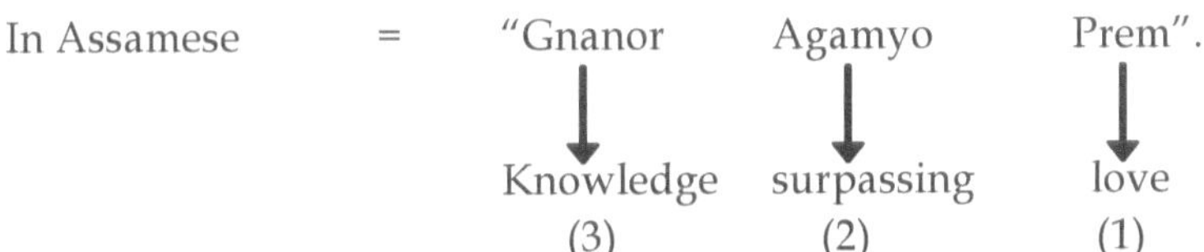

Illustration: As a boy Charles H. Spurgeon was daily reading the Bible for his grand father. When he came to Rev. 20.3 = referring to the "Bottomless pit". Again and again he read for days the same Bible portion. Suddenly this grandfather realised it and questioned him. His reply was "I was wondering   how long one falls in this bottomless pit". So too we can say no limits to the love.

The 3rd chapter ends in praise to God (i) in Christ and (ii) in the Church. God does far more than our thinking and asking.

Here below about Salvation.

Rom. 5.9 – Much more in terms of Justification.

Rom. 5.10 –Much more in terms of Reconciliation.

Rom. 5.15 – Much more in terms of the Gift.

Rom. 5.17 – Much more in terms of the Reign in life.

Rom. 5.20 – Much more in terms of the abounding Grace.

No stinginess with God's Grace.

Chapter – 4

4.1 – 6.9 Church's life in Society.

4.1-16: Church's vocation as Christ's Body.

v.1: 'Worthy of the calling' i.e., Practical outworking of this ideal in every day living.

v.2: The unity the Holy Spirit creates and Christian's responsibility – to maintain **harmonious relationship in the church.**

vs.3-7: **Unity Theme** – as 'One Body' already seen. **Unity does not mean 'uniformity'** but like a living organism, pulsating with life to be seen in growth and character.

The Purpose:for the Church to reach'Mature Manhood'{from infant to manhood: Heb.5.13-14}.

vs.2&3: 1. With all lowliness and meekness and patience.

2. Forbearing one another in love.

3. Eager to maintain the unity of the Holy Spirit in the bond of peace.

vs.4-6: Unity: **v.4** – Spirit;

v.5 – Lord; ⎫ Trinity = Oneness

v.6 – God

v.7: According to the measure of Christ's gifts.

Vs.8-10: Ref: Ps.68.18 – Christ's Ascension followed by the descent of the Holy Spirit on Pentecost day.

It's like the Lord returned to earth laden with gifts i.e., Christ's enthronement over the universe is a guarantee that nothing needful is lacking.

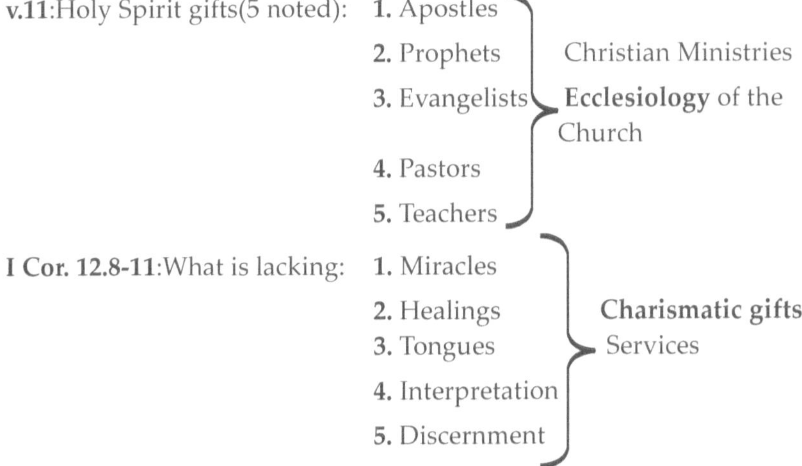

v.11:Holy Spirit gifts(5 noted):   **1.** Apostles

2. Prophets

3. Evangelists

4. Pastors

5. Teachers

I Cor. 12.8-11:What is lacking: **1.** Miracles

2. Healings

3. Tongues

4. Interpretation

5. Discernment

Purpose of Gifts of the Holy Spirit:

v.12: 1. To equip

2. To minister

3. To build up

v.13: a.   Unity of Faith

b. Knowledge of the Son of God

c.   Mature Manhood of Christ.

d. Measuring to the stature of the fullness of Christ.

v.14: No longer children   tossed to and fro by every word of Doctrine (Heb. 5.13-14).

v.15: We have to grow up.

Illustration: Indrampalem Peon of Kakinada town of Andhrapradesh (3 times baptized) changed 3 denominations.

vs.17-19: **The Gentiles**: 1.   Futility of mind

2.   Darkened in their understanding

3.   Alienated from godly life.

4.   Ignorance.

5.   Hardness of heart.

vs.22-24: Dressing analogy   1. put off old Nature   Rom.13.12-14

2. put on New Nature

v.25:   Speak the Truth (Jn. 8.44 – Devil – father of lies)

v.26: Be angry but forgive by evening.

v.28: Don't steal (vs. Decoity?)

v.29: No evil talk – but   1.   good for edifying

                           2.   grace to the hearers.

Illustration: Dan Nicklick: "Think before you Talk"

	T=	Is it True
THINK =	**H=**	Is it Helpful
	I=	Is it Inspiring
	N=	Is it Necessary
	K=	Is it kind?

v30: Don't grieve the Holy Spirit (sealed by Him).

v.31: All Bitterness, Wrath, Anger, and Clamor and Slander and Malice – put away.

v.32: Be kind to one another, tender hearted, forgiving as God forgave you in Christ. (Lord's prayer)

Gentle / Meek = 'PROUS' (Gk.) = 'Controlled Beast' etymologically like putting iron bridle in the Horse mouth, so control self.

Chapter – 5

5.1-20 – Christian Conduct in the World.

v.1: "Be imitators of me" (St.Paul).

"As I am of Christ"(I Cor. 11.1).

Almost impossible for any preacher to say so.

Lk. 11.13 – Men though evil give good things to children.

Illustration: U.C. College near Shillong (Meghalaya)– Principal caught a student drinking.

When questioned – he replied – I learnt it from my Father.

When questioned- the Father said– I do drink secretly (kept the bottle behind bath room shelf). The son found out and started to drink.

Illustration: Father's coffin – Mother asked the son to check if it is your father?

At funeral, however bad character becomes good in the preacher's reference. Why?

Probably Peter at Heaven's gate has to get certified by pastor.

v.1: God's children

v.3: "chosen people = saints vs. the world–a. Strangers to God

b. Enmity with God (Rom.5.10).

v.6: 'God's wrath' on them.

v.7: Don't associate with them   **Ref.** Dead Sea Scrolls: (Jn. 1.4-5 =Salvation =Light).

vs. 8: Children of Light

v.14: Christ shall give you light. Believers = Sons of Light

v.18: Not intoxication's inspiration.

But Holy Spirit's – a. Psalms b. Hymns c. Spiritual songs d. Sing and make Melody.

v.19: Encourage one another

USA.	vs.	India (Assamese)
Qn. How are You?		– Ans. "Ene Thene Asu".
Ans. Top of the world		= "Some how existing."

v.20: Give Thanks   a. always (in Christ's name) b. for everything- (good or bad –I Thes.5.18) (Rom.8.28-"Everything works for good and bad also").

Illustration: At lunch break, while he went to wash hands a dog ate lunch of a coal mine Believer – others made fun of him. He got upset, "why God allowed this?" He took half a day leave and went home. He gets in the evening news the mine collapsed and all his mates died. Then he knelt and thanked God for sending the dog, or else he would have been dead with his colleagues.

vs.21-33: Family Relations – Husbands and wives.

vs.26-27: Christ prepares the Church to be a Holy Bride(**II Cor. 11.2**).

Qn.: What about joint heirs **(I Pet. 3.7) v.21** – Be subject to one another (wife to husband and vice versa).

Qn. What about **v.21** – A man shall leave his parents and join his wife.

Illustration: Best man at a Meghalaya friend's wedding – he was crying and as I was his Best Man, I tried to stop him but on 3rd attempt he whispered to me to let him. Later I came to know – it was matrilineal tribe custom of Garos of Meghalaya where the wife takes to her house the husband.

The above v.21 (also v.31) seems to tally with the Matriarchal society in a literal sense.

v.22ff.: But from v.22 onwards it is based on patriarchal society as Christ head of the church so too wife to her husband be subject, where Paul adds "in everything" (v.24).

v25ff.: The Husbands to love their wives similar to Christ loving the church, adding that Christ "gave himself up for her".

On this basis Paul calls on the wives to cooperate with their husbands similar to Christ "who gave himself up for her ("the church") (v.25). This shows definitely reciprocity of love and honour between the couple envisaged.

So on the basis of the relationship between Christ and the church, here Paul brings out a profound truth of relationship to be really and newly formed between a couple (v.31):

a.   The Husband to love his wife as himself.

b.   The wife in addition to the mutual love, to respect her husband

Chapter – 6

vs.1-4: Family duties: a. Children have to obey parents,which is the 1ˢᵗ command with a promise:

  i.   long life

  ii. secured welfare to them.

  b. Fathers : Not to provoke the children, but to bring them up

  i.   in the discipline and

  ii. in the instruction of the Lord

vs. 5-9: Masters and slaves.

vs.6-8: Slaves: not as men-pleasures in the nature of eye-services but as servants of Christ

a. doing the will of God from the heart.

b. Rendering service with a good will, as serving the Lord.

c. Doing with the knowledge that in accordance one gets in return the same way from the Lord.

v.9: Masters : to be conscious, that how they treat their slaves, without any threatening, as they receive the same, from their Master (i.e., Christ) in Heaven.

vs.6,10-20: Christian Panoply.

A Roman soldier always guarding Paul. Paul seems to make spiritual analogy of Christian warfare (Eph.2.2etc.) Not against flesh and blood v.12.

v.10: Be strong in the Lord.

v.11: Fight against the Devil's vials.

v.12: Against the Principalities (Spiritual forces of the Devil)of the world rulers.

v.13: Paul calls on the believers to put on the whole armour of God.

    a.   To stand against (vs.13 and 14).

    b.   To keep alert (v.18b).

    c.   To pray at all times (v.18a).

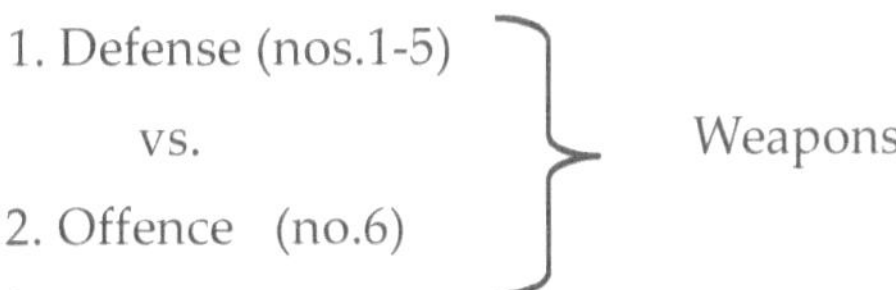

1. Shoes= Gospel of Peace

2. Girdle of Truth

3. Shield of Faith

4. Breast Plate of Righteousness

5. Helmet of Salvation

6. Sword of Spirit

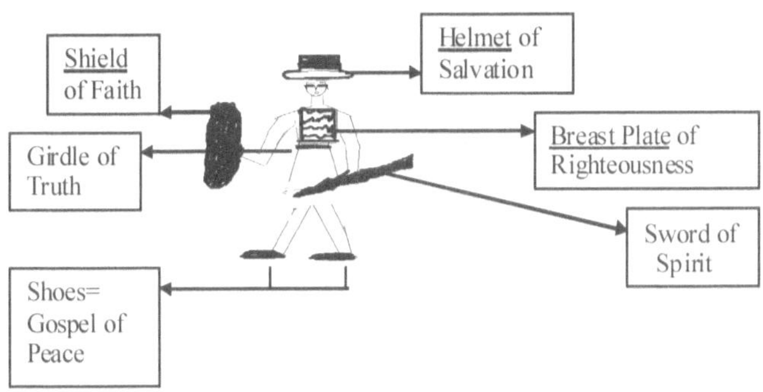

v.20 – Paul Ambassador (II Cor.5.20) of Christ (in chains) bold to speak.

Vs.21-22: v.21 – a. It seems the carrier of the letter Tychicus, was told to convey personally about Paul's welfare.

    b. Paul refers to him as i. beloved brother

               ii. faithful minister.

vs.23-24: Paul finally conveys in closing, peace and love undying from God the Father and Christ Jesus.

6
Philippians

MAIN DIVISIONS

1. 1.1-2   :   Opening salutations
2. 1.3-11   :   Thanksgiving and prayer
3. 1.12-26   :   The situation at Rome
4. 1.27-2.4   :   Incentives in Christianity
5. 2.5-18   :   The example of Christ.
6. 2.19-30   :   Approaching visits
7. 3.1-21   :   Warning against false Teachers
8. 4.1-9   :   3 final exhortations
9. 4.10-20   :   Acknowledgement of Gifts
10. 4.21-23   :   Closing salutations.

INTRODUCTION

I.1.   Before 360 B.C. Philippi a small village. Philip, father of Alexander the Great,gave its name.

2.   In 168 B.C. the Romans got it in the battle of Pydna.

3.   Then it became part of Macedonia, the Roman province.

4.   42 B.C. Anthony (with Octavian) won over Brutus and Cassius.

5.   Anthony then settled some of the disbanded soldiers there making it a Roman colony.

6.   In 30 B.C. Octavian defeated Anthony (and Cleopaatra) in the battle of Actium.

7.   Then some more disbanded soldiers from Italy colonized it.

8. So Philippi became a little place of Rome abroad.

9. It's language – Latin, Roman Law and Roman rules are used.

10. Taxes and public life carried like Rome abroad.

II.1. Though Thessalonica, capital of Macedonia, yet Paul knew Philippi's strategic importance. In the 2nd Mission Journey of Paul and Silas (49-52 A.D.), (Acts 16.9ff), Paul preached the Gospel there.

2. Paul was at Troas, when he had seen in a vision a man of Macedonia calling him to come there (Acts 16.8-12). So Paul and Silas decided to leave Asia Minor and go to Macedonia (Acts 16.10).

3. i. Finding no synagogue to preach on Sabbath day they went to the river side where some women were there. Paul preached and Lydia, a rich lady in cloth business, received the Gospel. She with her household were baptized.

ii. Next we find a young girl was used by some men for sooth saying. She used to follow Paul and Silas and for many days used to shout "These are servants of the Most High God who proclaim to you the way of Salvation" (Acts 16.17). Vexed with that Paul rebuked the evil spirit in her, which left her. Thus the gain of her masters stopped.

So they caught hold of them and dragged them to the city authorities saying, "They preach the Jewish customs contrary to the Roman customs and practice." They were caned and imprisoned.

In the prison both Paul and Silas began to sing and at midnight an earth quake occurred and the doors of the prison cells opened. The Jailor thinking the prisoners ran away was about to kill himself with his sword. But Paul shouted to him not to do so, as all prisoners were in. So the Jailor kneeled in front of Paul and asked him to tell how to be saved.

He took them to his house, washed their wounded bodies and fed them. Then he and his household believed the Gospel presented by Paul and were baptized.

In this way, Lydia, the Jailor and their households became the first members of the Philippian church there.

In the 3rd Mission journey Paul visited Philippi (53-57 A.D.).

Traditionally Philippian epistle associated with Ephesians, Colossians and Philemon and known as "the Prison Epistles".

Philippians was written by Paul from Rome from his prison in 62 A.D. or so. (Some like Adolf Deismann, associates it with Ephesus etc.).

THE PURPOSE (OF WRITING PHILIPPIAN LETTER)

1. To acknowledge the gifts sent by the Philippian church to Rome (4.10; 14-18).

2. To convey the News of his imprisonment and its circumstances.

   Not to think of his imprisonment as a set back for the Gospel proclamation (1.12-26).

3. The reason why he was sending back Ephaphroditus, though the Philippian church wants him to stay and serve Paul (2.25).

4. His plan to send Timothy and return back to him (2.19-24).

5. News brought to him of "party spirit" among the Philippians.

   Paul wanted them to be in unity and in that way to live, act and witness for Christ (1.27;2.1-11; 4.2f.).

6. He wanted to warn them of the danger of "the Judaizers".

   He wanted to warn them that legalism was danger to and contradicts the Gospel (3.3-11).

7. To warn of false perfectionism (3.12-16).

8. To encourage Philippian Christians to suffer bravely, to live in single-mindedness and to trust their lives to the Lord (1.22-30; 2.12-18; 3.17-21; 4.4-9).

THE SPECIAL FEATURES (of the Philippian Epistle)

1. Joy, a great theme in this letter (16 times mentioned) (800 times in the Bible).

   a. Rejoicing in prayer (1.4).

   b. Rejoicing in the fruit of one's own labours (4.1).

   c. Rejoicing in the knowledge of the preaching of the Gospel (1.16).

   d. Rejoicing in the sufferings and even death (2.17).

   e. Readers asked to rejoice in the Lord (3.1; 4.4).

   f. To have joy in believing (1.25).

   g. To have joy in fellowship (2.28).

   h. To rejoice, like Paul, even in trials and sufferings (1.29).

Chapter-1

COMMENTARY

v.1: Christians at Philippi referred as "Saints" adding "in Christ Jesus" i.e., they are made saints (=holy people of God) "not ethically or morally holy" but "in the imputed righteousness" of Christ.

v.2: "Grace and peace" conveyed like Jewish "Eulogies" = blessings.

v.3-11: "always" Paul remembers the Philippian Christians in his daily prayers like for the Ephesians, the Romans etc. (Eph. 1.16; Rom. 1.9 etc.).

v.4: Paul refers to "their gift" sent through Ephaphroditus as "their partnership" in the Gospel proclamation (In the case of the Corinthian church, Paul supported himself by "Tent-making" with Aquila and Priscilla (Acts 18.3;I Cor. 9.18).

v.7: The Philippian Christians also are partakers with Paul in the defense of the Gospel even to the extent of Paul's imprisonment.

vs.12-14: Paul's imprisonment, he says,

v.13: in a sense known even among the Roman guards; it was for the sake of Christ and the Gospel.

v.14–Some brethren became more bold because of Paul's imprisonment to proclaim the Gospel.

vs.15-18: Paul speaks of the Two categories of preachers:

v.15: a. some Evangelists do preach out of envy and rivalry out of partisanship (v.17) (Negative)

v.16: b. Others out of good-will and love (Positive).

vs.19-26: Paul was in a dilemma

   a.   To die – aznd be with the Lord, Vs.21 }In both he rejoices

   b.   To live – to continue preaching the Gospel} of both he rejoices
        (v.22).

But he knew it was not in his power. Only he hopes he will be released and he will visit the Philippian believers (v.24, 26)

Paul's view: a. to live is Christ, (but on the other hand,)

                   b. to die is gain }(v.21)

vs.27-30: Encourages Philippian believers

a.   to live worthy of the Gospel of Christ.

b.   to stand firm – in one spirit and one mind i.e., = unity (v.27).

c.   to suffer for the faith as they believe in Christ (v.29).

Chapter-2

vs.1-4: 5 points for Paul's appeal for unity (in humility).

    a.   In Christ himself is encouragement for unity.

    b.   Those knowing the blessing of love should manifest to others.

    c.   All should have the same spirit – to show affection and sympathy.

    d.   This will complete the joy (which Paul has already in him).

    e.   Selfishness and conceit – "enemies of fellowship" and unity.

2. Special ways to overcome them.

    i.   Count others better than yourselves.

    ii.   Cultivate the habit of thinking and speaking of the interest of others.

vs. 5-11: The best way to inculcate humility in others.

a.   To turn to the example of Christ – the condescension and self-giving -will shall change their attitude.

b.   A previously composed hymn – in praise of the pre-existent, incarnate and exalted Lord.

v.7: 3 Steps of Christ's Humility.

    7a. emptying himself. **7**b. as a **slave** than a lord.

    7c. Though Divine took upon our Humanity

v.8:c. His descent to depths, for having abased as a man – thus lived a life of utter obedience, to such depth of unimaginable pain and shame.

vs.8-11: Christ's Exaltation: (Heb 28)

a.   He is given a name which is above every name. i.e., Highest authority and honour over all creation (Eph. 1.20-22).

    i.   Is.45.23 quoted to express the above

    ii   The earliest creed stated that "Jesus is Lord" (I Cor. 12.3).

In the above light of Christ's life the Philippian disunity and the personal ambition should cease.

vs.12-18: Christ's example (not Paul's) such obedience the Philippians were called.

v.13: It is true –   a.   God-enabling – important than man's striving.

b.   God-pleasing – in Christian giving and desire.

v.14: Deeds: Not what is done but the spirit in which it is done, matters.

v.15: The Highest standard must be opted in the warped society they live in.

v.16: The Gospel they got is the word of life in the perishing world.

v.17: If Paul dies – that death – an offering to God sacrificed for their faith and life.

Paul rejoices to see the fruit in their lives.

v.18: Paul trusts that they too will rejoice with him in his fruitful service.

vs.19-30: Paul's future plans.

Paul speaks of his two fellow-workers – Timothy and Epaphroditus. His plans for them and his hopes for himself.

a. vs.19-24:   Timothy – commended

v.1.1: Timothy with Paul:

i.   When this letter was written.

ii.   When the Gospel 1st preached

Paul plans to send Timothy to the Philippians again.

Timothy –   a. to be cheered by the news of Christians there.

b. Timothy's mission at Philippi, Paul envisages.

vs.20-21: Paul speaks of Timothy in the highest commendation. Paul thinks of none except Timothy to send.

Timothy was genuinely anxious for their welfare.

To think sending others – they are all lost in their selfish ends.

Timothy, like a son, serving the father. Paul hopes Timothy will be able, by the time he leaves for Philippi, that which of the alternatives await Paul – release or death.

v.24: Paul hopes – it may be release for him. Then he can visit them.

vs. 25-30: **Epaphroditus**. (Nowhere we read about him in the New Testament). (Epaphroditus refers to goddess of love. The Greek form is Epaphrodite.

He must be a pagan convert. (Epaphras is the short form.)

a.   The Philippian church sent him with gifts to Paul (v.4.18).

b.   He was to stay at Rome and minister to Paul.

c.   **vs.26-28:** He got critically ill. So Paul decided to send him back.

d.   Paul refers to him as i. fellow soldier and ii. fellow worker,

e.   as his brother-in-Christ.

The news of Epaphroditus' sickness gave anxiety to the Philippian church. But by God's grace he recovered. So Paul decided to send him back as best for him as he felt longing to go home.

So Paul calls on the Philippians to receive him a. with gladness b. and with warm heart to welcome him. c. Also tells them to honour him for his costly service.

Chapter-3

vs.1-31: Spiritual ambitions.

As if to close the letter, Paul writes "Finally brethren, rejoice in the Lord", but it seems he suddenly remembered the problem created by **the Judaizers**. So he wanted to include **a warning about them.**

v.1-3: Warning against the circumcision party.

Lightfoot comments that Paul in effect was saying "Forgive me if I speak once more on an old topic. The warning was necessary".

v.2: The Jews regarded the Gentiles as "dogs", but Paul feels the Judaizers need this nick name more now.

They prowl round the Christian congregations and seek to win some Gentile converts. The rite they advocated was no longer spiritually valid, but a mere mutilation of the flesh.

vs.4-7: Paul's previous life and aims.

Paul if he chose he could argue on their own ground – on externals to argue he could make stronger case.

Paul tells of his previous background:

i.   Member of God's people

ii. of Benjamin tribe

iii. An Aramaic speaking Hebrew – a True Jew.

iv. His devotion to the law – a Pharisee

v.   His Jewish zeal shown by his persecution of the Christians.

vi. By his life's example of the Jewish religion he was blameless.

All these above, Paul puts on credit side, as long as his terms of reference were those of the Judaizers.

All such assets, Paul says 'I have written off because of Christ'.

vs.8-14: a. The renunciation of the old.

   b. The assuming of the new ambitions.

The gain of knowing Christ – all other things as – loss, refuse = dung.

1. To be accepted on the basis of righteousness which is God's gift offered on the simple thing of "believing".

2. He wants to live on that knowledge of Him which is fellowship, obedience and service.

   To have fellowship with Christ is to know the power of His resurrection daily.

3. His aim is to share Christ's sufferings.

Paul associated with Christ's death in two ways;
   a. The Baptism signifies – death to sin and new life with him and in him to   righteousness (Rom. 6.1-6; Gal. 2.20).

   b. In the whole of Christian life and service, sharing of Christ's sufferings and   death necessary.

v.11: Paul was never complacent – faith must endure to the end (Heb. 3.14).

It leads to **continued dying with Christ** and life in his risen power.

vs.15-16: Exhortation to Christian living.

vs.18-21: Warning concerning worldly living and a call to the heavenly aim.

Chapter-4

vs. 1-23: Exhortations, acknowledgement of the gifts of the Philippians.

vs.1-3:   Personal appeals.

Paul refers to the Philippian believers as

a.   whom I love and long for

b.   my joy and crown

c.   my beloved.

vs.2-3: Personal appeals

a.   Past : Euodia and Syntyche – Two important ladies joined Paul in evangelistic programmes in the past. Paul thinks that their names in the Book of Life (Rev. 20.12).

b.   Present: At loggerheads with each other – Paul asks them to reconcile. Paul asks Clement to help in their unity.

Appeal: Let their manner of lives be worthy of the Evangelistic ministry (1.27). Clement, it seems, a well known Christian at the church at Rome.

vs.4-7: A call to joy and prayerfulness. In their prayer Thanksgiving and requests to God.

So not to be anxious about any issue in life.

vs.8-9: A call to hold on to what is true and lovely.

v.8: True, honourble, pure, just, lovely, gracious, anything of excellence and worthy of praise.

v.9: Personal Life of Paul.

What you have i. learned ii.received iii.heard iv.seen in me that do (I Cor.11.1, 4.16).

Vs.10-20: Paul's response for the gifts from Philippi.

v.10: "Revived" the Philippian church concern for Paul; earlier they had concern but no opportunity to do so.

vs.11-13: Paul was used to be content whatever state:

a.   Plenty or hunger

b.   Abundance or want.

v.14: Paul says it was kind of the Philippians to share in his trouble.

v.15: It was only Philippians who entered into partnership with Paul in Macedonia (=in giving and receiving).

v.16: Even in Thessalonica the Philippians sent help more than once.

v.17: Paul sees this Philippian gift of help as it goes into their credit (before God, understood).

v.18: Paul says now he received the gift sent through Epaphroditus.

a.   a fragrant offering.

b.   a sacrifice acceptable] to God

c.   a sacrifice pleasing   ] to God

v.19: a. Paul prays in return for God to supply their every need.

b. According to God's riches in glory in Christ Jesus.

vs.20-21: Greetings.

7
Colossians

INTRODUCTION

St. Paul made Ephesus the Mission centre for Asia. He was presenting the Gospel from there for around 3 years (Acts 19.10;20.31) either himself or his helpers.

Colossae along with Laodicia and Hirapolis were in the Lycus valley bordering the river Lycus (Col. 4.13ff). Its about 100 miles from Ephesus. Paul has not seen the Christians of Colossae (Col.2.1). It was Epaphras of Colossae (and fellow-workers) who was sent by Paul to establish the church there (Col.4.12) and also at Laodicia and Hirapolis. Paul wrote also a letter to Laodicia (Col.4.16) which seems to have been lost. The Laodicia was one of the 7 churches of the book of Revelation (Rev.1.11). They seem to be luke-warm in their faith (Rev.3.14-15). The name Laodicia was given by a Roman official after his wife Laodicia.

Illustration: The Mizo Presbyterian Synod has a terminology of workers in their Mission field :1) Mission field workers and 2) other workers (locals). Epaphras comes under this second category, working on behalf of Paul (Col.1.7). He was a local man of Colossae (Col.4.12 – "one of yourselves").

The state of the church:

1.   Both Paul and Epaphras want the Colossian Christians "mature" in their faith (Col.1.28; 4.12).

2.   For 'building' up the 'Body of Christ' (Eph.4.12-13).

Paul seems to be getting the idea of "growth" in the 'building' metaphor. He brings in the metaphor of the 'physical Body', which has the possibility of growth (Col.4.13-14; I Cor. 14.20) – "That we may no longer be children" in the spiritual life.

St. Peter in his 1ˢᵗ epistle (IPet. 1.2-5) refers to "living stones", though stones were used for a building but they do not grow but as illustration for the "Church", he wants also "growth", thus the use of the term "living stones".

MAIN DIVISIONS

1.1-8	–	Salutations and thanks-giving.
1.9-16	–	Prayer for spiritual growth.
1.15-19	–	Believer and God; Universe and the church
.1.20-23	–	The reconciling work of Christ.
2.4-23	–	Warning and refutation of false teaching.
3.1-11	–	The New and old life.
3.12-17	–	Putting on the Virtues.
3.18-4.1	–	The Family Relationships.
4.2-6	–	Concluding exhortation.
4.7-18	–	Closing section (commendation and Salutations).

Chapter - 1

COMMENTARY

vs. 1-2: Greetings: Timothy associated much with Paul (IICor. Phil;Iand II Thes.).

v. 3ff. – Here his custom of giving thanks, with special reminders of their spiritual life.

vs 4-5 – shows the substance of Paul's thanksgiving.

a. v.4 – their faith and love (love in the context of other believers).

b.v.5 – 'Hope' being the motive for the faith and love.

i.e., A Christian's life is in relation to the future goal. That is, it is Heaven-bound life, though not fully known of the life in the Age to come. Here the Gospel Truth the Colossians received to be guarded against the false Teachings.

v.6 – The indication of spiritual growth or 'maturity', Paul says, is seen in bearing the fruit.

vs.7-8 – It was through Epaphras, that Paul, came to know of the state of the Colossian Christians.

Note: **Epaphras**. (His name is short form of Epaphroditus, the goddess of Love. Epaphrodite is the Greek term. He must be a pagan convert).

St. Paul did not found the churches of the 3 cities of the Lycus valley (Laodicea, Hirapolis and Colossea).

Qn. Then who preached the Gospel to these churches?

Qn. Why St. Paul was so concerned as to mention "How greatly I strive for you"? (Col.2.1).

Ans. 1. These 3 churches were probably established by Epaphras, who was mentioned as "fellow servant and faithful minister of Christ" (1.7).

2. He was referred as "one who worked hard for you" (Col.4.12).

3. As "who is one of yourselves" (Col. 4.12). This means he was a native of Colossae.

4. Epaphras' burden for the Colosseans can be seen in Paul's reference to him "always remembering you in his prayers" (Col.4.12b).

5. From Acts 19.10; 20.31 we find that for 3 years St. Paul evangelized the whole of Asia Minor (the present Turkey). Colossae was around 100 miles from Ephesus and must have come under the campaign of Paul. Though Paul himself could not go, yet must have sent Epaphras to his own home town, "on our behalf" i.e., on Paul's behalf (Col.1.7).

6. Epaphras thus must have worked under the direction of Paul.

Illustration: Dr. E. Clark, the pioneer American missionary to the Hill Tribes (Ao Nagas chiefly) of Nagaland worked earlier through Gadhula Brown, an Assamese Christian of the plains

Illustration: The Friends Missionary Band calls upon the committed Christians either to go out as a missionary or support some one to go out as a missionary.

7. The following verses show the burden in the prayer of Epaphras for the Colossian Christians.

    "That you may stand mature and fully assured in all the will of God" **(Col. 4.2).**

8. "He has 'worked hard' for you and those in Laodicia and Hirapolis" **(Col.4.13)**. This shows that those who pray are also those who work hard.

Illustration: O.T. – 1.   Samuel (I Sal. 12.23);

                    2.   Jeremiah (Jer. 9.1-3);

                    3.   Nehemiah (Neh.1.4-6).

N.T – St. Paul himself shows such prayer and burden for the Jews (Rom. 9.1-3; 10.1ff).

vs. 9-14 – The prayer of Paul for the spiritual growth of the Colossian Christians

1. (**v.9**)– They may be filled with all spiritual i) wisdom {"Sophia" (Gk.)} – divine wisdom and ii) knowledge {Gnosis" (Gk.) = understanding this world.

2. **(v.10)** – God-pleasing and God- worthy

3. **(v.10)** – Fruit-bearing (in good works)

4. **(v.10)** – Increasing in spiritual growth.

5. **(v.11)** – Endure the trials of life a. with patience and joy

                                        b. strengthened

                                          in   i. all power

                                        and   ii. glorious might.

6. **(v.12)** –To give thanks to God for the future sharing of the divine inheritance with the saints.

7. **(v.13.7)** –God has delivered us from a. the dominion of darkness (Satan's) and b.transferred to the Kingdom of Christ (the Divine Son).

8. **(v.14)** In Christ a.   the believers have got Redemption (from bondage / evil).

                              b.   Through the forgiveness of our sins.

The above concluding section refers to deep Theological terms. It also portrays like the picture of a victorious ruler who overcome his enemies. Here Christ vanquishing Satan and establishing His glorious kingdom. The kingdom of Darkness of Satan overthrown and the righteous rule of the Divine Son (Christ) established. By this the believers can be rest-assured of their future state in the Kingdom of Christ, their Saviours.

vs.15-20 – The supremacy of Jesus Christ.

One N.T. scholar comments that in this passage we get "profound Theological ideas" (about Christ). Another N.T. scholar, R.P. Martin, suggests that whether St. Paul "incorporates an existing Hymn to Christ" here.

v.15 – Christ Jesus

Jesus is the visible expression to mankind while he lived and ministered on earth. One can be reminded of Jesus' reply to Philip (Jn. 14.8-10). Philip wanted Christ to show him "the Father God", i.e., The "Theophany" i.e., the physical manifestation of God. To this Jesus' reply was "He who has seen me has seen the Father". This tallies with Christ's statement in **Jn.10.30** "I and the Father are one".

To the preaching of the Gospel by the Serampore Missionaries (William Carey, Marshman and Ward)– the Serampore Mission Trio – at the beginning of 19th century, Raja Rammohan Roy of Calcutta disagreed. Rather the ethical teaching of Christ he appreciated and wrote a booklet titled "The Precepts of Jesus, a Guide to Peace and Happiness". In this 82 page treatise he never referred to Jn.10.30 which affirms the Christian faith of Jesus' Divinity – He is the incarnation of God, i.e., God coming to us in human form. Some parallel to Vaishnavite "Avatara" idea, Vishnu taking physical form from time to time to earth to destroy the wicked, to help the saints. Many Christian thinkers do not equate to avatara" the physical manifestation of the divine, as "Avatara" not to save sinners and also in around 9 forms from sub-human to human, while Jesus had once for all time appearance.

a.   Jesus is the image {"Eiskon" (Gk.)}of the invisible God (v.15)

b.   The 1st Born {Protokos (Gk.)} of all creation (v.15).

This raises the question if Jesus was a "created being" like the similar statement in **Rom. 8.29**, be it the first, of all the created beings. This aids the argument of Arius of the early church fathers, who was rightly condemned as "Heretic" by the 325 A.D. Nicene council of the churches.

So Jesus being divine could not be a creature like us all though 1st Born. He is of the category of Creator not of the creatures. So it should be understood not as "born before" all of us but as a supreme being only. The next verse (16) clarifies it.

c. i. For in him, all things were created, visible and invisible (v.16) and adds "through him and for him".

This clarifies Christ as the Creator, thus Divine.

  ii. His earthly existence for man's salvation only. He is before all things (created ones), which shows not only his divinity but also, here expresses, his pre-existence. Jesus' incarnation presupposes both his divinity and his pre-existence.

d.   In Christ all things hold together, i.e., the God who created the universe, did not leave it to turn on its own, though the laws of Nature laid to run the universe, yet like a clock wound and left to run for itself, He did not do so. This means the Creator God is actively involved in running the universe to go in an orderly manner, i.e., God is a caring God in each of our lives on earth. That is the reason when man fell into sin God was actively involved in sending his Son for our salvation. The Scriptures of the church (the Bible) is a record of the Acts of God for man's salvation, in finally sending His Son for our Redemption (Gal. 4.4).

e. Christ is the Head of the church, or the headship of Christ as "My church" (Matt.16.18). This ownership or the very existence of the church is based on Christ. Not only that but it also refers that under his direction the Church runs. No one can replace Christ in the working of the fellowship of believers or the church. It is Christ's church; not any one's church.

Thus the one (Christ) who is supreme in the world also claims that same status in the Church also.

f. Christ is the first-born from the dead (Col. 1.18b).

This refers to Christ's Resurrection.

In I Cor. 15th Chapter St. Paul holds that the basis for the Church's belief in the Resurrection of the believers is firmly based on Christ's rising from the tomb (where his dead body was laid), on the third day. Even if this is impossible to believe by many, it does hold true.

If Christians deny the Resurrection, St. Paul says then

   a. our faith is futile

   b. we are still in our sins.

   c. Those dead Christians have perished.

   d. Christians to be most pitied (I Cor. 15.17-119).

   e. This way in everything Christ is pre-eminent.

   f. In Christ dwells all the fullness (PLEROMA (Gk.) of God-head. This means in every aspect and every respect Christ is fully divine.

   g. All things, on earth and in Heaven, reconcile to Christ (Col. 1.20).

This last statement deals with the Colossian heresy, where they were trying to add to the atoning death of Christ – for man's salvation, something more, like the angel-worship, self-abasement etc (Col. 1.20). This will effect the all-sufficiency of Christ's Atoning death to man's salvation and the supremacy of Christ.

vs.21-23: v.21 – Before " **a.** estranged **b.** hostile in mind **c.** doing evil deeds.

v.22 – Now (in Christ) **a.** to be holy **b.** blameless **c.** irreproachable Reconciliation involves a Transformation.

v.23 – There is a condition: they have to continue in the faith.

Again in **Col.2.6** refers to the above v.23 –

i.   **1st part:** Those who **accepted** Christ (past tense used)

ii. **2nd part:** "They have **to continue** to live in him" (the present continuous verb used here).

The continuation of their faith involves a. stable b. steadfast c. not shifting from the hope of the Good News in Christ, i.e., salvation.

v. 23b – "The Gospel for all humans". It refers not the actualities, that all heard it but the Gospel meant for all.

vs.24-29:

1. **vs.24-25** – Now Paul turns to his own self and his share not only in the ministry but his share in the suffering for Christ's sake.

2. **v.26** – He then talks of the Hidden Mystery now revealed to Christ's servants.

3. **v.27** – this mystery is associated with the plan of God. That is, the riches of God's glory – to bring in the Gentiles, now to participate in the saving activity of God in Jesus Christ.

4. **v.28–**   a.   The end result is salvation to every man (= Jews and Gentiles).

          b.   Not only initiation into it, but also to lead to maturity in this hope and experience.

Note: v.28– "warning every man"   This is opposite to the Gnostic
          "Teaching every man"   heresy, where only the "
          "present every man"   initiated" given the "isoteric"
                                          knowledge with special
                                          passwords to reach God above.

Qn.: Why this emphasis on "every man"?

Ans.: Here Paul was denouncing the Intellectual aristocracy in salvation, like that of

          1. Gnostic heresy

          2. The Jewish prejudice against the Gentiles (Col. 1.26, 27).

This is opposite to the Gnostic heresy, where only the initiated given the "isoteric" knowledge with special passwords to reach God above.

Chapter - 2

vs.1-5 – Salutation and Thanks-giving

v.1 – Introduces himself as an Apostle, on the basis that the resurrected Jesus called him for the proclamation of the Gospel, specially to the gentiles, on the road to Damascus incident (Acts 9.1-9). (The Corinthian Christians seem to question him as he was not in the 12 chosen by Christ in his life time (I Cor.9.1-2). The Colossian Christians addressed as "Saints" normal to Paul's reference to the Christians in other letters, in the sense of those in trusting Christ get the "imputed righteousness" in Christ as "set apart" people.

v.3 – Paul informs the Colossians of his upholding them in his prayers with thanksgiving.

v.4 – Paul commends them for   a. their faith in Christ

b. their love for the "saints".

v.5 – "for the hope laid up for you in Heaven".

vs.6-7 – a.   The receiving of Christ is the starting point of a believer – The verb "you have received" is in the past tense.

b.   The next step is "to continue to live in Christ" which is the follow up – in the present continuous verb.

Two metaphors used here: i.   "rooted – Tree symbolism.

ii.   "built up"–building symbolism.

i.   Tree symbolism

When I visited Mt. Sinai, from Jerusalem, beyond Elath port of the Red sea, it was alluvial land and brazen mountains. Hardly any tree grew there, except 'Acacia' tree here and there. (That must be the reason, Moses was asked to make furniture for the Tabernacle in the wilderness journey from the wood of the Acacia with thin tree trunks (Ex.26.26; 27.2ff etc.).

I was told by the Swiss guide, that when the Suez canal was built along side of Egypt on the other side of Sinai, the roots of Acacia was found at 150ft. That's the secret of its survival in that barren region.

ii. The Building Symbolism

When I visited New York (USA), I was taken to climb by electric lift the Empire State building, the tallest building in the world then. It was 104 stories high. One can see like from an airplane, the Atlantic Ocean to the east, the statue of Liberty to the north, the suspension bridge connecting New Jersey State to New York and so on. We asked the guide, how the Americans could build such high building. The guide asked us not to get out at the ground floor. So we went down to the basement, 8 stories, below the ground then we came out to a large brazen rock connected to the Atlantic Ocean. The guide said that rock foundation was the strength of this tall Empire State building.

Ephesians 3.17-19 adds love along with faith referred here in Col. 2.6-7, the quadratic dimensions of love adds strength to one's faith in Christ as a believer.

So it is not only for a believer to receive Christ forgiving one's sins, but also to continue to live a victorious life all along his life of Christian faith.

Col.2.16-23: Problem - I: Legalistic and Religious approach to Religion.

    a. **2.16** – Food, drink and external observances.

    b. **2.18** – Angel worship.

    c. **2.23** – Ascetic practices.

a. i. **The Food Laws** of the Jews – clean and unclean (Lev.11.1-47)

Illustration: "Cosher" meat in diet is strictly observed today by the Jews. The injunction is "Don't add a kid's meat in the mother's milk" (Ex. 23.19).

Illustration: In some churches in North East India hills eating dog meat is strictly prohibited (even excommunication).

  ii. **Drink regulations** added here though the Levitical law was silent on it, probably found in Judaism of a later stage.

  iii. **Observance of Days:** Rules and regulations made concerning the festivals (Passover, Tabernacles and Dedication).

Illustration: a.: 7th Day Adventists and the 7th Day Baptists observe the 7th day-Sabbath for worship.

b. Many Christians make their Sundays like a Sabbath observance these days.

Ex.20.10 – There are 39 'Abboth' (=prohibitions) of labour and also 'Toldoth' of minor degree works.

Christ was often questioned for healings on the Sabbath day. But Christ replied:

a. Sabbath is made for man and not man made for Sabbath, i.e., the end is man, not means (Mk.2.27).

b. God never rested, so no Sabbath rest. So Christ is working (Jn.5.17).

c. When good work done, that counts even it be Sabbath (Mk.3.4).

d. The Son of Man is Lord of the Sabbath (Mk.2.25).

Problem –1: The False Teachings and the Answer by the Believers. The Jewish Influences:

Antiochus Epiphanus, the Great, transported 2000 Jews from Babylon to this area, Phrygia. Many more joined later. These were concerned for the rules and regulations concerning the Jewish festivals like the Passover, the Feast of Tabernacles, the Feast of Dedication etc. v.11 refers to the rite of circumcision.

Paul holds, at best, these are shadows of the real (v.17; Heb.10.1).

Problem – II: Ascetic Practices (vs.21-23)

Paul says those like "touch not", "taste not", "handle not" are "sense perceptions" of human precepts and doctrines.

v.23–a.   promotes rigour of devotion

b. Self-abasement.

c. Severity to the body.

Dangers: This leads to false pride and rejects the humanity of Jesus.

Chapter – 3

I.   **Paul's advice:** "Put to death what is earthly" (Col.3.5)

"Mortify that which keeps you from fulfilling God's will", i.e., not just of the flesh only (Rom.8.12).

Self-indulgent pleasures, desire for more from others, these are all self-centered . These must end. This is idolatry.

Illustration: Dr. E.Standly Jones held "Anything which makes self center of one's life and not God, is **off-centre**, and is **"eccentric"**, i.e., Eccentric Religionists.

II. Paul's Advice:

a.   vs.8-9 – "Put away" old life (Rom. 13.12 – cast away)

b.   v.10 – "Put on" new life (Rom.13.14 – put on)

This above refers to dressing analogy of a person.

II Cor.5.17 – "If any man be in Christ, he is a new creation, the old things are passed away."

a.   3.5-9 – The past life of sin to be put off Paul records many acts of sin.

b.   3.11-16 – The new life in Christ to be put on. Paul records many virtues of a believer.

v.15 – The old nature to be "put off" is "what is earthly in you"

v.10 – The new nature, "after the image of its Creator".

3.11: "There cannot be" – i.e., the old hostilities not possible based on –

    a.   Greek or Jew=Racial

    b.   Circumcised or uncircumcised= Religious

    c.   Barbarian or Sythian=Civilization

    d.   Slave or free=Citizenship

Chapter - 4

Col. 4.1 - To Masters (Philemon 10, 12)

To Philemon about Onesimus (the slave) as "faithful and beloved brother".

Qn. How do we treat our servants at our homes?

Important
The important thing to note here is that there are obligations on both sides:

1. Wives towards husbands and vice versa (Refer Eph. 5:21-33).

2. Parents towards children and vice versa (Refer Eph. 6: 1-4).

3. Masters towards slaves and vice versa (refer Eph. 6:5-9).

III. The Society (Col. 4:5-6) - towards the outsiders:
St. Paul's advice   a. "Conduct yourselves towards outsiders"

                b. "Let your speech be always gracious ... to answer everyone".

                c. To redeem the time (' Kairos in Greek), i.e. not to miss for action in any opportunity.

A quote : "The most effective testimony to the power of the Gospel is the life and conversation."

VS. 7-9; Paul refers to :
1. Tichicus, referred as a faithful minister and beloved servant in the Lord and to Paul a beloved brother (ref. Eph. 6:21 f.). Seen as linkman between Paul and the believers of Colossia.

2. Onesimus, also a faithful and beloved brother, both supposed to convey the Ephesians situation and ministry Paul was involved in. Helped specially when Paul was seized by a mob. (Acts 19:29).

3. Aristracus, (s 10-11). He was also a fellow prisoner with Paul.

4. Mark, as the cousin of Barnabas, only mentioned here, though we find him associated with Barnabas, in his Mission journey (Acts 15 : 36ff). Later Paul seems to be reconciled with Mark, as Paul opposed him in joining the second mission journey, for leaving halfway in the Ist mission journey (Acts 13:13).

5. Justus, Nothing known about him (v. 11).

All these above seem to be from the Jewish background engaged in Paul's ministry and Paul seem to be happy for their participation in his ministry.

6. Epahras, was the linkman serving at Colossia, being the local man. Paul refers to him as a man of prayer -

    i.   Always praying for the Colossians

    ii.   To see them to come to maturity in their faith. (same as Paul's wish, Col. 1:28).

    iii.   He was entrusted to the service also at Laodicea and Hierapolis fellowships (Col. 4:14).

Vs. 14-15: Greetings from a. Luke. b. Demas.
Greetings from -i. Paul to brethren at Laodicea,

               ii. To Nympha and the fellowship in his house.

v.16: to exchange letters between Colossians and Laodicians.

v.17 - special note to Archippus to carry his ministry faithfully referred in Philemon - v. 1 (Refers to Philemon letter for fuller infromation of this.)

8
Philemon

INTRODUCTION

Philemon here as one of the 4 prison Epistles the others being Ephesians, Philippians and Colossians).

Out of the 13 letters or epistles of St.Paul, there are 3 letters addressed to individuals (not to churches). These are:

1. to Timothy (2 epistles)

2. to Philemon (1 epistle)

Of the 3 noted above, the third one, to Philemon, is different as it is a private letter or personal letter entirely dealing with a private matter.

1st Qn.: How could this get into the New Testament Canon of Paul's epistles, while so many other personal letters of Paul were not included?

Ans.: 1. The probable answer seems to be that Ephesus was St. Paul's Mission Center in Asia Minor (present Turkey) (Acts 19.10; 20.31). From here for about three years he reached out with the Gospel to most of the places there.

2. The matter of this letter to Philemon deals with the returning of Onesimus, the slave of Philemon, and Paul requesting Philemon to accept him (vs.12 and 15).

3. Ignatius, 50 years later, when he was taken from Antioch of Syria for his execution at Rome,he wrote a letter from Smyrna on the way in Asia Minor to the church at Ephesus. In that letter he refers to their renowned Bishop "Onesimus".

4. That was the time the first collection of Paul's letters were made at Ephesus. It is very probable that though the letter to Philemon was a personal one, yet as a Bishop Onesimus there he must have insisted or prevailed on them to include it in the list of Paul's letters, to let the other churches know what way God in his great grace turned this former slave of Philemon into their beloved Bishop now.

2nd Qn.: In Col. 4.16, Paul asks the Colossians "you read also the letter from Laodicia". We don't have the letter in the New Testament. Was it lost?

Ans.: First we have to note, that from vs. 12 and 13, we find Epaphras, who was under St.Paul's guidance, was able to establish Colossian church (v.12). He also seems to have worked hard for the closeby two churches of Laodicia and Hierapolis (v.13).

These 3 churches seem to be localized closely in the Lycus river valley. That's how they were asked to read each others' (Colossian and Laodicia letters in exchange) (Col. 4.16).

Now the question of where exactly Philemon, (the master of Onesimus) resided? In Philemon v.2 Paul refers to "i. Appia, our sister and ii. Archippus, our fellow soldier".

Col.4.17 refers to Archippus, who was exhorted "to fulfil the ministry, which you have received in the Lord".

This means Archippus was getting this advice after series of references to Laodicia (Col. 4.13, 15, 16). So it is possible Archippus was the Pastor of the church at Laodicia and he seems to be the son of Philemon, and Appia, his wife.

The reference in Col. 4.17 "say to Archippus" indicates verbal, person to person talk, as such, Philemon must have his residence at Laodicia most probably, as he is Archippus' father. If that be so, as Goodspeed, the New Testament scholar, argues, Onesimus must also be a Laodicean, being Philemon's slave. Then this letter to Philemon (of Laodicia) could well be "the letter", the Colossians were asked to read also, as these 3 towns – Colossea, Laodicia and Hirapolis are of close proximity of Lycus valley.

3rd Qn.: Why the Colossians and the Laodicians were asked to exchange their' letters?

Ans.: For Onesimus' return acceptance issue belongs not only to Philemon's family alone but also to the two churches there, as he is now "a believer" and to be accepted as such in the church also.

COMMENTARY

vs.1-7: Here we find Paul was not using his usual title "an Apostle" of Christ. In its place refers to himself as "the prisoner of Jesus Christ" This shift in dropping his title, is probably as it is a personal letter addressed to Philemon.

He includes Timothy's name (with Paul). The last letter before his execution we find was to Timothy (IInd letter). When he takes up Bishop's post at Ephesus, [some time later where John (the Apostle) was released from Patmos island during the time of Emperor Nerva]

v.2: We have noted Archippus, as Philemon's son and Appia, Philemon's daughter-in-law (being Archippus' wife).

The reference to the "church, in your house," we have to note at the initial stages, "house churches"were common. (Act 3.46; Rom. 16.5; I Cor. 16.19; Col. 4.15; Phil.3).

v.3: "Grace and peace," we note, are the common Jewish eulogy (=blessing); Paul uses in most of his letters.

v.4: "I remember you in my prayers." Paul was a man of prayer and as he established churches, he has a burden for them and their problems, which he used to place before God in his daily prayer time (Rom. 1.9; I Cor. 1.4; Eph. 1.16).

In the II Corinthian letter, Paul refers to his sufferings and includes in the list "the daily pressure for his anxiety for all the churches" (II Cor. 11.28).

v.5: The love towards Christ, and "the love towards the saints (= believers).

a.　Here we find the extension of and response in a sense to Christ's saving love for the believers of the church.

The vertical relationship with Christ, to be extended in the horizontal relationship with the fellow-believers. Paul often addresses believers as "saints" in the sense of being sanctified or "made holy" in Christ. This is not moral holiness as such but "imputed" in Christ, our sins being forgiven in Christ's atoning work.

b.　It is not only love but also "faith" added "in sharing" in the next verse (5).

v.5: The sharing of faith, Paul says in v.5 is to promote "all in the knowledge of the good that is in Christ Jesus."

The Greek "KOINONIA PISTEOS" = the "fellowship in faith" sharing may most probably refer to prayer support or it may refer possibly to sharing one's Christian witness.

v.7: The practical side of Philemon's life, how he looked after the fellow believers and servants of Christ.

"Refreshed by you" has a connotation of hospitality to the "local" as well as "visiting servants of God" to his house church.

vs. 8-17 – v.8: Here Paul makes the distinction of **a.** what is Philemon's "duty" (or requirement) and Paul's command.

v.9: But Paul was in his condition of **i.** an Ambassador of Christ and **ii.** in a prisoner state.

v.10: Paul makes an appeal (or request) to Philemon.

4th Qn.: What relationship Paul has with Onesimus?

Ans.:   a. Paul has become Onesimus' Father ("in faith") (understood)

b. Onesimus, is referred as Paul's "child".

It is a family's concern of a father for his son's welfare.

v.11: Paul refers to Onesimus' changed life.

The name in Greek means "Profitable". Paul makes "pun" "in saying not only by name but also by nature".

a. Before Onesimus was useless to you.

b. Now Onesimus is useful to you and to me (added).

vs.12-13: Paul now comes to the main issue:

a.   Paul is sending him back to Philemon but adds In a sense Onesimus has become very dear to Paul.

b.   It is like sending Paul's very heart.

5th Qn.: Why Onesimus became so dear to Paul?

Ans.:   a. Onesimus proved a useful helper to Paul

b. Specially in the context of   i. Paul's confinement in prison and
ii. Onesimus' conversion.

v.14: This above wish of Paul is conditioned by Philemon's good will

    a.   not by compulsion

    b.   but by Philemon's consent.

vs.15-18: The conversion of Onesimus was given here.

It is possible that Onesimus ran away from Philemon, his master, for which Paul's reference to him.

a. "If he has wronged to you" at all, or Probably "a theft" case.

b. "owes you anything."

Onesimus thus "a run away slave" of Philemon.

Onesimus' background: A run away from Lycus valley town of Colossea or Laodicia.

He finally seems to have ended up at Rome, the Imperial Roman Capital, where it is said, for every 4 citizens one seems to be a slave. It is said there were 60 million slaves in the Roman Empire then.

Some how he might have been introduced by one of his acquaintances at Rome or met by one of the believers and brought to Paul and his life was transformed – **1.** he became a Christian. **2.** He started to help Paul at Rome.

Paul now felt it was his responsibility to send him to his master. It is probable Epaphras of Colossea recognized him as Philemon's slave or Onesimus himself revealed his identity.

Normally slaves are the property of the master who buys him and the punishment for running away could be severe, to thrash him or to brand him with iron rod on his forehead etc.

vs.16-17: Paul asks Philemon to receive him in his new condition.

v.15: He was   a. parted for a short time,

                b. but you can have him "for ever".

v.16: a. No longer a slave but

     b. as a beloved brother.

As "beloved brother" – Paul says a. "more to me" b. "How much more to you?"

Onesimus now a Christian.

This "beloved brother both in the flesh and "in the Lord."

v.17: Paul asks Philemon to receive Onesimus as he would receive Paul himself.

As Paul's convert naturally Philemon owes much himself to Paul.

v.19: Paul writes him that with his own hand he was writing, i.e., not using any secretary like in other letters. This being very special and important matter involved – to accept Onesimus "now returning to Philemon his master."

v.20: To oblige to Paul's request in this regard Paul feels it amounts to getting some benefit from Philemon now in this regard.

Paul feels it is "refreshing his heart in Christ."

vs.21-22: Paul feels that he was confident of Philemon.

v.21: a. obliging to his request in this regard.

v.22: b. Paul adds here   i. his hope of release from prison

ii. asks for a place to prepare for him as he hopes to visit Philemon and the fellowship in his house.

v.23: Paul conveys the greetings from those who are with him and must be known to Philemon and the church there.

These are 1. Mark 2. Aristarchus 3. Demas 4. Luke.

Demas earlier he refused to be with Paul and left him for the love of the world (II Cor. 4.10).

Luke, seems to be also in the prison there with Paul; he was his fellow-missionary Doctor.

v.25: Final benediction of Christ's grace conveyed to Philemon and the church too.

6th Qn.: The question asked that why Paul had not condemned the "slavery" and ask Philemon to release Onesimus?

Ans.: It would have been disastrous, as the Roman society built on slavery, and also as Christians under persecution, it would be a good cause to destroy them if demanded so.

Probably at a later stage the church go to that extent. Right now one can note that – no distinction in Christ made between citizen and a slave.

The church emphasis at this stage of Paul's time was rather put the categories of the then society – citizen versus slave – along with other categories in a new relationships as being now members of the one body, the church:

a. **I Cor. 12.13:**   i.   Jews or Gentiles

                     ii.   Freeman or slaves.

b. Gal. 3.28: There is   i.   neither Jew nor Greek

                     ii.   slave nor freeman

                     iii.   male nor female

c. Col. 3.11: There is   i.   neither Jew nor Greek

                     ii.   neither circumcision nor uncircumcision

                     iii.   neither barbarian nor Scythian

                     iv.   neither slave nor freeman.

Onesimus ran away as a slave and now he was returning again as a slave.But now he returns to his master as a Christian and thus "a beloved brother" in Christ.

Thus the very social distinction of Master and slave becomes meaningless – a new relationship established in Christ.

a.   Onesimus now has to serve Philemon as he would serve Christ.

b.   Philemon should treat Onesimus as Christ would have treated him.

The centrifugal place of Christ transforms now the relationships between the different former "man-made" sections of the society in relation to common allegiance to Christ now, as members of his one body and brothers in Christ.

9
I Thessalonians

INTRODUCTION

The city Thessalonica was the capital of Roman province of Macedonia. It connected Rome with the East by the military road. St. Paul visited it in 49 A.D. in the 2nd missionary journey, 49-52 (Acts 15.39-18.22) with Silvanus (referred in Acts of the Apostles as Silas) and Timothy. It was a populous city, already by then .There was also a synagogue (Acts 17.1). A fellowship of followers of Christian faith was formed into a church there (I Thess. 1.1; Acts 17.1 ff). From Col. 4.10f. we come to know Aristarchus comes from Thessalonica and he was a Jewish Christian (Acts 20.4). Otherwise the members of Thessalonian church were mostly Gentile converts (Acts 17.4 points "a great many of the devout Greeks and not a few of the devout women followed Christ"). But the Jews got jealous and set the city in an uproar which led to the believers sending away Paul.

They then went **to Beroea**, where they had good reception. But here also opponents came from Thessalonica and disturbed them (Acts 17.13f). Paul left but Silas and Timothy stayed back. St. Paul refers to the believers at Thessalonica as example to the church at Macedonia and Achaia (1.7f.). Paul called for Silas and Timothy to come soon to him to Athens. It seems they met Paul at Corinth. Paul came from Athens (Acts 18.1,5).

The Date

I Thessalonians seems to be written from Corinth. It seems Silas and Timothy were with Paul (I Thess. 1.1; 3.6 – though I Thess. 3.6 shows Timothy was with Paul at Athens).

Generally the date was shown as 50 A.D. As it deals with topics of the 2nd coming of Christ, it's Theme is said to be both – Soteriological and

Eschatological (the End time references are prominent). The II Thessalonians' date is also given as 50 A.D. It's theme same as the I Thessalonians.

THE MAIN DIVISIONS

Chapter – 1

v.1 :   Addressed by Paul and others with him; and greetings to the church.

vs.2-10 : Thanksgiving for their faith in Christ.

Chapter – 2

vs.1-12 : Paul defends his Evangelistic work at Thessalonica.

vs.13-16 : Paul recapitulates the Readers' mind.

vs.17-19 : Paul's desire to visit them and renew the fellowship.

Chapter – 3

vs.1-10 : A portrayal of Paul's past relationship with the church

vs.11-13 : Paul's intercession for them.

Chapter – 4

vs.1-12 : Paul reminds them as Christians their moral duties.

vs.13-18 : The hope of and details about the Parousea at the 2nd coming of Christ.

Chapter – 5

vs.1-11 : (Continuation) of believers to be diligent for the 2nd coming and Parousea.

vs.12-22 : Series of directions to the believers.

vs.23-28 : Closing prayer, greetings and benediction.

Chapter – 1

COMMENTARY

vs. 1-2: Greetings to the church.

Along with Paul, Silvanus (=Silas in short used) and Timothy greet the church at Thessalonica.

a.   In the name of God, as Father and Jesus Christ, as Lord.

b.   In Grace and peace greetings conveyed to them.

vs.2-10: Thanksgiving for their faith in Christ.

v.2: i. Giving thanks to God always for Thessalonian believers.

ii. Constantly mentioning them in prayer.

v.3: iii. Remembering   a. their work of faith.

b. their labour of love.

c. their steadfastness of hope in Christ.

v.4: Paul reminds them i. God has chosen them (being beloved of God).

v.5: a.   The Gospel proclamation done:

i. not only in word = their preaching.

ii. but in the power of Divine strength.

iii. in the Holy Spirit = Holy Spirit's guidance.

iv. with full conviction = their firm faith.

b.   From their preaching the Thessalonians must have come to realize the true selves of Paul and his fellow-workers.

v.6: The Thessalonians received the Gospel

i. in much suffering

ii.with joy – by the inspiration of the Holy Spirit.

In this way the result was: They have become followers

i.   of Paul and his Colleagues.

ii.   and of Lord Jesus Christ.

I Cor.11.1: (I Cor. 4.16): Paul calls on the Corinthian believers to be "imitators" of Paul, or close followers and in transformed lives in Christ, as Paul adds " as I am of Christ" (imitation). In other words, Paul's life is an example of full surrender to Christ. Thus his preaching tallies with the surrendered life he lives.

This is a great challenge to our Christian workers, for often their lives do not match their ministries.

v.7: Qn.: Why Paul calls on Thessalonian believers to be imitators of living a life in effect worthy of a follower of Christ, so that the spreading of the Gospel message to Macedonia (of which Thessalonica is the capital and Achaia (or present Greece) which is the neighbouring state (as Thessalonica situated in the middle between the two states).

v.8: Pa ul gives the reason for his call to be "imitators' of Paul and colleagues, (who brought the Gospel to them) and Christ; their faith has come to be known already

a.   in these two states, Macedonia and Achia,

b.   the news of their faith gone forth every where, Paul adds.

Chapter – 2

vs.1-2: St. Paul defends his evangelistic work at Thessalonica.

v.1: Paul defends his visit to Thessalonica, and says it was not useless or fruitless.

v.2: Paul refers to what happened to them at Philippi of Macedonia state. There they suffered and shamefully treated. Likewise at Thessalonica, (after that incident at Philippi) Paul testifies that he and his colleagues (Silas and Timothy) had **i.** courage in God **ii.** in the face of great opposition.

v.3: Paul maintains that their Gospel appeal, does not originate from

  i.   delusion or error

  ii. or impure purpose or motive

  iii. nor in fraud or   deceit

(This implies probably some do so indulge).

v.4: Paul and colleagues claim God being the witness:

  i.   They have been approved by God and so entrusted with the Gospel proclamation.

  ii. So preach not to please men but to please God, who tests their hearts.

v.5: iii. a. so never used either flattering words,

       b. nor their preaching a cloak for greed.

v.6: iv. a. Never did Paul and his colleagues sought glory from men. This above Paul clarifies,

       b. Paul and companions might have made demands as Apostles of Christ.

Qn.: What does it; mean?

Ans.: Paul makes it clear in I Cor. 9th chapter.

i.　As an Apostle he has right to food and drink (v.4).

ii.　As a soldier or owner of a vineyard or a shepherd (v.7)

iii.　A farmer (vs.10,11)

iv.　The priests at the Temple service (v.13) have a right to a share of the fruit etc.

v.7: On the other hand Paul testifies they were gentle like a) a nurse taking care of the children.

v.8: so having much affection for them, willing to share **a.** not only the Gospel **b.** but share themselves all because now in Christ, the Thessalonian believers have become very dear or loving to them.

vs.9-12: v.9 – "You remember"　　　　refers to fresh recollections
　　　　v.10– "You are witnesses"　　of Paul here.

v.9: a.　Paul says "night and day" he and his colleagues worked among the Thessalonians.

　　b.　but without taking any financial help from them i.e., free- service.

　　c.　for this other churches like the Achian (Greek) churches came forward and supported the team (II Cor. 9.1-5).

v.11:d. Paul says he acted like a father towards the children (the Thessalonians); i.e., not taking any financial help from them. In I Cor. 4.12 Paul refers to labour with his own hands, so too his colleagues.

In I Cor. 4.15b Paul says he became a father to them in the Gospel. So too to the Thessalonians he refers himself as a father to them (v.11).

So Paul in this fatherly state　　i.　He was exhorting each one of them

　　　　　　　　　　ii.　He encouraged them

　　　　　　　　　　iii. He charged them personally.

v.12: All the above to lead a life worthy of God.

God calls them i. into the Divine Kingdom

　　　　　　ii. into His glory.

This is their privilege, if they respond to God's call to them through the Gospel preaching.

vs.13-16: Paul seems to have visited Thessalonian church twice or more times – to see if they stand firm in the new found faith. Paul rejoiced that they stood firm in their faith.

v.13: 1st – These received the Gospel "as the Word of God" (i.e., not of men). Really as Word of God it is at work in them.

v.14: In this way they became same sufferers from your own people like the Christians of Judea at the hands of the Jews and also the Judaizers and the Gnostics.

v.15: As for the Jewish opponents, they killed Lord Jesus, and the prophets and now drove out Paul and his fellow workers. In effect they displease God in opposing Paul and his colleagues.

v.16: It is to fill up the measure of their sins – by hindering Paul and his co-workers from preaching the Gospel to the Gentiles.

v.17: Paul felt God's wrath will certainly come upon them, the Jewish opponents.

vs.17-20: Paul's portrayal of his relations with the church.

vs.17-18:   a.   Paul and his colleagues wished very much to see the Thessalonian believers.

        b.   i. Paul personally tried again and again to visit them but feel sorry it did not materialize.

           ii. Paul feels it is Satan who hindered them.

        c.   This was at a time of it's going through tribulation and persecutions (3.2).

vs.19-20: Paul refers to them

v.19 – a.   as hope, joy and crown of boasting.

v.20 – b.   Paul repeats "You are our glory and joy".

Chapter – 3

---

vs.1-10: A recounting of Paul's past relationship with the church.

v.3: shows the believers at Thessalonica were passing through afflictions, "our lot" indeed.

vs.1-2: For this from Athens Timothy was sent who was "our brother" and "the Lord's servant" to establish them in their faith, by his exhortation so that no one be moved away from their faith.

Paul gives highest commendation to Timothy seen in the letter to the Philippians (2.19). Here also Paul plans to send Timothy to them, again.

vs.4-5: v.4 – Paul refers to the caution already given that afflictions will surely come to them.

v.5: a. As such to know how they were faring, and to encourage them, Timothy was sent to them.

    b. The tempter ('Satan' used earlier) tempting you and Paul and his colleagues' "labour of Gospel work may be in vain" was "Paul's fear".

vs.6-10: a. Timothy returned from visiting Thessalonian church and brought good news of their faith, i.e., they were in their faith.

    b. Timothy also reported of i. theThessolonian Christians always remember them kindly ii. and long to see Paul.

v.7: The result was Paul and his co-workers a. were comforted for their faith. b. at a time of distress and affliction of Paul and colleagues.

v.8: Paul adds: a. now we live if they stand fast in the Love.

v.9:   b. all the joy Paul and colleagues feel before God.

    c. what thanksgiving Paul and colleagues can render before God.

v.10: a. At the end Paul expresses the wish to visit them face to face.

b. and adds what is lacking in their faith to offer to them.

vs.11-13: This seems Paul's prayer

a. for God the Father and Lord Jesus to direct Paul and co-workers to Thessalonica again.

b. i.   for the Lord to increase their brotherly love for one another in the church.

ii.   and to all men (i.e., Non- believers around them)

iii.   and establish their hearts in holiness (i.e., unblamable)

Chapter – 4

---

vs.1-12: Paul reminds them as believers their moral duties.

vs.1-2: Paul exhorts them – to continue following what they are doing as instructed:

i.   how you ought to live.

ii.   how thus to please God which they are doing but to do more now.

vs.3-5: Moral instructions now:

1.   a. To abstain from unchastity.

      b. each one to have his wife i. in holiness

                                    ii. in honour

                                      iii. not in the passion of lust, as heathen do.

This is the will of God and their sanctification.

vs.6-8: 2. a. No person wrong his brother in this above matter.

           b. as fore warned by Paul and co-workers,-

              i.   the Lord is the Avenger in this matter.

              ii. for God's call is for holiness, not uncleanness.

v.8: so any one disregards the above instruction

              i.   disregards God, not man.

              ii. also disregards the Holy Spirit.

vs.9-12: This is about brotherly love in the church-fellowship.

v.9: a. this is taught, in the scriptures, by God – to love one another.

v.10: b. i.   The Macedonian believers throughout that region love one another.

          ii.   The instruction here is to love "more and more"(like in vs.1-2).

v.11: i.   To aspire to live quietly.

ii.   To mind your own affairs.

iii.   To work with your hands (i.e., not burdensome to others).

v.12: By this way they will be respected by the Non-Christians.

vs.13-18: The Hope about the Parousia at the 2nd Coming of Christ and its details (4 and 5 chapters).

Here Paul seems to answer about the reports he got freshly from the Thessalonian Christians about the state of the believers dying and what happens to them in view of the delay in the immediate expectation of the 2nd Coming of Christ which they thought will take place in their own generation.

v.13: Paul's clarification about the state of the dead believers.

Paul says not to grieve for the dead relatives, as the Heathen do who have no hope like the Christians.

v.14: Paul's answer in the above respect:

a.   Christ will bring with him those believers who died as he is the one who died and rose again.

v.16:b. The Lord will descend from Heaven

i.   with a cry of command

ii.   with the Archangel's call

iii.   with the sound of the Trumpet of God.

v.16: c. Then the dead in Christ will rise first.

v.17: d. Then those believers, who are alive, next,

i.   They will be caught up together with the former ones (those already dead) in the clouds

ii.   to meet the Lord in the air (this is Parousia).

In this way Paul encourages the Thessalonian believers that "we shall always be with the Lord".

This is the comforting message of Paul to Thessalonians.

Here we have to note, as shown also in detail in the book of Revelation, that two phases involved in the hope of the 2nd Coming of Christ.

v.11: Paul calls on the believers to comfort one another with this hope.

Note: 1ˢᵗ Stage a. The Parousia, where the dead and the living believers caught up to the air where they meet the Lord.

b. That was also the time of Great Tribulation on earth for 7 years or so.

c. Satan is said to be bound after that for a 1000 years. As per the book of Revelation being 1000 years, it is called the Millennial reign of Christ after parouria

2ⁿᵈ Stage: then Christ and his followers come to earth and the Armageddon battle with Satan now released from the bottomless pit. He with his armies fight and Christ will defeat and send him and his followers to eternal punishment.

3ʳᵈ Stage: There will be the Final judgment for all the dead who will be brought back alive to stand before the judgment seat of God and those alive too come there.

a.   Heaven – for the followers   seems to be the final end

b.   Hell - for the evil doers   of the end time.

Chapter – 5

---

vs.1-11: The believers cautioned to be diligent for the 2nd Coming of Christ and the Parousia.

vs.1-2: a. As the 2nd Coming of Christ will be like a thief entering into a house, which will be secret, so no need of specification of the exact time(Matt.24.42-22 – Jesus also uses 'thief').

   b. It is also like people saying 'peace' and 'security' then comes the sudden destruction.

   c. It will be like a woman in travail of child birth and she has to give birth – the emphasis here was no escape from it.

In Mk.13.32 – Christ himself tells that the exact time that no one knows, except God the Father.

vs.4-5: Paul says as believers are "sons of light", so not in darkness, to surprise them like a thief breaking into a house.

vs.6-8: Paul refers to **slumber** versus being **awake**. He refers:

   a.   the believers to the latter, being awake, for the day of Christ's 2nd Coming.

   b.   In **v.7** he also refers to the drunkards, who usually used to get drunk at night. So believers not of darkness represented by Night.

v.8: c.   to be awake as in the light of the day and so be sober (i.e.,) not be drunkards of the night.

   d.   Paul here in **v.8** brings out the analogy of the panoply   or soldier's war dress seen in Ephesians 6.13-17: of the Ephesians two versus 6.16-17 only, Paul brings out:

Here Thessalonian:

   a.   the breast plate of faith (**love** added).

   b.   The helmet of salvation (**hope** added).

v.9-11: v.9 – Christ's coming is for man's salvation, i.e., it is for sinners to be saved Christ came into the world (Mk. 10.45 and Matt.9:13)

This is, as we have to note, different from the Hindus.

a.   'Avatar' concept, where Vishnu said to take forms to save the saints and destroy the evil. So the use of 'Avatar' term for Christ's incarnation not favoured , by some, while some in favour

    i.   The Indian Christian thinkers like A.J. Appasamy favours use of 'Avatar' with certain safeguards.

    ii.   V.Chakkarai uses this 'Avatar' concept in the sense of "Jesus of history is the Avatara of God".

    iii.   Keshab Chandra Sen of Brahmasamaj, vehemently opposed to use 'Avatara' term for Jesus, as he calls it "a lie of Christian Avatarism". Etc.

b.   The term **'wrath' of God** St. Paul deals with it in the opening section of his famous epistle to the Romans (1.14). There the concept is shown opposed to the righteousness of God. It is shown not a personal factor of divine, as his nature, but like the Chinese proverb, though the sun shines yet 'shadows' fall, for which sun not responsible but some object in the way. So too God being a Saviour God, it is man's fault for God's wrath.

In v.9: Paul here states "God has not destined us for wrath".

v.10: Jesus Christ died for our sins so that **i.** we might obtain salvation.

ii. and 'night or day' we might live with him.

v.11: So calls on the Thessalonian believers **i.** to encourage one another and adds "as you are now doing" **ii.** to build up one another.

vs.12-22: Series of directions to the believers.

v.12:   1. to respect those who minister among them.

    2. who are "over you", as those work among them.

v.13: 3. To esteem them highly in love because of their labour.

    4. Be at peace among yourselves.

v.14: 5. To admonish the idlers.

    6. To encourage the 'faint-hearted'.

    7. To help the weak.

8. To be patient in their dealings with others.

v.15: 9. None of them to repay evil for evil.

10. but seek to do good to one another, i.e., "to all".

vs. 16-22: Paul deals with spiritual matters from now on.

v.16: a. To rejoice always, i.e., in all circumstances.

v.17: b. to pray constantly (i.e., without ceasing). Paul himself does pray always.

v.18: c. To give thanks in all circumstances, i.e., good or bad. (Rom. 8.28 in every situation good or bad God works for our good). Paul adds here "This is Christ's will for you".

v.19: d. Not to quench the Holy spirit, i.e., His activity.

v.20: e. Not to despise prophesying.

v.21: f. but to test everything

g. and to hold fast what is good.

v.22: h. To avoid every form of evil.

v.23: Prayer of Benediction:

a.   The God of peace to sanctify them wholly.

b.   At the 2nd coming of Christ, the 3 constituent parts of a person – the life spirit(= 'nephesh'), soul and body be kept sound and blameless.

v.24: St. Paul adds the assurance of being called by Christ is faithful and He will do it.

It means God never fails to do what he promised (The Old Testament resource with proofs).

vs.25-28: Final requests, greetings and closing prayer.

v.25: Paul requests for the Thessalonian believers' prayer for him and his colleagues.

v.26: to greet the believers with a holy kiss.

v.27: Paul on oath calls on them to read this letter before all believrs. (In the Colossian letter even to exchange letter with Laodicians in reading each church's letter by the other church).

v.28: Final benediction, closing with the grace of Christ on them.

10
II Thessalonians

INTRODUCTION

The city Thessalonica was the capital of Roman province of Macedonia. It connected Rome with the East by the military road. St. Paul visited it in 49 A.D. in the 2nd missionary journey, 49-52 (Acts 15.39-18.22) with Silvanus (referred in Acts of the Apostles as Silas) and Timothy. It was a populous city, already by then .There was also a synagogue (Acts 17.1). A fellowship of followers of Christian faith was formed into a church there (I Thess. 1.1; Acts 17.1ff). From Col. 4.10f. we come to know Aristarchus comes from Thessalonica and he was a Jewish Christian (Acts 20.4). Otherwise the members of Thessalonian church were mostly Gentile converts (Acts 17.4 points "a great many of the devout Greeks and not a few of the devout women followed Christ"). But the Jews got jealous and set the city in an uproar which led to the believers sending away Paul.

They then went to Beroea, where they had good reception. But here also opponents came from Thessalonica and disturbed them (Acts 17.13f). Paul left but Silas and Timothy stayed back. St. Paul refers to the believers at Thessalonica as example to the church at Macedonia and Achaia (1.7f.). Paul called for Silas and Timothy to come soon to him to Athens. It seems they met Paul at Corinth. Paul came from Athens (Acts 18.1,5).

The Date

I Thessalonians seems to be written from Corinth. It seems Silas and Timothy were with Paul (I Thess. 1.1; 3.6 – though I Thess. 3.6 shows Timothy was with Paul at Athens).

Generally the date was shown as 50 A.D. As it deals with topics of the 2nd coming of Christ, it's Theme is said to be both – Steriological and

Eschatological (the End time references prominent). The II Thessalonians' date is also given as 50 A.D. It's theme same as the I Thessalonians.

1. Only we can note here that it was dated 50 A.D.

2. It was written from Corinth.

3. It's emphasis was both Sotereological and Eschatological themes.

4. **a.** Harnack (N.T. Scholar), held that the readership of II Thessalonians was Jewish Christians (while that of the I Thessalonians, it was for the Gentile converts).

   b. Though F.C. Burkitt, modified it in suggesting that as seen in 3.17 though meant to show the whole letter written by Paul, but inreality the 'autographed' post-script of Paul, suggests that there is additions to Paul's writing by others. There is a letter falsely ascribed to Paul circulating among the Thessalonians with regard to the 2nd coming of Christ.

THE MAIN DIVISIONS

Chapter – 1
vs.1-2: Introduction and greetings.

vs.3-12: Paul commends for their endurance in suffering; praises and prays for their faith and love; reminds again of the Parousia and final judgment.

Chapter – 2
vs.1-12: Advises them against soon expectation of Parousia.

vs.13-17: Advises to stand firm in their faith.

Chapter – 3
vs.1-5: To be steadfast in faith.

vs.6-16: Special instruction to the disorderly getting lazy.

vs.17-18: Paul's own hand written greetings and conclusion.

Chapter – 1

1.1.1-2: To the Readers: Paul with Silvanus and Timothy to the believers there.

2.1.3-12: Thanksgiving and Encouragement.

v.3: Paul feels (and his party) is bound to give Thanks to God for you.

It seems these Thessalonian Christians most probably commented that why too much commendation in the 1st letter? So the reply of Paul, it is the least he can do, specially

    a.   their faith is growing much

    b.   their brotherly love is increasing.

v.4: For this above state of the church, Paul says,

    a.   they are boasting before others about them

    b.   this in the face of   i. persecutions they suffer

                                  ii. afflictions from the others.

vs.5-12: Encouragement from Paul and colleagues.

v.5: a.   they can be made worthy of the Kingdom of God.

    b.   Which is the righteous judgment of God for them.

v.6: As Paul refers to Divine judgment above, now turns his attention on their enemies.

God in relation to their Adversaries, (like "tit for tat") will afflict them himself.

vs.7-9: At the 2nd coming of Christ as a judge

    a.   He will grant rest to the Thessalonian believers

    b.   But vengeance upon their Adversaries

    i. who do not know God

    ii. who do not submit to the Good news.

v.9: c. These above Adversaries also suffer

      i. the eternal destruction

      ii. exclusion from the presence and the glory of the Lord.

v.10: As for the Believers on that day of the 2nd Coming of Christ

    a. to be glorified by his saints

    b. to be marveled at, by the believers.

vs.11-12: So Paul points to the Thessalonian Christians the chief emphasis in their prayer was:

v.11: a. God may make you worthy of his call.

    b. God may fulfil   i. every good resolve

                      ii. every work of their faith by his power.

v.12: The end result will be i. the name of Christ be glorified in them

                             ii. the name of you in Christ.

All these in terms of the abundant grace of Christ.

Chapter – 2

---

vs.1-12: The Events associated with "the Day of the Lord".

The believers of Thessalonica some how began probably based on a letter ascribed to Paul but penned by some one else as noted above, to think that the Day of the Lord had already begun.

a. St.Paul here had to instruct them to the contrary.

b.   St. Peter (in II Pet. 3rd chapter) too had to deal with the so called "Scoffers" who held since their fathers died, all things continued as before, since creation.

a. **II Pet 3.6:** By flood the then world perished.

II Pet. 3.7: Now by fire the present world will be destroyed.

b. **II Pet. 8-10:** Peter gives few reasons for the delay.

Divine counting: i.   1000 years of man is like 1 day before God.

ii.   God in delaying is giving opportunity for sinners to repent.

c. **II Pet. 11-13:** So Peter was telling the believers

i.   the fire will melt the heavenly bodies and earth.

ii.   New earth and New Heaven will be formed by God then.

St. Paul in similar manner

II Thes. 2.2: Not to be shaken in mind "quickly" or excited either

a. by spirit

b. by Word,

c. by letter

as if from Paul, conveying the Lord's Day has arrived.

v.3ff.:   Did St. Paul give some sure signs for the Final Day, (most certainly drawing imagery from Daniel and Zechariah, plus Apocalyptic passages of the Gospels).

i.   1st the Rebellion comes

ii.   next the Man of Lawlessness will be revealed i.e., "the son of perdition".

Christ himself warned in **Mk. 13.6**, that many will come in his name saying "I am He" They will lead many astray.

Christ himself spoke in **Mk.13.7-8** of wars and "rumours" of them, but the End not yet. Also earthquakes, famines etc., all these are like the birth pangs of child-bearing only.

Mk. 13.9-13 shows – Persecution of believers takes place. Next Christ talks of the Fall of Jerusalem and the persecutions.

Mk. 13.24-27 – the cataclysms in the heavenly bodies – sun and moon darkened and the stars falling etc.

After these only takes place the 2nd Coming of Christ.

St. Paul too in similar manner cautions the believers.

II Thess.2.3: 1st – the Man of Lawlessness gets revealed; also called "the son of perdition".

v.4: Paul says he takes his seat in the Temple, at Jerusalem.

(In Mk.13.14 Christ referred already to the desolating sacrifice at Jerusalem).

Paul refers to him proclaiming himself as God.

v.5: Paul reminds that when he visited the church he already told the believers about it.

The historical background for this was a. the Seleucid king of Syria, Antiochus Epiphanus, who ruled in the 4th century. He sacrificed swine on the Altar and erected a great statue of the Olympian God, Zeus, in the Temple at Jerusalem. For this the Temple was closed. When Judas Maccabees defeated him the Temple was rededicated in 165 B.C. Then they started to observe this annually as the Feast of Dedication (Jn. 10.22).

b.   Emperor Gius in 40 A.D. tried to set up his statue in the Jerusalem Temple.

vs.7-8: St. Paul says already this Lawless one at work; When Christ appears he will destroy him with the breath of his mouth.

v.9: a. This above Lawless One will be assisted by the power of Satan.

b. He will be also with pretended signs and wonders.

v.10: c. with all wicked deception for those who are to perish.

These above i. Refused to love the Truth.

ii. They had pleasure in unrighteousness.

v.11: The above such people   i. came under strong delusion

ii. to make them believe what is false.

v.12: The end result of the above group is i. as they did not believe the Truth ii. they had pleasure in unrighteousness.

vs.13-15: Paul says "we are bound to give thanks always for you".

He refers to them as "brethren, beloved by the Lord".

v.13: a. "God chose you from the beginning".

b. "to be saved through sanctification".

c. by the Spirit and "belief in the Truth".

v.13 – sounds like "pre-destination" idea, propagated by John Calvin of Geneva (Switzerland) in his famous volumes, the Christian Institutes.

What Paul means here probably of those who responded to Paul's preaching at Thessalonica must be seen in retrospection: it is all God's gracious work among their hearts to respond positively to the Gospel, while many just rejected it.Same way the prophets felt for their task (Jer 1:5) or Paul felt for his ministry (Gal 1:15) God chose them.

v.15: Paul advises them to   a. stand firm

b. hold to the tradition (taught by Paul and colleagues)

i. by word, ii. or by letter.

This refers to the continuity of the truth of Christian faith, transmitted by the servants of God.

vs.16-17: verses 16 and 17 look like a Benediction but coming as it does, before another chapter indicates probably Paul felt to close or saw it as a climax for his above message. Then he had one more section to deal with, so he began again, may not be an after thought.

Chapter– 3

vs.1-5: call for prayer support and encouragement.

vs.1-2: Paul seeks the Thessalonian church's prayer support

v.1:a. Positive: That the Gospel proclamation may be carried on successfully and triumph as it did among the Thessalonian church.

v.2: b. Negative: that Paul's team may be delivered from wicked people, who in effect are unbelievers to the Christian faith.

vs.3-5: Paul informs then that the Lord will strengthen you;

v.3: as he is faithful and will guard them from all evil.

v.4: Paul conveys to the Thessalonian Christians

    i.   We have confidence in the Lord about you.

    ii.   you are doing and will do the things which Paul commanded.

v.4: In a sense Paul seems to be boasting, even a bit excess: "We ourselves boast of you".

This was questioned by the Thessalonian believers as "too much".

In a sense it expresses Paul's over joy of the end result of the church there in the face of the strong opposition from the Jewish opponents (I Thess. 1.3-4).

v.5: Paul calls on Christ to lead their hearts **a.** to the love of God, **b.** to the steadfast endurance in their faith in Christ.

vs.6-15: The need for the Disciples: **i.** To keep away from the idle person.

Qn.: Why so?

Ans.: Such person becomes burdensome to others for his daily needs of food etc.

To support it, Paul refers to his own case.

v.8: i.   We did not eat any one's bread without paying.

ii.   Paul and colleagues toiled "night and day", so as not to burden any.

In **I Cor. 9.15-26:** Paul at Corinth laboured as Tent-maker joining with Prisquilla and Aquila, he earned his labour, of which he boasts, he preached freely to those at Corinth. We notice he also shows from the Old Testament examples like the Ox threading out the grain not to muscle his mouth, the farmer, the vineyard owner, must enjoy the fruit of his labour. He brings in here examples of the soldier, the labourer et.al. who do their jobs and they deserve their wages.

v.9: Paul points out, surely Paul and his colleagues have the right as the "labourer is worthy of his hire", yet they set an example for the Thessalonians to emulate from us as their leaders.

v.10: On the above basis, while Paul was at Thessalonica, he gave the command: "If any one will not work, let him not eat".

v.11: Being idle Paul shows that such idle people will also become "busybodies".

This is the result of not doing any work.

v.12: Now positive   **i.**   command of Paul to these people.

                   ii.   also the command of Christ.

                   iii.   and exhortation of Paul

                       a.   "To do their work in quiteness".

                       b. "To earn their own living".

v.13: Paul also exhorts in addition of working, not get tired of doing good deeds.

It is possible that being not engaged in any work may be also connected with the early belief of the Christians of the return of Christ in their own generation. For this Paul was spending quite a portion of the Thessalonian 1st letter chiefly, (so too Christ in his time, to wait for the definite signs), and not to run here and there of hearing the news of his coming and the parousia.

Illustration

In the early 15th century, of the New Hampshire Baptist Association of USA, some congregations led by one of their leaders, left their worldly possessions, resigned their jobs and waited in tents on the hill top with their leader announcing Christ's return on Oct 1844. But it never happened. That way from time to time, some church leaders misled the Christians like in South Korea in the recent past. The point is when Christ himself clearly stated in **Mk. 13.32** – "even the Son of Man will not know the exact date of the 2nd Coming", how any one can claim he knows the exact date.

vs.14-15: Paul warns the church there, if any one does not obey to what Paul wrote, not to have any dealings with him, which will make him ashamed. It is not serious like the one ex-communicated for serious sin (I Cor. 5th chapter).

v.15: Paul not to be confused with excommunication person, as such not to treat him as an enemy but as a brother warn him.

v.16: Benediction – with peace of the Lord on them

i.　in all things　　　　on all of them.

ii.　in always

v.17: Paul's stamp in terms of　　i.　signing with his own hand.

ii. Paul calls it was his mark (or stamp) in some of his letters.

v.18: Conclusion: The Grace of the Lord Jesus to be upon them all, Paul's prayer in closing.

11
I Timothy

INTRODUCTION

The two letters to Timothy, one each to Titus and Philemon are personal letters, unlike the letters to the different churches.

The letters in general are addressed to a person yet we get also some idea of the person addressed, like his work and the problems he was facing if any or the success of his career and so on. These letters being written by Paul, a Roman citizen, naturally includes the Roman pattern of greetings first and salutations last and in between, the main contents like a topic of the other's achievements or abilities and issues involved; the suggestions or advices given for the betterment.

Though they are written with personal feeling and sympathy; here these are unlike the secular letters, are Ecclesiastical or pastoral letters – i.e., dealing with matters of the church. In the case of both letters of Timothy (also to Titus) these are according to the Muratorium Canon, the earliest official list of the New Testament Canon, "they are still followed in the respect of the Catholic church and in the Ecclesiastical discipline".

The name as Pastoral Epistles they first appeared in the 18th century. A famous scholar by name Paul Anton gave series of lectures in 1726 under the title "Pastoral Epistles" for 1st and 2nd Timothy and Titus. From that time on this designation for these 3 epistles kept.

Date and Place:

a.   I Timothy was written from Macedonia in around 62 A.D.

b.   II Timothy from Rome in around 64 A.D.

(This is the last letter of Paul, before his execution).

These two letters deal in a sense the matters of church governance and its discipline.

THE PERSON TIMOTHY

Ref.: Acts 16.1-5; Phil. 2.19-24; I Cor. 16.10; II Cor. 1.1; I Thes. 3.2; Heb. 13.23 etc.

Timothy was a native of Lystra of Asia Minor. His mother was Eunice and his grand mother Lois. He was the son of a mixed marriage. His mother was Jewish but his father was a Greek. When Paul visited in his II mission journey (Acts 16.1-3) he found Timothy and his mother and grand mother as believers.

Paul stayed in their house and Timothy was treated as Paul's son in faith. As per the Jewish custom Timothy was circumcised. By this way Paul felt Timothy can work among the Jews (As per the Gentiles Paul was against this observance).

Paul began to treat Timothy as "his son in faith" (I Tim. 1.2, 18; II Tim. 1.2 etc.).

Timothy was with Paul at Corinth when he wrote the letter to Rome (Rom. 16.21). Later Timothy was sent to Corinth when there was trouble there (I Cor. 16.10). He was with Paul when he wrote the II Corinthian letter (II Cor. 1.1, 19). Timothy was also sent to Thessalonica on behalf of Paul to find out how the believers there were faring (I Thes. 1.1; 3.2-6).

Timothy when he was with Paul in prison at Rome, he planned to send him to Philippi (Phil. 1.1;2.19). He was with Paul at Rome when Paul wrote letters to Colossae church and to Philemon (Col. 1.1; Phil. 1.1).

Paul had great trust and esteem in addition to his affection for Timothy. We see this in his letters to Corinth and Philippians:

1. I Cor. 4.17: "My beloved and faithful child in the Lord".

2. Phil. 2.20-22: "I have no one like him; as a son with the father, he has served me in the Gospel".

Paul thinks of Timothy in the highest commendation. He was genuinely interested for their welfare.

It is said later Timothy was made the Bishop of Ephesus.

MAIN DIVISIONS

CHAPTER - 1

vs. 1-3   –   Address to Timothy from Paul and the Jewish Eulogy of grace, mercy   and peace to the reader.

vs. 12-17   –   Paul's conversion.

vs. 18-20   –   call to Timothy to keep the Christian tradition.

CHAPTER - 2

vs.1-7   –   Advice to conduct worship, keeping in mind, the universality of the Gospel.

vs. 8-15   –   Qualities required for the post of a Bishop or pastor.

CHAPTER - 3

vs.1-7   –   the qualities required for the Bishop or pastors, the Deaconesses.

vs. 8-13   –   How the above offices to be kept and the call to Timothy about keeping these instructions.

vs.14-16   –   All this applies to the church, the guardian of God's plan and purposes.

CHAPTER – 4

vs. 1-10   –   Instructions to keep in control the false Teachers.

vs.11-16   –   Reminds Timothy to keep the spiritual gift given to him in his ministry.

CHAPTER – 5

vs 1-6.2   –   Directions to various stages of living and with regard to men and women.

CHAPTER- 6

vs.3-10   –   Warning against false Teachers and love of money.

vs.11-16   –   Exhortation to Timothy to uphold the faith.

vs.17-19   –   for pastoral care of the rich.

vs.20-21   –   final warning against false knowledge and benediction.

COMMENTARY

vs.1-3: a. Paul often refers to himself as an "Apostle" though not "the Twelve" of Christ's time but as one who personally had an encounter with the risen Christ on the road to Damascus and received his call to be "an Apostle" in the sense of being "a sent one" on Christ's mission (Acts 9.1-19; specially v.15).

vs.4-11: To the preachers – a. Not to teach to be something, leading to wrong tenets of Christian faith.

b. Neither to indulge in idle (i.e., unprofitable) stories.

c. Nor turn to genealogies which will have no end.

These above, not only waste time in endless speculations, in effect devoid of promoting faith.

Paul rather reminds Timothy of his instructions which if heeded produces faith in terms of a. issuing from pure heart, b. issuing from a good conscience, c. an understanding of faith.

Paul here refers to those engaged in instruction of the Law.

He says these false teachers a. do not know the actual meaning of the doctrines they talk b. nor do they know the real meaning of it.

Paul says the Jewish scholars may waste time that way but what is important is instruction of Christian life.

Many scholars think this may refer to "Gnostic" teaching, where the initiated few only are privileged to have the knowledge to reach Heaven.

vs. 12-14: St. Paul refers to his pre-conversion period, when he, a. blasphemed, b. persecuted and c. insulted Jesus.

All this he did against Christians yet after his encounter with Christ on the Damascus road, he heard directly from Christ it was against Christ himself (Acts 9.5) what all he did against the Christians.

vs.15-17: Paul refers here to the 1st Advent of Christ, which was to save sinners (v.15).

This is opposed to other religions where like in Hinduism's Vaishnava faith in their Puranas that the so called "Avatars" or Vishnu taking physical forms from time to time, it was to destroy the wicked and rescue the saints. But in the Gospels we find the coming of Christ was to save the sinners (Matt. 9.13).

As such Paul says he was saved, though he was "the foremost sinner" (v.15f).

vs.16-17: Paul is now saved – this exhibits the perfect patience of Christ as a Saviour, as seen from the transformation of Paul, an enemy of Christ to be his devoted disciple now engaged in the ministry of the salvation work of Christ.

vs.18-20: This is a call from Paul to Timothy to maintain the Christian tradition.

The Greek form of Timothy is Timothius, which is a combination of "Timo" = honour and "Theos"= God. Thus it means "honouring God" which is the charge entrusted to Timothy. So he cannot let down God and man. By rejecting their conscience about their faith they received, Paul says that they have like the sea faring people shipwrecked their Christian faith.

v.20: Two persons mentioned here – 1) Hymaneus and Alexander. In II Tim. 2.17 – Hymaneus mentioned again 2) In II Tim. 4.14 – Alexander was mentioned again. These two seemed to have gone back to their old life, renouncing their Christian faith.

Paul says both of them "delivered to Satan", which may refer to "Excommunication" from the church. It may also seem to the worldly way of life where Satan's sphere is.

Chapter – 2

---

vs..1-7: Here the church's responsibility to those in secular authority like "kings and all those in high authority" (v.2).

1. At this time the claim of some Roman Emperors "as Divine like Caligula – 38-41 A.D.; Claudius – 41-54 A.D. Domitian – 81-96 A.D. etc.). "The divine right of kings to rule" was brought out from this above Biblical passage.

Paul was a Roman citizen (from his native place "Tarsus" in Asia Minor, held Roman citizenship). Then "the Caesar worship" was not that prominent, for which here Paul was supporting the secular rulers. Much later the Baptist group under Thomas Helwys A.D. 1612, in England and Leonard Busher, called for religious liberty or "liberty of conscience" from secular rulers in, 1614 in England.

2. The second point to note is the universality of the Gospel:

   v.1 – Prayers made "for all men".

   v.4 – to be saved "all men".

   v.6 – Christ, a ransom "for all".

Illustration: Once I attended a church service at Edinburgh, Scotland, where Presbyterian church is the official denomination. The preacher spoke on the theme of "Predestination". After the church service I had a big argument with a Scottish Medical student. I told him the missionaries preached the Gospel for all and not to a section, for Christ died for all and not for a certain section of the people. This doctrine of Predestination propagated by John Calvin, the Protestant Reformer in Geneva, Switzerland. He wrote 4 volumes titled as Christian Institutes. In that he held to this double predestination, i.e., some destined to Heaven and some to Hell by God. I asked this student, then what is the need for preaching. His reply was "To collect the select". I said "as far as the Gospel we know Christ died for all".

Of course when we look back we can say it is divine work for being able to respond to his call.

It is the characteristic of the Gospel "salvation offered for all". If any reject it, they are responsible and not God. Paul emphasizes this here.

v.1 Talks of different types of prayer

a. Supplications – "deesis" (Gk.). it means "requests" here made to God for our needs.

b. "Prayers" – "Proseuche" (Gk.) used exclusively towards God, for these needs only God can fulfil.

c. Intercessions – "Erteuxis" (Gk.). These are petitions, in the sense of "intimate conversations with God". Like taking a petition before a ruler, we approach God for help.

d. Thanksgiving – "Eucharistia" (Gk.). This shows prayer always does not mean making requests to God but also to express one's gratitude for what God graciously helped in certain situation. It is to praise God for his gracious help in our needs.

vs.5-6: v.5: These verses refer to the Redeeming work of Christ for mankind.

Christ is referred as the "Mediator" between God and men. In the Old Testament we see **a.** the prophets – Mediators from God to men.**b.** the **priests** – Mediators from men to God at the Jerusalem Temple. But in the case of Christ he fulfilled both aspects,.

v.6: The "Ransom" term used for Christ saving work (in Greek "Apolutrosis "). It is a metaphor of "slave market", where a slave is bought (or redeemed here by Christ) by paying "the slave price" ("Lutron" (Gk.). Likewise the sinner redeemed by the blood price made by Christ (Rom. 3.24).

v.9 is contrasted with v.10.

In **v.9** Paul talks of the over adorning of women both in dress and in ornaments, against his advice.

In **v.10** was of a. modest adornment befitting religious women added with good deeds.

In **vs.11-12:** Paul asks the women **a)** to learn in all submissiveness, and **b)** to be silent and learn but not to preach or show authority over men.

This injunction Paul brings out the spiritual authority in vs. 13-14.

v.13 – Adam was 1st made and Eve next.

v.14 – It was Eve who first fell into sin, then only Adam

For **v.13**   i.   Paul was using only **(the later) the "P" source** (Gen. 2.7ff.).

                      ii.   While Gen. 1.27, (**the "J" source**), where both male and female were shown created in the image of God, Paul does not refer it.

v.14: Of course falling into Temptation and sin, Eve was shown first and Adam later through her, fell into sin. We find in I Cor. 11.2-16 Paul deals with the issue of women wearing veil for the worship services. And takes the "P" source of Gen. 2.7f. for support.

Two conditions were shown for women's redemption:
i.   Through child bearing.

ii.   Through modesty and religious faith.

These above in i. faith   ii. love   iii. and holiness.

Chapter – 3

The Qualities and Character Traits Needed for the Offices of the Church

The Bishop: His qualities or character that is,

v.2: a) beyond criticism, as it is referred safeguards noble task.

b) The husband of one wife.

c) Temperate

d) Sensible.

e) dignified

f) hospitable.

g) an apt teacher.

v.4: he must manage his household well.

i) Keeping his children

1) Submissive

2) Respectful in every way.

v.3: Negative side to himself

a) No drunkard

b) Not violent (i.e., gentle)

c) not quarrelsome

d) No lover of money

v.6: e) he must not be a recent convert lest he puffs up and fall into temptation

v.4: i) Qualities in the household management.

v.5. ii) the church management to be foreseen by the household management first.

v.7: He must be well thought of by the outsiders, lest he fall into reproach and snare of the devil.

Thus these are two spheres of management and the later (the church) dependent on the former (household).

If we look to the above qualities for appointing a pastor for the church, most probably we may never get one. The head of the Roman Catholic Church, the Pope most probably, is regarded as "Infallible" "he can do no wrong" based on the above qualities required for a Bishop.

Illustration : Once a pastor got up in the pulpit and said that his topic was Christian "perfection" based on Matt. 5.48 and he challenged that no one can say he/she is perfect. If so "you can stand". None got up but at the back a lean man slowly got up. The pastor asked him "Then you claim, you are perfect, no fault in you?" That member replied "Not me, but I am standing for my wife's first husband". Though like the sermon on the Mount (Matt. 5-7 chapters) its ethical code too high to attain, yet Christ was giving it as ideal to look for one to reach it.

vs.8-13: The office of the **Deacons** and **Deaconesses**

v.8: Deacon: Qualities required of him for his job

Positive	**Negative to avoid**
a. Must be serious	a. Not double-tongued.
v.9: b. Must hold the mystery of faith clear conscience.	b. Not addicted to in much wine. c. Not greedy for gain.
v.10:c. Let them be testified first.	
d. The husband of one wife.	
v.12:e. Manage the house and children well.	

v.11: If the Deacons thus prove of the above qualities and blameless then they can be used for this ministry in the church.

From the Greek "Diakonia" verb referring to "to serve" or service, got the name "Deacon" i.e., one who serves.

The early church appointed 7 "Deacons" to serve the tables, to help the poor in the church; from then on this term used as a second category of service from that of the Apostles earlier (Acts 6.1-6), who wanted to give their time for preaching God's word.

v.11: For the women, as Deaconess, though some churches leave it as women's ministry without the designation of the "Deaconess". We find St. Paul sending the letter to the church at Rome through Phoebe, of

Cenchrea port as he wrote it from Corinth and this is the port for it. She is referred in the RSV translation as "Deaconess", though some versions do not do so. These days when women are even ordained in some churches, there will have no problem of the "Deaconess" designation.

The men and women for this job:

Positive	**Negative to avoid**
v.11: a. Must be serious	a. No slanderers.
b. Temperate.	
c. Faithful in all things.	

v.13: In **conclusion on** this post of Deacons "(plus Deaconesses) Paul commends, if they serve well, they receive good standing in the church understood, and also great confidence in the Christian faith.

vs.14-16: All this applies to the church, which is the guardian of God's plan and purpose.

To serve in the church is both a privilege and responsibility.

v.14: St. Paul hopes to visit Timothy; but in case he delays, he is telling Timothy how to carry on his work in the church.

St. Paul refers to the church: a.   The church of the Living God.

b.   The household of God.

c.   The pillar and bulwark of Truth.

v.16: Paul concludes in this section in referring to Christianity as that what we confess is great, the mystery of our religion, in terms of the Truth about Jesus Christ (I Jn. 4.2) the founder.

a.   Christ – he was manifested in the flesh (I Jn. 4.2).

b.   Vindicated in the Spirit (I Cor. 15.3-8).

c.   Seen by angels (I Cor. 15.3-8).

d.   Preached among the nations (Acts 1.8; Matt. 28.18f).

e.   Believed on in the world (Acts 1.8; Matt. 28.18f).

f.   His Ascension into glory (Acts 1.9-11).

This above sounds like the Christology of the Pauline church, which he spread all over the world then. It also sounds like "the Kerygma" or Creed of the early church.

Chapter – 4

vs.1-10: Instruction to keep in control the false teachers.

v.1: Paul cautions Timothy of what happens in the later times:

a.   Deceitful spirits   through these some will depart

b.   Doctrines of demons   from true faith (ref. Col.2.22).

v.2: c.   liars whose consciences are   This applies to those

        scared

v.3: d.   who forbid marriage (Col. 2.16) who think everything

e.   who forbid to eat some foods   from the body evil.

1.   Paul says these are God's creation and have to be taken with thanksgiving by those who are believers and who know the Truth.

2.   Paul also adds if this food is consecrated by prayer, and thanksgiving (i.e., Grace offered before eating) and by the Word of God it is good.

This above situation is similar to that referred in Col. 2.16-23 and also I Cor. 10.23-30.

This specially applies to the Jewish converts who have food laws (and also the new converts against idol worship) to observe and probably demanding from the Gentile converts.

vs.6-10: This passage deals with instructions not only to Timothy but also to all servants of Christ engaged in the church service.

It tells also how to lead, not ordering in instructing in terms of teaching, and what to seek and what to avoid, given here by Paul.

v.6: Paul refers here to the good doctrine based on the words of faith, (as against the doctrine of the demons referred in v.1), Timothy will become good minister of Christ Jesus, if he observes it.

v.7: a.   **Positive**: Train yourself in godliness.

    b.   **Negative**: Avoid godless and silly myths.

v.8: a.   Bodily training – has some value.

    b.   Godliness – has value both for the present life and for the life to come (the future), the Eternity.

vs.9-10: Paul was trying to convey – the present life and striving

a.   for physical- the sports and sexual desires common in Hellinistic culture has limited time in this world.

b.   while the spiritual, the God-fearing life – guarantees the life of eternity in the Divine presence.

Paul asks Timothy to command and teach as per advice.

vs.12-16: St. Paul's series of instructions to Timothy.

v.12: i.   Being youthful, to be careful not to be despised on that account.

    ii.   To set an example before the church congregation

        a. in speech   in total personality

        b. in conduct   in terms of   i. love

                                           ii. faith

                                           iii. and purity.

v.13: As in 3.14, Paul here mentions of his plan to visit Timothy.

Again series of instructions – now about the church worship services.

i. Scripture reading   ii. Preaching and iii.Teaching. .

v.14: a. This seems to refer to Timothy's ordination before he took up the pastorate,where the elders laid their hands, most certainly as Timothy knelt before them.

    b. This was also the occasion when Timothy received gift of the Holy Spirit when (may be) one of them pronounced about it.

v.15: Timothy encouraged to move ahead, to mature in his ministerial task.

Here we find Paul's encouragement to Timothy.

a.   Not to neglect the spiritual gift (v.14).

b.   To practice and devote in his tasks (v.15).

c.   To be careful to give attention to himself and to his teaching (v.16).

Finally in heeding to St.Paul's advice, Timothy will both benefit

a.   himself

and b.   his audience in the church.

Chapter – 5

St.Paul's directives to Timothy to various stages and age relationships of life with regard to men and women.

vs.1-2:lays down the rule for younger people as to how to behave or show respect to the elderly people:

Illustration: I always appreciate the Bengali society (so too other Nothern people) that whenever I meet my former students at Kolkata, they bend down and touch my feet called "Pranaam" and I lay my hand on their heads to bless them.

Timothy being a young man, St. Paul makes sure to show respect to the elderly members:

v.1: I. A. i. Elderly man if done wrong – a. Not to rebuke

b. but like a father treat and
to exhort him.

v.19:   ii. Never to admit a charge against elder except with 2 or 3 witnesses.

v.20:   iii. Paul adds in case any one persists in sin, to rebuke in the presence of others, so they may fear to sin in that way.

To Treat

B. Older women like mothers.

II. a.   Younger men like brothers.

b.   Younger women like sisters.

v.17ff: a. The elders who rule well – to give double honour.

b. specially those engaged in preaching and teaching in the church.

Paul quotes from O.T. Duet. 28.4, where the Ox that treads out the grain is not mussled, i.e., by this it gets the privilege of eating the grain as it treads. St. Paul used this illustration earlier in I Cor.9.8-12 that this illustration was given for humans that the labourer is worthy of his hire, so it applies to those elders engaged in the ministry of the church, as above, as well in evangelism.

vs.3-16: It is a long section about widows in the Society.

v.3.5: a. Paul talks of "a real widow" more than once, as one who

v.9: is "over 60 years of age", wife of one husband.

v.10: Who is well attested for

a.   her good deeds.   In this way devoted

b.   who brought her children   herself in doing

c.   washed the feet of the saints   good in every way.

d   relieved the afflicted.

In **vs.4-5** Paul refers to the "real widow" not only taking good care of her own children but also her grand children and later hand them over to their parents.

v.4b: Paul says this is acceptable in the sight of God.

v.5: The widow who left all alone, gets the opportunity to spend time in supplications and prayers night and day, as she sets her hope in God.

v.6: A widow who is self-indulgent, even while she lives is dead.

vs.11-13: Paul is advising Timothy, to refuse the younger widows for they get wanton against Christ, they wish to marry.

v.12: These have broken their earlier pledge to serve Christ.

v.13: Having free time these widows go around visiting neighbours' houses to gossip and gadding as busy bodies, and thus indulge in unnecessary talk.

Thus these are: a. idlers   All these unnecessary

                 b. busy bodies   talk and thus breaking their

                 c. gadding   earlier pledge to serve Christ.

                 d. gossiping

v.14: For this situation, the best solution St. Paul advises

a. for the younger widows better marry again.

b. To bear children

    c. thus give no occasion for the enemy to revile them.

v.15:d. Some younger widows have already strayed after Satan.

v.16: St. Paul advises that if these are relatives to the above

    a. such widows, they should come forward to look after them

    b. so that the church can be relieved from such burden to care for them.

vs.21-22: St.Paul strengthens this above charge to Timothy sealing with Divine oath.

v.21: a. In the presence of i. God ii. Jesus Christ and iii. the elect Angels (here the Holy Spirit missing) give these rules

    i.   to keep them without favour

    ii. or any partiality.

v.22: Paul adds, that Timothy   a. not to be hasty in laying of hands

                                       b. nor participate in another person's sins.

In that way Timothy to keep himself pure.

vs.24-25: Paul says a. some persons' sins known already b. some others' sins will be revealed later.

v.23: There is a personal note about Timothy's health.

Timothy seems to have frequent ailments, specially his stomach problem. So Paul advises to drink wine now and then in place of water. The Jews have wine at their dinner but it always 3:2 proportions of water and wine to avoid intoxication.

Chapter – 6

vs.1-2: In the general admonition, series of instructions given:

v.1: a. The slaves to hold their master worthy of respect, i.e., the slave should not take advantage because his Master is a Christian. By this way God is not dishonoured and Christian faith upheld.

v.2: The Master being a Christian brother he should not be shown less respect. On the contrary now as believers and beloved the slaves are benifitted.

vs.3-10: Warning against i. false teachers

ii. and money.

v.3: Teachers; their teaching   i. must agree with what Christ taught

ii. it must lead to godliness.

v.4: If it is contrary to the above – he is a false teacher

    a.   He is puffed up with conceit.

    b.   He knows nothing

    c.   He has great craving for controversy.

    d.   for dispute for words, which produce

           i.   envy

           ii.   dissensions

           iii. slander

   and   iv. base suspicions.

v.5: Also creates wrangling among men

   i. who are depraved in mind

   ii. who are bereft of the Truth

These see that through godliness they can make gain.

v.6: St. Paul instead thinks godliness with contentment is the real gain.

vs.7-8: Paul shows that in our life in the world;

- a. We humans brought nothing into the world when we came.
- b. We humans likewise take nothing from the world when we leave.
- c. so we should be content if we have

  i. food to eat

  ii. cloths to wear

vs.9-10: So Paul observes a. "The love of Money is the root of all evil'. But if contrary one desires to be rich, they fall

- i. into temptation
- ii. into a snare
- iii. into many senseless desires.

The senseless desires, plunge men at the end into ruin and destruction.

v.10: St. Paul concludes this section in stating that many have

a. wandered away from the Faith i.e., ruined their lives.

b. pierced their hearts with many pangs

vs.17-19: To the rich, Paul cautions

a. not to set their hopes on uncertain riches

b. but on God – who richly provides all things to enjoy in life.

v.18: They have to be rich in good works – it lays foundation for life – eternal.

vs.11-16 : Exhortation to Timothy to uphold the faith.

v.11: Paul addressed Timothy as "Man of God"

This is one of the great titles in the Old Testament:

- a. applied to Moses – Deut. 33.1; Ps.90. It is also the title for the prophets and messengers of God.
- b. to Eli – I Sal. 2.27;
- c. to Samuel – I Sal. 2.27; 9.6.

The qualities of the Man of God:

i.   Righteousness – the man who does his duty to God and man.

ii. Godliness – all life time lived in the presence of God.

iii. Faith: In all states of life loyal to God.

iv. Love

v.   Steadfastness – It is victorious endurance.

vi. Gentleness – shows the spirit *of gentleness yet knows the pride* of one's high calling.

v.12: St. Paul calls on Timothy a. to fight the good fight of faith.

> b. to take hold of the eternal life to which Timothy was called.

vs.13-14: St.Paul's final charge to young Timothy in the presence of

> a. God – who is the source of life to all beings.

> b. Christ Jesus – who made good confession before Pilate (during the Roman trial).

v.14: Paul gives charge to Timothy till the time of the 2nd coming of Christ to keep the commandment (of Paul's charge to him)

a.   unstained

b.   free from reproach.,

vs.15-16: v.15 – The result known at Christ's return.

Christ is referred as i. the blessed and only sovereign

> ii. the King of kings and Lord of Lords i.e., He is supreme over all rulers.

v.16: Paul adds to the above, Christ as i. immortal ii. dwells in unapproachable light, (whom no man can see or approach)

It is held most probably Timothy has a confession of Faith like that of our present churches, and reminded by Paul. It does this way:

"I believe in God the Almighty, Creator of Heaven and earth, and in Christ Jesus, who suffered under Pontius Pilate, and will return to judge; I believe in the Resurrection from the dead and in the life immortal".

vs.20-21: As closing words of advice Paul calls on Timothy

a. to guard the ministry task entrusted to him.

b. to abstain from so called "knowledge" which is nothing but chatter and contradictions. For many engaged in such discussions finally missed the core of Christian faith.

BIBLIOGRAPHY

1. Ellis, E.E.   -   "Paul and His Recent Interepreters", pp. 49ff. 1961

2. Guthrie, D.   -   The Pastoral Epistles, (MC:E)

3. NTS., 2, 1955-56.   -   "The Pastoral Epistles and the Duncan Ephesian Theory'

12
II Timothy

INTRODUCTION

1. This letter to Timothy was written from Rome. Timothy was pastoring the church at Ephesus.

   As the letter to the Galatians was the 1st letter of Paul fromAntioch in 48 A.D., this 2nd letter to Timothy was the last letter of Paul from Rome in A.D..64, just before his execution.

2. It was one of the 3 letters, which form "the pastoral letters" of Paul (I and II Timothy and Titus), its theme being Ecclesiastical dealing with regulations of church offices, tasks etc.

3. Timothy was like a son in faith to Paul (I Cor. 4.17; Phil. 2.20,22 etc.) since he got him from Lystra of Asia minor in the 2nd Missionary journey (Acts 15.39- 18.22). [The reader can refer to Introduction section of I Timothy for further information].

St. Paul's Affairs at Rome (as per II Timothy letter)

1. II Tim. 4.16 and 18f.: Paul feels he was close to his death.

2. Only Luke with him (4.16); the others sent on errands and some have forsaken him.

3. Paul had to defend himself, forsaken by all.

4. a. Crescens had gone to Gaul

   b. Titus to dalmatia.

   c. Tychicus to Ephesus, sent by Paul.

   d. Demas has forsaken him.

   e. Phygelus and Hermogenus of Asia forsaken him (1.15f).

5.   a.   Paul calls on Timothy to come soon (f.9,20).

      b.   Paul warns Timothy against a Coppersmith, Alexander, who did much harm to him.

6.   Timothy was asked a) to bring Paul's cloak, his books and parchments left with corpus at Troas (4.13).

7.   Paul also told Timothy about Trophimus, who was ill, left at Miletus (4.20).

N.T. scholar W.G.Kummel, about St.Paul asking Timothy to bring his things left at Troas, but as per Acts 20.2ff, Timothy was with Paul then. It is possible some years passed by now, Paul requesting Timothy.

It was not certain if Timothy was still pastoring the church at Ephesus. Priscilla and Aquila, by this time still at Ephesus. Earlier they were at Corinth when Paul visited them (Acts 18th chapter).

MAIN DIVISIONS

CHAPTER – 1

vs.1.1f.   -   Letter addressed to Timothy

v.3-5   -   and prayer for him.

Vs.6-14   -   call to him to maintain the charismatic gifts given at his dedication.

Vs.15-18   -   St. Paul's experience with his Associates.

CHAPTER – 2

Vs.1-2   –   The instruction got by Timothy to pass on to others to teach.

Vs.3-7   –   The illustration of the soldier, the Athlete and the farmer.

Vs.8-13   –   The life of Christ, how he suffered, so too Paul suffers for the Gospel.

Vs.14-19   –   The correct handling of Truth and avoiding wrong ways.

Vs.20-26   –   Advice to a Christian leader

CHAPTER – 3

Vs.1-9   –   Caution against false teachers who specially lead astray weak women.

Vs.10-17   –   Timothy should continue what he learned from Paul and the Scriptures.

CHAPTER – 4

Chapter – 1

THE COMMENTARY

vs.1-2: The letter addressed to Timothy:

We have noted this was the last letter Paul was writing. It was to his beloved son in faith – written from Paul's Roman prison to Timothy, pasturing the church at Ephesus. The date is given 64 A.D. After this Paul was executed.

    a.   Paul always refers to himself as an "Apostle" based on his encounter with the risen Christ and his call, on the road to Damascus.

v.2: b.   Paul also uses the Jewish pattern of eulogy, referring to grace, mercy and peace.

    c.   He does not fail to refer to Timothy as "my beloved child (or son)".

vs.3-5: a. Paul was a man of prayer and in many of his letters he does not fail to mention his prayers for the recipients of his letters (Rom. 1.9; Phil. 1.3 etc.).

    b. i. Paul refers to Timothy's mother Unice and his granny Lois, both from Jewish background turned to Christian faith, based at Lystra of Asia Minor.

      ii. Their faith Paul feels bequeathed to Timothy, who too accepted Christian faith; "in tears" Paul adds, conveying his sincere conversion.

Though his father was a Greek, yet Timothy was circumcised as per the Jewish custom, so that he can freely move and serve among the Jewish community

v.4: Paul longs to see Timothy, a young man, specially that Paul was approaching his martyrdom at Rome (4.6), so asks him to come to him soon (4.9).

vs.6-14

v.6: Paul reminds Timothy of his initiation to ministry; chiefly Paul laying his hands on him, i.e., dedication to rekindle that spiritual gift, probably of Timothy's teaching ministry.

v.7: The Holy Spirit offers **a.** a spirit of power (not timidity). **b.** a spirit of love. **c.** a spirit of self-control.

v.8: So Paul calls on Timothy not to be ashamed, but in Divine power,

    a.   in his testimony for Christ, or Paul, the prisoner

    b.   share in the sufferings for the Gospel proclamation.

v.9: God a. saved us.

        b. called us with a holy calling.

        c. Not by virtue of our good deeds .

        d. but in virtue of God's own purpose.

        e. by the grace in Christ Jesus (long ago planned).

v.10: a. Now God's purpose (i.e., salvation) shown in the coming of Jesus,
            our Saviour.

        b. i. Jesus abolished death now;   reference to the saving

                                                 Work of

            ii. he brought life and immortality.   Christ in the world – "the
                                                 Gospel".

v.11: Paul claims that he was appointed by Christ for this Gospel.

a.   As a Preacher – to know the Truth and act upon it.

b.   As an Apostle – in general to one who is sent to preach like the 12 Apostles appointed by Christ.

c.   As a Teacher – to convey knowledge and enlighten one.

v.12: St. Paul's testimony a."I know whom I have believed" for that he is willing to suffer. b. He is certain that he will guard him till the final Day of reckoning.

vs.13-14:

v.13: What advice Timothy heard from Paul?

    a.   The pattern of the sound words.

    b.   of Christ Jesus – in the faith and love.

v.14:   c. to guard the Truth, which has been entrusted to Timothy.

d. through the indwelling of the Holy Spirit.

vs.15-18: St. Paul's experience with his Associates.

v.15: Phygelus and Hermogenes, among them of Asia, who turned away from him when opposition against Paul rose up.

v.16: In contrast Onesiphorus and his family.

a.   They were not ashamed of St.Paul's chains.

b.   They cared for his needs.

v.17c.   He searched for Paul, after reaching Rome, till he found him.

d.   Earlier he looked after Paul while at Ephesus.

v. 18: For this above service and care Onesiphorus took for, Paul blesses him in saying "May the Lord grant him mercy on the final Day of reckoning".

Chapter – 2

Vs.1-2: v.1: Paul begins with encouragement to Timothy to be strong in the grace in the Lord Jesus.

v.2: Then instructs him.

a.   Timothy got instructions from Paul in the presence of many witnesses.

b.   Timothy was to entrust in turn to faithful workers.

c.   These then can teach others.

Here we find the Christian ministry like chain link from Paul to Timothy, and from Timothy to other ministers.

v.3-7: Three illustrations Paul uses to explain the Christian ministry: the soldier, the athlete and the farmer.

vs.3-4: i. The Soldier: a. His aim is to satisfy him who entrusted him b. Not entangled in civilian pursuits. (Ref. I Cor. 9.7)

About runner uses analogy in terms of pressing to the point, "a labourer worthy of his hire".

v.5: ii.   The Athlete, not crowned unless he competes as per the rules (Ref. I Cor. 9.25 – Paul refers to self-control.)

v.6: iii.   The Farmer, whom Paul refers as "hard working"who has to have the first share of the crop.

In I Cor. 9.7 – Paul makes the same point with regard to the vineyard owner for the share of the fruit.

v.7: So Paul at the end, calls on Timothy to understand what he meant by these three analogies he brought here.

vs.8-13: Paul suffers for the Gospel's sake as Christ too suffered to convey the same.

v.8: The proclamation of the Good News or Gospel is

i.   a.   Jesus descended from David's family i.e., as per the prophesies about him.

      b.   He died but resurrected from it the Messiah fulfilled in him.

ii.   For this Gospel proclamation Paul in fetters, as a criminal suffers, yet the Gospel not in fetters, he says. (Matt.2.4-6, cf. Micah 5.2 Is. 53.4-5)

iii.   Paul suffers for the salvation of people, the elect or the chosen, he says.

vs.11-13: He adds: i.   If we die with him, we also live with him.

                      ii.   a. If we endure we shall also reign with him.

                           b. If we deny him, he will also deny us.

                      iii.   If we are faithless, he remains faithful for he can not deny himself.

This reference is precious to the 1st Century Christians, for at the occasion of their persecution the Christian church put the above words in a song.

Polycarp, the early church Father, gives two lines, which reads "If we walk worthy of him So shall we reign with him"

Some think these lines also go along with the above words, indicating Paul was quoting only a portion of a longer hymn, sung in the early church.

vs.14-19: The correct handling of Truth:

v.14: 1. St. Paul cautions Timothy "to avoid" disputing of words. This is what we call as "literary criticism".

Qn.: Why to avoid such literary discussion?

Ans.: Paul feels **i.** it does no good. **ii.** it ruins the hearers (i.e., their faith).

v.16: 2. To also avoid, what Paul calls "as godless chattering".

Qn.: Why so?

Ans.: Paul says "It leads people to more ungodliness".

vs.17-18: 3. a. "It will eat its way like gangrene" (harming a person's body).

              b. Paul brings as example, the cases of two persons so effected

                 i. Hymenaeus

                 ii. Philetus.

v.18: These above two Christians hold wrongly their faith that the Resurrection has already past. By this wrong faith, they disturb the true faith of others.

v.19: But Paul says i. With God's firm foundation, God knows those who are ii. with God's seal on them.

These should depart from inequity, i.e., wrong faith.

v.15: For guarding the above situation, Paul advises Timothy, to do his best,

a.   to present himself to God as one approved;

b.   a workman who has no need to be ashamed;

c.   rightly handling the word of Truth.

vs.20-26: Advice to the Christian leaders:

v.20: The two categories of vessels in a great house.

a.   Some for noble use: like vessels of gold and silver.

b.   Some for ordinary use: like wooden and earthen utensils.

v.21: Comparing humans to these vessels, Paul says if one separates himself from contaminating and corrupting influences, he will be like a vessel set apart useful for honourable and noble purposes, consecrated and profitable to the Master, fit and ready for any good work. (From Amplified N.T.).

v.22: Paul now commands: "shun youthful lusts and flee from them and aim at and pursue **i.** righteousness **ii.** faith **iii.** love and **iv.** peace.

Peace in terms of harmony and concord with others and fellowship with Christian believers, who call upon the Lord, out of a pure heart (from Amplified N.T.).

v.23: Paul calls on believers now,

a.   to shut the mind of believers of stupid or unedifying controversies over   ignorant questionings.

b.   as they foster strife and breed quarrels.

v.24: Paul now refers to the Lord's servant

Negatively: He should not be quarrelsome.

Positively: He should be i. kind to every one.

           ii.   apt teacher, i.e., skilled teacher.

           iii.   patient and forbearing.

           iv.   willing to suffer wrong.

v.25: He should correct the opponents with gentleness. By this way it may result that the opponents

     a. repent

     b. come to recognise the Truth.

v.26:   c. thus escape from the snare of the devil, (held captive till then).

     d. from now on to do God's will.

In Conclusion we can say it is transformed life in Christ (II Cor. 5.17).

Chapter – 3

vs.1-9: Caution against false teachers.

v.1: It is referred as "the last days", i.e., End time, described as

    i.   perilous times

    ii. of great stress and trouble.

    iii. hard to deal with and to bear.

v.2: a. People of these days are described as

    i.   lovers of self and self-centered.

    ii. lovers of money and greedy for wealth.

    iii. proud and arrogant.

    iv. contemptuous boasters.

v.3: b. They will be:

    i.   without natural affection.

    ii. relentless, not for appeasement.

    iii. slanderers.

    iv. trouble-makers.

    v.   intemperate.

    vi. loose in morals and conduct.

    vii. uncontrolled and fierce.

    viii. haters of good.

v.4: c. i. They will be treacherous.

    ii. rash.

    iii. inflated with self-conciet.

iv. a. lovers of sensual pleasures and amusements.

  b. more than lovers of God.

v.5: d. i. The form of piety or true religion they deny.

  ii. thus they are strangers to the power of piety.

  iii. their conduct contradicts their religious genuineness.

St. Paul's advice to Timothy is to avoid such people.

vs.6-9: Seduction of weak women in the name of religion by the false teachers.

The women in the Hellenistic culture earlier were not allowed to move freely, like for shopping or for attending pubic meetings. With the coming of Christian religion they were in a sense emancipated. But then this emancipation brought its own problems now for the church, as the Christian women did not know how to deal with their new liberty in the face of false teachers taking advantage of this situation.

v.6: The weak women are captured, as they are

i) burned with sins

ii) swayed by various impulses.

v.7: i. They listen to anybody

  ii. but never arrive at the knowledge of the Truth.

vs.8-9: St. Paul brings from the so called Apocryphical books of the Old Testament (found in R.C. and Anglican Bibles now).

For illustration two persons:

a. Jannes

b. Jambres.

  i) Their minds were corrupt and

  ii) Their faith was counterfeit.

St. Paul was trying to say that the folly of the false teachers was as clear as those of the O.T. imposters.

In the Inter-Testamental period (around 200years) many Jewish books appeared, which expanded the O.T. stories. These two were shown as magicians of Pharaoh's court. These magicians were able to match the wonders which Moses and Aaron did before Pharaoh. But at the end they were defeated, proving as Imposters (Ref. Ex. 7.8-13).

vs.10-17: Timothy has to continue what he learned from Paul and the Scriptures.

vs.10-11: These verses refer to St. Paul's life and the call to Timothy to learn from it as trusted disciple. The Greek "Parakuluthein" means to follow one with unwavering loyality.

v.10: Paul about himself –

I .   My teaching

ii.   My conduct

iii. My aim in life

iv.   My patience.

v.   My love

vi.   My steadfastness

v.11: vii. My persecutions

viii. My sufferings

 ix. What befell me at Antioch, Iconium and Lystra.

Paul concludes "What persecutions I endured yet from them all the Lord rescued me".

vs.12-13: v.12: Paul draws the conclusion with two lessons:

   i.   All followers of Christ who live a godly life – persecutions   come to them.

        In contrast

   ii. Imposters and evil men – go from bad to worse, as deceivers and being deceived.

vs.14-15: Paul turns to Timothy's life.

v.14: i.   To hold to things that Timothy learned,

        ii. of which he was convinced (as they are from Paul)

v.15: i.   from childhood Timothy was acquainted with the scriptures.

        ii. These scriptures a. instruct him

             b. give understanding for his salvation

             c. through faith in Christ Jesus.

vs.16-17:

v.16: Paul urges young Timothy to be fully acquainted with the scriptures, as it is inspired by God. The Law, the prophets and the writings used to form the scriptures of the Old Testament, with the 39 books (Jn. 5.47; 8.53; 12.34).

St. Peter tells "No prophesy ever came by the impulse of man, but men moved by the Holy Spirit spoke from God" (II Pet. 1.21).

This last passage deals with divine inspiration, by which the authority of the scriptures held.

But the scholars are divided in its interpretation,

1. **Dictation theory** – i.e., every word was dictated, thus translations into vernacular insufficient.

2. **Dynamic theory** – where the inspiration by Divine Spirit but the Language words the writer's own.

By 200 A.D. the 27 books of the New Testament were canonized or accepted and closed with Revelation as the last book and added to the Old Testament.

The division is seen in holding the Bible

a.   as the Word of God (i.e., the DictationTheory)

b.   It contains the Word of God (i.e., the Dynamic Theory).

We emphasise the authority of the Bible. But we notice that during the Revival period some sections of the church in preference of the Holy Spirit gifts in operation, chiefly Prophecy and Tongues, the Bible is relegated to a secondary place, as God's Spirit is seen directly leading. But we have to recognize that the Holy Spirit interprets the redemptive work of Christ. So the Holy Spirit's operation confirms Christ's work as given in the Bible. (Jn.16.13-14).

The Old Testament is referred by the Jews as the "Torah", i.e., instruction. The church refers to the written word of God as the "Bible", from the Greek "Bibilion"=book, in the plural thus in English as the "Bible".

v.16: Being divinely inspired book, naturally Paul refers to it as profitable

     a.   for teaching

     b.   for reproof

c. for correction

d. for training righteousness.

v.17: By this way the man of God is completely equipped for every good work.

Chapter – 4

THE DIVISIONS

vs.1-5	:	Timothy called on to give sound teaching.
vs. 6-8	:	St. Paul feels his martyrdom approaching near.
vs.9-12	:	St. Paul's reference to a number of his fellow workers.
vs.13-15	:	St. Paul calls on Timothy for certain works for Paul.
vs.16-18	:	Paul conveys the seriousness of his condition.
vs.19-21	:	The greetings.
v.22	:	The benediction.

COMMENTARY

v.1: Timothy called on to give sound teaching

St. Paul was coming to the closing section of his letter. He seems to challenge Timothy about who Christ is, whom he was serving:

i. Jesus the coming Judge of all – the living and the dead. The believer has to so live and carry on his tasks, so it can be acceptable to Christ, when he tests it.

ii. Jesus will appear as a warrior. Whenever the Roman Emperor plans to visit a place, it will be put in order. Likewise for Christ's visit next time one has to be fully prepared.

iii. Jesus will be a great sovereign when he visits next . The kingdoms of this world will become his.

So Paul asks Timothy to be ready, prepared to welcome the King of kings.

v.2: Paul advises Timothy   i.   to preach the Word (of God).

                           ii.   be urgent, in season and out of season.

                           iii. convince, rebuke and exhort.

What St.Paul seems to advise Timothy was to keep the sense of urgency in preaching.

    a.   Whether the occasion is favourable or not.

    b.   Whether the occasion is convenient or not.

    c.   Whether the occasion is welcoming or not.

To be unfailing in patience and in teaching.

vs.3-5: In the future Paul shows how it turns out.

    a   People will not endure sound and wholesome instruction;

    b.   but having itching ears to hear something pleasing and gratifying ears.

    c.   they gather to hear one after another teacher.

v.4: d.   To hear their own likings and turn to myths instead of the Truth.

v.5: In contrast to the above situation, St. Paul advises Timothy

    a.   to do the work of an Evangelist.

    b.   to fulfill his ministerial task

    c.   to be steady and endure the suffering.

v.6-8: St. Paul feels his martyrdom near:

v.7: In view of his impending death, St. Paul testifies;

  a.   I have fought the good fight.

  b.   I am (now) finishing the race.

  c.   I have kept the faith.

    i.   It is in the metaphor of a gladiator in the Roman amphitheatre he fought a good fight.

    ii.   As a Track runner at the Olympic games he did run well.

    iii. St. Paul feels it is like a sacrifice his life going to be offered or poured out like the wine poured from the cup at the Roman meals as an offering to the gods.

v.8: So Paul awaits for the crown of righteousness to be given to him in that final Day, the Day of Judgment.

In Cor. 9.25 – Paul refers to the wreath of leaves, given to the Olympic winner, which perishes, but what Christ offers is a crown which does not fade.

St. Paul was conscious that there are others also similar to his case, so he adds that this recognition not only for him but for all fellow martyrs like him.

vs.9-12: St. Paul refers to a number of his fellow-workers (refer to Introduction page)

vs.9,21b: Timothy was asked to come soon.

v.10:   a. **Demas**, deserted Paul and left for Thessalonica.

b. **Crecense**, has gone to Galatia.

c. **Titus** has gone to Dalmatia.

v.11:   d. **Luke** alone with Paul at Rome.

v.20:   e. **Erastus** remained at Corinth.

f. **Trophimus** got ill and left Miletus.

v.12:   g. **Tychicus** was sent to Ephesus.

vs.11a and 13b: Timothy was asked to do certain works

i.   he was to bring Mark with him.

v.13: ii. Timothy was asked to bring Paul's cloak, the books and specially the parchments Paul left at Troas.

vs.14-18: Paul refers to Alexander the coppersmith who did him great harm.

In Acts 19.23-40, we have an account how Demetrius, a silversmith, who lived on making idols for Artemis, the goddess of Ephesus, roused his fellow workers and created a great furor against Paul.

In **vs.33ff.,** we find one Alexander, put up by the Jews to look into this uproar, at the end it being religious issue involved and also the courts are there to appeal, made the crowd to disperse.

This above we know from Acts but not of any coppersmith by name Alexander. We have no record. Anyway Paul was asking Timothy "beware of him".

Few things Paul notes:

v.15: 1. Alexander strongly opposed the Gospel.

v.16:2. No one sided with Paul in his defence and they all deserted him.

v.17: 3. a. But the Lord stood by Paul.

> **b**. so that he was strengthened , to proclaim the Gospel message fully.

> **c.** By this way Paul was rescued from the lion's mouth, he says.

v.18:a. On the above experience of getting God's help.

> **b.** Paul now was confident that in the future also He will rescue him for the Heavenly Kingdom.

vs.19-21: Greetings.

I. a. Greetings sent to Pricilla and Aquila.

b. Greetings sent to the household of Onsiphorus.

c. Greetings sent to Timothy.

II. From all the brethren at Rome and specially from Eubulus, Pudens, Linus and Claudia.

v.22: Benediction: i. The Lord be with your spirit.

> ii. Grace be with you.

FOR FURTHER REFERENCE:

1. Ellis, E.E.   -   "Paul and His Recent Interpreters", pp. 49ff. 1961

2. Guthrie, D.   -   The Pastoral Epistles, (MCE)

3. NTS.,2.1955-56   -   "The Pastoral Epistles and the Duncan Ephesian Theory"

13
The Letter to Titus

INTRODUCTION

Titus Epistle was written by Paul from Ephesus (or Corinth) in 62 A.D.

1. In Titus 1.4, Paul addresses (in this letter) as "my True child" (i.e.,
    son). This is similar to Paul's reference to Timothy as "his son in faith"
    (I Tim. 1.2; I Cor. 4.17; Phil. 2.22). This indicates most probably he was
    Paul's convert.

2. The fact this letter to Titus, placed under the section of "the Pastoral
    letters" indicates Titus has responsibility in the respect of the leaders
    or elders of the church at some place. It is Crete, an island south of
    Italy.

    a. In Titus 1.5 we find Titus was sent or left there at Crete by St.
        Paul "to appoint elders". This conveys that he must be given
        administrative or organizational responsibility there. The fact
        not one town or village of Crete but "in every town" of Crete.
        This certainly gives us the idea that he was made a Bishop of
        Crete. It is an island, below Italy, with many towns and villages.

    b. Titus 2.7 refers to not only administrative but also "Teaching"
        responsibility. This is pastoral task.

    c. In Titus 2.7 Paul asks him to show himself as a model not only
        in teaching but as in

    i.   doing good work   All these are qualities

    ii. in integrity   of great leadership task.

    iii. in gravity

The church today commemorates Titus, the Western wing on 4th January,
while the Eastern Section of churches on 25th August.

3.   What was the background of Titus (other than the above we noted) in terms of his earlier Association with Paul's ministry.

   a.   Gal. 2.1: Paul visited Jerusalem church, a lapse of 14 years after his conversion, some of the Apostles and church leaders like Peter, John and James (the Pastor of the church there) were suspicious of him as he was earlier persecuting the Christians. It was Barnabas who introduced him to the church leaders there. At this juncture Paul took Titus with him to Jerusalem, like a trusted companion to him.

II Cor. 8.16

   i.   The church at Corinth started to split with 4 different groups I Cor. 1.11-12 shows and reports about its problems reaching Paul. Paul wrote "a severe letter" (II Cor. 10-13 chapters). Paul could think of no one but Titus to go there and deal with the situation.

   ii.   II Cor. 8.17 – Paul says Titus was going on his own accord to raise funds from the Corinthian church for the poor at Jerusalem.

   iii.   II Cor. 8.23: Paul also names Titus to go with his group to faithfully hand over the collections from Macedonia and Corinth to the poor at Jerusalem church. He refers to Titus as "My partner and fellow –sharer in your service".

This almost raises Titus to equal status with Paul.

In II Cor. 8.18 there is a reference here by Paul to another"famous among all and the churches".

II Cor. 12.18 Some speculate this for Luke, who was a physician, who accompanied Paul in his missionary work. Both are constant companions of Paul and some speculate if Titus could be Luke's brother. Not sure indeed.

MAIN DIVISIONS

CHAPTER – 1

vs. 1-4   –   The purpose of the letter.

vs.5-9   –   rules for installation and the character of the Bishop, elders etc.

vs.10-16   –   Jewish myths etc., spread by false teachers.

CHAPTER – 2

vs.1-10	–	The teaching of all sections in the church.
vs. 11-15	–	salvation brought by Christ is God's grace.

CHAPTER – 3

vs.1-2	–	Obedience to authorities and good conduct to all.
vs.3-7	–	In Christ shown goodness and God's kind.
vs.8-9	–	Good works
vs.10-11	–	Warning against false teachers
vs.12-15	–	Final greetings.

Chapter – 1

COMMENTARY

vs.1-4: The purpose of the letter.

v.1: a.   To further the faith of God's elect.

    b.   To further their knowledge of the "truth".

1.   The word "elect" expresses that in our context, as we are "believers", in terms of the Old Testament concept, God's action precedes man's response. Like the Israelites "the chosen race", the church seen as New Israel. St. Peter uses the same for New Testament believers – I Pet. 2.9. Even man's "faith – response" to divine action and offer of salvation is divine work; in the theological terms it is "prevenial grace" – God's Holy Spirit boding us to accept the Gospel when preached to us.

2.   The second reference to knowledge, following our faith. The fourth Gospel's emphasis on knowledge, like in Hindu marga (=ways), the "Gyana marga" is one of the ways of approaching God (the other two "ways" (= "Margas") being "Bhakti" (=Divotion) and "Karma" (=works).

The above two – faith and knowledge – results in "godliness" which leads at the end to Eternal life.

    i.   Godliness is seen in the sense of living constantly in the presence of God.

v.2: ii. the hope of Eternal life i.e., to live forever with the Lord.

This Eternal life was God's promise long past and it does happen as God is dependable, as true to his word. On the contrary it is Satan who is referred as a "liar" (Jn.8.44).

v.3: St. Paul since he was commissioned to the ministry, was preaching the Coming of the saviour and offering salvation in him.

v.4: to Titus, (as the recipient of this letter) who shares the same faith with Paul, who was sending this letter.

It closes with the eulogy of grace and peace, normal with the Jews.

vs.5-9: The rules for installation of the elders to church office at Crete.

   i.   To appoint church elders in every town. This is Paul's directive to Titus.

   ii.   also to amend the defective actions in this regard.

P.S.: This shows something went wrong in some earlier cases. Paul seems to have laid down some rules in this regard.

I Tim. 3.1-7 already shown the list of necessary qualifications for Ecclesiastical positions, so no need to repeat here. We can see in brief only. We note from the book of Acts every place where people responded to the Gospel the "house churches" were formed. Paul and his colleagues appointed "elders" to care for those fellowships (Acts 14.23; Philm. 1.2; Rom. 16.5; I Cor. 16.19).

The Qualities needed for the church office

v.6: 1.   The husband of one wife.

     2.   i. His children should be believers

           ii. They should not be profligate or insubordinate to the parents.

v.7: 3. The Bishop should be blameless.

A. Personal – i. Negative

   a. He should not be arrogant or quick-tempered.

   b. He should not be drunkard or violent.

   c. He should not be greedy of gain.

v.8: ii. Positive

   a.   He should be hospitable.

   b.   A lover of goodness.

   c.   A master of himself.

   d.   He must be upright, holy and self-controlled.

v.9: B. Church Ministry – for instruction of God's Word.

   a.   He must firmly hold to the Word of God as he was   taught.

b. i. so that he will be able to give instruction in sound doctrine.

ii. so that he may be able to confute those who contradict the Truth.

vs.10-11: The "Judaizers" or the False Teachers, added by Gnostic philosophy:

v.10: a. There are insubordinate men – many of them.

b. There are empty-talkers and deceivers (the Judaizers chiefly)

v.11: a. These are upsetting whole families

b. their teaching is for base gain.

c. They have no right what they teach.

These "Judaizers" (of circumcision group) were persuading the Gentile converts that to be saved these need more than the grace of Christ and their faith. It is not enough.

They insist these converts must observe the rules and regulations of foods and absolutions of Mosaic Law etc.

The Gnosticism: This is the oriental religious product where the matter is evil (the world) while the spirit is good. As such the body or some foods polluted. One needed to be initiated through knowledge.

vs.12-14:

v.12: Paul refers to the Cretan poet who tells them, that they are liars, evil beasts and lazy gluttons.

v.13: This above testimony   being true, Paul tells Titus they need to be rebuked, calling on them to heed to sound Christian faith.

v.14: They should desist from giving heed to

a) the Jewish myths or commands of men.

b) and they in effect rejecting what is Truth.

vs.15-16: Here Paul makes a distinction between the pure and the impure.

v.15: a. **The impure**: "Deluktoi" (Gk.) which comes from the references to idols which was seen as an abomination. From this came the idea of repulsive or impure mind.

In this context Paul says to such impure minds every thing is bad.

b. **The pure**: In contrast, "to the pure" (in mind understood) all things are pure (being God the creator of these, these food products, or days etc., have come from God).

v.16: These above impure conscience type of people though they prefer to be religious and accept God yet in their living, they deny God.

So Paul's **final observation** of these as:

i.   detestable.

ii. disobedient

iii. unfit for any good deed.

Chapter – 2

SECTION-1

St. Paul deals with "**the Christian character in action**" of different sections of the community.

Divisions

1. vs.1-2:   The elderly men.

2. vs.3-5: i. The elderly women.

and ii. the younger women.

3. v.6:   The younger men.

4. vs.7-8:   The Christian teacher.

5. vs.9-10:   The Christian slaves.

SECTION-2

1. vs.11-14:   The salvation work of Christ.

2. vs.1and 15:   The three aspects of Titus' office.

COMMENTARY

I. v.2 :The senior men in the community.

This elderly society of men, Titus was asked by St. Paul – to be temperate or sober, instead of continuing in self-indulgence of youthful stage.

To be serious not in terms of being gloomy, but of heaven-bound behaviour.

To be sensible in terms of being able to control his instincts as a senior.

To be sound in a) faith, b) in love and c) in steadfastness.

II.   vs.3-5: The elderly women:

These have to be i. reverent in behaviour.

ii. a. not slanderers.

b. or slaves to drink

iii. a. to teach what is good

Younger women i. to love their husbands and children i.e., their family. ii. submissive to their husbands.

v.5 – to be a. sensible b. chaste c. domestic d. kind.

All the characteristics needed so that Christian preaching may not be discredited.

v.6: Younger men: As it is the stage of prime life and youthful urges at zenith, such stage of "trial and error" of life it needs to be lived in 'self-control".

vs.7-8: The Christian Teacher:

v.7: The one who teaches others, must also **exhibit in one's practical life** what he teaches.

It is shown by Bornkam (a N.T. scholar) that in the life of Christ, he taught what he lived i.e., there is no difference between his preaching and his life. This gives moral authority to one's teaching. So Paul urges here that these teachers should show in their life.

a.   a model of good deeds

b.   in teaching show

     i. integrity (= it is to keep one's word)

     ii.gravity (= being serious of what is said).

v.8: a. A sound speech that cannot be sensured.

     b. so that an opponent   i. finding no evil in the speech.

                            ii. will be put to shame, as nothing evil to say against it.

Illustration: Often after church worship services, the talk centered among the departing members is criticism of the sermon preached. (Of course at times appreciation also there). So much, many lay members hesitate to occupy a pulpit when the pastor is out or on leave.

Once the church leader placed in this situation to preach next Sunday, asked the members to come with papers and pens to note the mistakes they find in his preaching and at the end added, "the one who has the mistakes of a greater number will win, he will be asked to preach the following Sunday". That settled and none submitted any of his mistakes the next Sunday in his preaching.

vs.9-10: The Christian **slaves**–   a. to be submissive to their Masters

b. to give satisfaction in their work.

c. Not to talk back.

d. Not to steal.

e. to show entire and true fidelity with hearty good will.

In the above way they may adorn the teaching given by Christ our Saviour. The only question raised in this context was, if true to the Christian faith and teaching, if a Master asks the slave to do a wrong thing, should he as a believer obey his master or Christ his Saviour. It is natural the Master will get angry for the slave's disobedience, but as a Christian Master certainly later he will realize his mistake and have more respect for his slave as a trustworthy person.

II. The Second Section

vs.11-14: The saving of Christ and its influence on man's morality.

I.   a.   to renounce godlessness

b.   to renounce worldly desires for forbidden things

c.   to await the second coming of Christ our blessed hope.

II.   That is who gave himself for our redemption.

i.   from the power of lawlessness.

ii.   to purify us as his special people.

III. To live a) a sober b) upright c) and godly lives in this world

We find there are 4 motifs for ethical demand in the New Testament.

1.   the a, b and c in the above list we find are based on the second coming of Christ which is "Eschatological motif" (as in Rom. 13.8-10).

2.   In the ii above as a special people of God, which is "Fellowship motif".

3.   the a, b, c to be sober, upright and godly above refers to the "Holiness motif".

4.   v.14 – To purify a people and zealous for good works – here we find both fellowship and personal motif.

v.15: Paul's advice looks homiletics arena of "the art of preaching"

1. Titus to realize he is Royal Ambassador of Christ (II Cor. 5.20). Not to treat this authority over others cheaply; as such along with proclamation and encouragement, to rebuke those going wrong.

Chapter– 3

---

vs.1-2	:	Christian's citizenship duties
vs.3-7	:	The two fold Christian life.
vs.8-11	:	Good deeds; To avoid foolish speculations.
vs.12-15	:	The final greetings.

COMMENTARY

vs.1-2: Christian's citizenship duties.

We have already seen in I Timothy 2.1-2f. the reference of Paul about the rulers and the citizenship responsibilities of the Christians.

If we refer there, we note, few points in this regard.

a. St. Paul, a citizen of Tarsus, of Asia Minor, becomes automatically a Roman Citizen. As such calls for obedience to (Roman) Government is natural.

b. i. By then the Caesar worship as divine was not very prominent.

   ii. Even when it started, yet the Jews were exempted then.

c. In the Synagogue, the Jews offered prayers for the rulers, as such Paul most probably felt to continue that practice in the church services. I Tim. 1.1 – as prayers made for all men, it could include the rulers, who have the task to run the government in a smooth way.

d. Even Christ was not totally against paying taxes to Caesar, the Roman ruler (Mk. 12.17).

v.2: Paul adds "to be ready for every good work". So it is not only law abiding but ready for

   i. every good or honest work.

   ii. To be tolerant, not start a quarrel for any small matter.

   iii. To be kind i.e., ready to help others.

   iv. To be gentle, the Greek word "prous" refers to control anger.

vs.3-7: The two fold Christian life.

1. In the past: **a.** i.   senseless

              ii.   disobedient

              iii. misguided

              iv. slaves to all kinds of desires and pleasures

       b. living in i. maliciousness

              ii. envy

              iii.detestable selves

              iv hating each other.

These **above qualities** are **opposed** to the **Christian living**.

v.4: But when the saviour God appeared with i. his goodness and ii.his love.

Men realized it was not by i. righteousness, through works.Salvation came to Men but by ii. his own mercy

   This was the problem of the Jews (Rom. 10.3).

v.5: 1.   The washing away of sins which is the work of the Holy Spirit (Jn.3.58)

   2.   the rebirth and renewal sent by Christ (as promised) after his ascension (Jn.14.15-17;15.26 etc.Acts 2.1-4etc)

vs.6-7: The Aim (of the above work of Christ)

   1.   To put us back into right relationship with God

        (which was broken by sin).

   2.   It is done through Divine Grace.

   3.   To realize our hope of righteous relationship with God, the salvation as "Atonement" – to unite man to God.

vs.8-11: To avoid speculations and give attention to good deeds:

   St. Paul advising Titus

v.9: To avoid a. foolish speculations: b.genealogies c. contentions and logistic battles.

These do i) no good to any one ii) serve no useful purpose.

v.8: Paul wants first a)   to have faith in God.

next b) to i. think and plan

ii. how to practice good deeds

iii. these are excellent and profitable to men.

vs.10-11: Advice about a quarrelsome person: A man who is factious i. he is perverted and sinful. ii.he is self-condemned .

Titus was asked   i. to admonish him, once or twice

ii. after that have nothing to do with him

i.e., such a character who does not heed to correction, no need to waste one's precious time on him.

Not that a preacher give up on a sinner, but a person in wrong views, who thinks he is right and all others wrong. This is the character of a heretic. Not much hope can be put on such a person and waste one's precious time.

vs.12-15: Final greetings

Here in closing as usual Paul gives **i.** personal messages in addition to **ii.** greetings

v.12:1:   1.   **Artemas** – Not known who he is.

2.   **Tychicus** – we know he was the bearer of letters to the Ephesian (Eph.6.21) and Colossian churches (Col. 4.7).

Nicapolis town was in the Roman province of Dalmatia, where the Stoic philosopher Epictetus has his school. Paul wishes to spend his winter there and asking one of them to come there.

v.13:   3.   Zenas, one of them to come there;

4.   **Apollos** : He was the active preacher from Alexandria who came to Ephesus, and later went to Corinth. Aquila and Priscilla taught him more of the Christian faith (Acts 18.24-19.1).

Paul was asking to help these two leaders in their journey for their travel fares and other needs.

v.14: Let the Christians learn to come forward to help, specially in cases of urgent needs of others.

v.15: Final greetings of all those with Paul, he conveys here and ends with the benediction of Grace to Titus and those with him.

FOR FURTHER REFERENCE

1. Ellis, E.E.   -   "Paul and His Recent Interpreters", pp. 49ff. 1961

2. Guthrie, D.   -   The Pastoral Epistles, (MCE)

3. "The Pastoral Epistles and the Duncan Ephesian Theory' NTS., 2, 1955-56.

4. Scott, E.F.   -   The Pastoral Epistles (MCE)

Bibliography

1. Anderson, Scott   1932   Christianity According to St. Paul, Cambridge University Press.

2. Baker, J.C.   1980   Paul: the Apostle, Philadelphia.

3. Barret, C.K.   1932   A Commentary on Romans, London:ISPSK.

4. Barret, C.K.   1985   Freedom and Obligation, London: ISPCK.

5. Bornkamm, Gunther, 1971   Paul, London: H. & Stoughton, England Tr.

6. Brown, Roger,   A Guide to Romans, Delhi: ISPCK.

7. Bruce, F.F.   1980   A Guide to Apostle of the Free Spirit, (Exeter).

8. Bultmann, Rudo,   1967   The Old and New Man, England: Richmond.

9. Dodd, C.H.   1960   The Epistle of Paul to the Romans, London: H & Stoughton.

10. Fuller, R.H.   1975   A Critical Introduction to the NewTestament, London.

11. Hanson, A.T.   1987   The Paradox of the Cross in the Thought of St. Paul, Sheffield.

12. Kasemann, Earnest, 1971a   Perspectives on Paul, London, Eng. Tr.

13. Kittle, G. (Ed.)   1974   Theological Dictionary of the NewTestament,London: Erdmans.

14. Longenecker, Richard 1971   The Ministry and Message of Paul, Grand Rapids: Zondervan

15. Longernecker,Richard 1976 Paul: Apostle of Liberty, Grand Rapids: Baker.

16. Richardson, P.   1979   Paul's Ethics of Freedom,
                                    Philadelphia.

17. Ridderbes, H.   1977   Paul: An Outline of his Theology,
                                    London, Eng.Tr.

18. Ryrie, Charles C.   1959   Biblical Theology of the
                                    NewTestament, Chicago:
                                    Moody Press.

19. Sanders, E.P.   1977   Paul and Palestinian Judaism,
                                    London.

20. Sanders, E.P.   1983   Paul the Law and the Jewish
                                    People,Philadelphia.

21. Wright, N.T.   1988   'Paul', in the New dictionary
                                    of Theology, Ed. By S.B.
                                    Ferguson et.al. Illinois: Versity
                                    Press.

22. Zeisler, J.A.   1972   The Meaning of Righteousness
                                    inPaul,